Modern Literary Theory

Modern Literary Theory

A Comparative Introduction

Edited by Ann Jefferson and David Robey

with contributions from David Forgacs, Ann Jefferson,
David Robey and Elizabeth Wright

Barnes & Noble Books
Totowa, New Jersey

First published in paperback 1984

First published in the USA 1982 by
Barnes & Noble Books
81 Adams Drive
Totowa, New Jersey, 07512

ISBN: 0-389-20469-2

Printed in Great Britain

Contents

Contributors

David Forgacs is lecturer in Italian at Sussex University. He did an undergraduate degree in English and an M.Phil. in comparative literature at Oxford University and a diploma thesis in Italian at Pisa University. He has recently jointly published an edition of Gramsci's cultural writings in translation.

Ann Jefferson is research fellow in French at St. John's College, Oxford. She did an undergraduate degree and a D.Phil. in French at Oxford University. She is the author of *The Nouveau Roman and the Poetics of Fiction* (1980) and of a number of articles on modern French fiction and literary theory.

David Robey is lecturer in Italian at Oxford University and fellow of Wolfson College, Oxford. He did undergraduate and graduate work in modern languages at Oxford University. He is the editor of *Structuralism: An Introduction* (1973) and has published articles on aspects of Italian Renaissance humanism and on Dante.

Elizabeth Wright is at the time of writing lecturer in German at St. Anne's College, Oxford. She did an undergraduate degree in German at London University and a D.Phil. at Oxford University. She is the author of *E.T.A. Hoffmann and the Rhetoric of Terror* (1978) and has published articles on psychoanalysis and literary criticism and on rhetorical discourse in Goethe and Schiller. She is about to become lecturer and official fellow in German at Girton College, Cambridge.

Introduction

Ann Jefferson and David Robey

Literary theory has developed in the course of this century into a branch of literary studies that is studied and taught as a distinct subject in its own right. It is not, of course, a totally new subject. Philosophers, writers, critics and scholars alike have always been inclined to speculate about the theoretical implications of literary practice, and most literary theorists of the twentieth century are conscious of belonging to a tradition that goes back at least as far as Plato and Aristotle. Modern literary theory has a great deal in common with, and owes a great deal to, such antededents but it differs from most of them in a very important respect; the place it occupies within the discipline of literary studies.

To make clear what is usually meant by modern literary theory, we need to distinguish it from two areas of thought to which it is closely related: philosophical speculations about poetry and literature that fall under the heading of aesthetics, and reflections by practising writers about the nature of their art. When one speaks of literary theory one must evidently mean something that overlaps with and draws on these areas of thought; but the term usually concerns a somewhat different set of interests, and it is in relation to these interests that we shall be using it in this book.

The distinguishing feature of modern literary theory is its connection with practical literary criticism and scholarship. Aesthetics is concerned with literature from a philosophical point of view, in relation to the general concepts of art, beauty and value. Its relevance for practical literary study has thus been rather limited, although criticism has drawn on it in the past from time to time. Modern literary theory has far more extensive and specific relevance for practical literary study, because it has grown up in close connection with it, and has thus tended to be directly concerned not only with the distinctive properties of literature, but also with the distinctive objectives of literary criticism or scholarship.

For the same reason modern literary theory is different from writers' speculations about their art, although such speculations may often have influenced it. What writers think about literature in most cases has a limited bearing on the way in which critics and scholars approach the subject. In dealing with a given author, literary studies have traditionally paid considerable attention to his views on writing,

1

but only as part of the 'background' to his work. These views have been used to explain his motives or intentions, and to account for the peculiar character of his texts, but on the whole they have not fundamentally affected the *way* in which these texts, or those of any other author, have been treated. While Mallarmé's views on literature, for instance, have often been studied in relation to aspects of his poetry, very few critics would make his views their own to the extent of allowing them to influence the general principles and methods on which their activity as critics is based. In contrast modern literary theory has a much more vital relationship with critical and scholarly practice; its purpose is both to illuminate and to call into question the very discipline, literary studies, that encompasses it. It is above all a way of thinking about the practice of literary study, and as such what it has to say may frequently challenge the established forms of that practice.

We can understand better the need for literary theory if we consider two highly influential approaches to literature which, in their different ways, can be said to be antitheoretical. The first is a form of scholarship that goes by the name of positivism; the second is a form of criticism which has acquired more fame or notoriety than any other in this country in the last few decades, that of F. R. Leavis. Together the two approaches are responsible for a great deal that is taught under the name of literary studies in our universities.

To clarify the issues involved here, we first need to explain the distinction we have been making between scholarship and criticism. The distinction, it should be said, is not one to which we attach much weight, and since it tends to disappear when literature is approached from a theoretical point of view, in the rest of this book, except where the opposition between the two terms is particularly relevant, by criticism we shall mean scholarship as well. But in common usage criticism generally stands for discussions of literary works that focus on the experience of reading. It is concerned with describing, interpreting and evaluating the meaning and effect that literary works have for competent but not necessarily academic readers. Scholarship, on the other hand, stops short of, or goes beyond the experience of reading, in that its concern is with factors in one way or another external to this experience: the genesis of the work, its textual transmission, or elements within it that the non-specialist reader need not necessarily take an interest in. Criticism is not exclusively academic, and often may be personal and subjective, though it is of course capable of a detachment and rigour of its own; scholarship is a specialist activity which aims for the same detachment and rigour that characterize other academic disciplines.

In modern literary scholarship positivism usually means a general attitude of mind rather than a specific method or school of thought;

but originally—as well as in some of its more recent forms such as the 'logical positivism' of A. J. Ayer—it stood for a distinctive philosophy of knowledge, first formulated in the work of the French philosopher Auguste Comte, who published between 1830 and 1842 a monumental *Cours de philosophie positive*. In brief the object of this philosophy was to extend to the 'arts' subjects the methods and principles of the natural sciences. The positivist philosopher was concerned with perceptible facts rather than ideas, and with how these facts arise, not why; all knowledge not wholly founded on the evidence of the senses was dismissed as idle speculation. In the later nineteenth century this kind of positivism became a major influence on European thought in general, and on the study of literature in particular.

What positivism means in literary scholarship is summed up in its most extreme form in the introductory chapter of the history of English literature by the French scholar Hippolyte Taine, published in 1863. A literary text, Taine argued, must be regarded as the expression of the psychology of an individual, which in its turn is the expression of the *milieu* and the period in which the individual lived, and of the race to which he belonged. All human achievement can be explained by reference to these causes, summarized by Taine in his famous three-term formula 'la race, le milieu et le moment' (Taine 1863: iii-xlviii). Literary scholarship must therefore take as its object the causal explanation of texts in relation to these three factors; by doing so, according to Taine, it will become a form of scientific history comparable in its status and methods to the natural sciences.

This extreme scientific optimism now seems very dated, but in an exaggerated way Taine expressed assumptions about the character and purpose of literary study which guided the greater part of European and American scholarship in the late nineteenth and early twentieth centuries, and have been and still are an important influence on the British academic world as well. In its pure form positivist scholarship studied literature almost exclusively in relation to its factual causes or genesis: the author's life, his recorded intentions in writing, his immediate social and cultural environment, his sources. To use a common distinction, it was an extrinsic rather than an intrinsic approach to texts. It was not interested in the features of the literary text itself except from a philological and historical viewpoint. That is, it used linguistic history to interpret the meaning of individual words, and other branches of history to explain references and allusions; but it disregarded questions concerning the value or the distinctive properties of literature, since these could not be dealt with in a factual and historical manner. Or more exactly, while it took for granted that literary texts possessed a special value, in practice it treated them as if they were indistinguishable from other sorts of historical document.

3

INTRODUCTION

We must leave readers to decide for themselves exactly how widespread this approach is in British literary scholarship today. Where it does persist it undoubtedly takes a more qualified form than that which we have just described. Modern scholars make greater allowance than their nineteenth-century predecessors for the special character of literary texts, and are probably more cautious in their attempts at historical explanation. Yet the positivist influence can still be seen, surely, in the strong preference among many scholars for the historical, factual and extrinsic treatment of texts, coupled with a strong disinclination to discuss problems concerning literary value or the nature of literature in general. The most obvious consequence of this tendency is that a great deal of scholarship fails to satisfy many readers' feeling that the academic study of literature should somehow reflect and account for the special status which literature enjoys in our culture.

The same disinclination to discuss the nature or value of literature has meant that much modern literary scholarship has failed to meet another kind of demand, in this case one that can reasonably be made of any academic discipline: that it should provide an adequate definition of its subject-matter, in order to ensure clarity and consistency in its methods and, equally importantly, to explain and justify itself to the world at large. If asked to define the subject-matter of literary study, modern positivist scholars will argue that a general academic consensus exists as to which texts are worth studying as literature and which are not, and that there is no reason why they should call this consensus into question. They take their object of study, literature, as already given, and concentrate on explaining it by reference to its historical genesis, rather than discussing its intrinsic properties.

Yet one may well question whether a real consensus exists as to which texts are worthy of study as literature. It is true that as far as the educational system is concerned there is an established canon of works officially certified as meriting academic attention, but such a canon is merely the product of custom and institutional pressure, neither of which would seem a very satisfactory basis for intellectual choice. In any case inside and outside the educational system there is a growing variety of conflicting views on the subject of literary value and on the difference between literary and non-literary texts. The criterion of consensus by which positivist scholarship selects its subject-matter is thus increasingly called into question by intellectual developments in other areas of literary study. But even if such a consensus really did exist, it still would not provide scholarship with a truly adequate definition of its subject-matter. Almost every other academic discipline can say in exact general terms what its subject-matter is. All literary scholarship of the positivist kind can do is point to a wide variety of individual texts and hope that everyone will agree that together they constitute a special category. A discipline that can only define its subject-matter in this way cannot but seem inadequate and confused in its methods, and will be incapable of providing a convincing account of its character and aims.

Since most literary theories are concerned with the special properties or the special value of literature, what they can offer literary scholarship is a basis on which to build a more rational and systematic discipline, which will be more able to do justice to the peculiar status which literature has traditionally enjoyed. Criticism can also benefit from literary theory in the same way, but its need for literary theory may appear in a somewhat different light, mainly because it is far less inclined than scholarship to neglect the specific value or properties of literature. This is true, at least, of our second antitheoretical approach, that of F. R. Leavis, whose criticism always focused firmly on those aspects of texts that he considered most significant from a literary point of view. Since we have no room here for a full discussion of this criticism, we shall have to limit ourselves to discussing a single exchange of views between him and René Wellek, the author, with Austin Warren, of the influential *Theory of Literature*. This exchange of views, which took place in 1937 in Leavis's journal *Scrutiny*, is important both because it provides a convenient summary of the principles underlying Leavis's criticism, which has had such an enormous influence on the study of English literature in this country, and because it helps to clarify further, in a different way from our discussion of positivistic scholarship, the point of literary theory.

The exchange was started by a letter which Wellek wrote to *Scrutiny* about Leavis's book *Revaluation*. Wellek admired the book and for the most part agreed with it, but criticized it on one important score, that it failed to state explicitly and defend systematically its assumptions concerning the nature and value of poetry. On his behalf Wellek formulated Leavis's assumptions as follows (Wellek 1937a: 376):

> Your poetry must be in serious relation to actuality, it must have a firm grasp of the actual, of the object, it must be in relation to life, it must not be cut off from direct vulgar living, it should be normally human, testify to spiritual health and sanity, it should not be personal in the sense of indulging in personal dreams and fantasies, there should be no emotion for its own sake in it…

To a large extent, Wellek said, he shared these assumptions; he asked of Leavis only one thing, 'to defend this position more abstractly and to become conscious that large ethical, philosophical and, of course, ultimately, also aesthetic *choices* are involved'.

Leavis's answer is a powerful defence of a point of view widely accepted in British criticism today. On the whole, with certain reservations, he agreed that Wellek's formulation of his critical principles was correct, but he disagreed very strongly that such a formulation was necessary or desirable. Wellek, he argued, was writing as a philosopher, not as a critic, and philosophy and criticism are wholly distinct disciplines. The aim of the critic is for the most part the same as that of the good reader, to 'feel into' the experience of the text in its 'concrete fulness' (1937: 61). Apart from this all he has to do is communicate the experience to his readers, and he must do so in a manner appropriate to the essential nature of poetry: through the use, that is, of language which is not abstract and general but concrete and particular, to describe, compare and evaluate the text in question. 'My whole effort,' Leavis wrote, 'was to work in terms of concrete judgments and particular analyses: "This—doesn't it?—bears such a relation to that; this kind of thing—don't you find it so?—wears better than that", etc.' (1937: 63). The kind of abstract formulation of standards that Wellek required is, he says, too clumsy and inadequate; it distracts the reader from the essential concrete experience of the text. The critic should not try to argue his case in conceptual terms, but attempt to convey directly this experience to the reader.

Now in at least one way Leavis has the best of this argument. Criticism that is couched in direct and concrete language is a good deal more readable and frequently much more stimulating than abstract discussions of the kind that Wellek called for and illustrated in his first letter. But to say that Leavis's criticism is stimulating is not necessarily to hold it up as a model for literary study. As Wellek pointed out in his rejoinder (1937b), however much a critic aims, like Leavis, for the direct communication of his 'complete response', he cannot avoid invoking norms or standards, and he cannot avoid using concepts. If his reader shares these norms or standards, and if he understands and agrees with the critic's use of concepts, then perhaps no difficulty arises. But the weakness of Leavis's model of criticism is that it cannot cope adequately with disagreement. The point has been made of Leavis himself, that despite the apparently open-minded way in which he formulated his approach to the reader ('This—doesn't it?—bears such a relation to that; this kind of thing—don't you find it so?—wears better than that'), his reaction to a negative response in discussion was simply to ignore it. Given his resolute opposition to theorizing, it would have been difficult for him to do otherwise, for many, perhaps most differences of view in criticism are differences of principle, concerning the nature of literature and the purpose of the critic. What Leavis calls philosophy, and we would prefer to call literary theory, will certainly not always be able to resolve such differences, but it does at least allow one to understand them and to discuss them intelligently. Given the multiplicity of critical approaches that characterizes the academic study of literature today, it would seem essential to be able to do this.

To sum up the points that have arisen so far, we can say that literary theory provides not only a means of dealing with differences of critical opinion, but also the basis for constructing a more rational, adequate and self-aware discipline of literary studies. In saying this, evidently, we are still emphasizing the connections between literary theory and critical and scholarly practice, and we must also emphasize that these connections go in both directions. That is to say, not only does theory illuminate or improve practice, but it also draws very heavily on it; the questions that critics and scholars ask of individual texts are ultimately of the same order as those that literary theory asks of literature in general. Literary theory is not something that has developed in a vacuum, but has arisen for the most part in response to the problems encountered by readers, critics and scholars in their practical contact with texts. Thus when we proceed, as we shall now do, to list in more detail the different kinds of question to which literary theory proposes answers, we shall simply be listing questions that critics and scholars have long been accustomed to ask in a less systematic way about individual literary texts. One might simply say that the point of literary theory is to draw attention to these questions and to make them more problematic, to show that they can be answered in a number of different ways, and that established ways of answering them should not be taken for granted.

At its most basic level literature is commonly regarded as a kind of communication between author and reader. Just as in ordinary linguistic communication a speaker sends a message to an addressee, so an author sends a literary text to a reader. Filling out this scheme, we can add that the message-text is about something (content, reality) and that it is written in language. The first addition is designed to account for the fact that the literary text is assumed to be a specially motivated form of discourse, that it is written because it has something to say; the second addition serves to distinguish literature from other art forms which, of course, do not have language as their medium. So a preliminary definition of literature could be formulated like this: the *author* sends a literary text about *reality* to the *reader* in *language*.

This definition is, in a sense, a pure fiction. It covers a range of *possibilities* only; all its component elements are open to challenge, and in practice most theories will concentrate on some more than others, or even to the exclusion of others. It would seem more judicious, therefore, to recast this basic framework into a set of questions which one might ask of any theory of literature: (1) how does it define the literary qualities of the literary text? (2) what relation does it propose between text and author? (3) what role does it ascribe to the reader? (4) how does it view the relationship between text and reality? (5) what status does it give to the medium of the text,

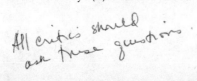
All critics should ask these questions.

7

language? Let us take these questions separately and consider them in more detail.

(1) *The text as literature*. Although the word 'literature' tends to be used as if it were precisely and unproblematically definable, in fact definitions of the term vary widely in their scope and premises. The modern definition of literature is an extremely narrow one; in seventeenth-century France, for example, the texts which we now call literary were part of a much larger sphere called 'letters', which did not include the distinctions that we now make between literary and non-literary writing. One conclusion that can be drawn from such differences of meaning is to adopt the so-called 'institutional' definition of literature; that is, to see it as essentially similar to any other sort of social or cultural institution and therefore as changing its character and function as the society that produces it changes. Most literary theories do not adopt such a historicist attitude, but attempt instead to devise universal definitions of literature or related categories such as poetry, verbal art, etc. Such definitions vary in a number of ways. They will differ in the degree to which they want to establish the specificity of literature: the Russian Formalists, for example, staked everything on literature's distinctive qualities, whereas certain 'vulgar' Marxists regarded literature as just one element of the superstructure. The nature of the terms in which literature's distinctiveness is defined will vary too: the Russian Formalists define it in relation to ordinary language, and Pierre Macherey in relation to ideology.

Most theories will, however, include an evaluation of the formal properties of the literary text, since some notion of form usually enters even the sketchiest definition of literature; literature is generally regarded as a more patterned or organized kind of message than those of ordinary communication. But the function attributed to the formal elements of literature will vary from theory to theory. A view of literature which puts great emphasis on the content is not likely to regard form as anything more than ornamental or ancillary. A slightly more complex model would shift the burden of representation onto form itself, defining content not just as what is said but as the way in which things are said. The New Critics are a typical example of just such a view. Other theories which disregard literature's non-literary content will privilege formal features over any representational function in the text, thus making literature's content as incidental as form is for the content-biased theories. A preoccupation with form tends to be the mark of those theories most anxious to establish the distinctiveness of the literary, so that to ask of a theory what status it gives to the formal elements in the text is another way of homing in on this basic but very vexed question.

(2) *Text and author*. Biography has traditionally played a large role in

literary studies, but ever since the American New Critics raised the issue of the 'intentional fallacy', it has been thought that biography may actually constitute an obstacle to the study of literary texts. The importance given to the author by literary studies tends, roughly speaking, to be in inverse proportion to the importance given to specifically literary qualities. Theories which concentrate on these qualities are apt to attribute only an incidental role to the author: for instance, both the New Critics and the Russian Formalists felt it necessary to downgrade the author, in order to guarantee the independence of literary studies, and to save them from being merely a second-rate form of history or psychology. Those theories for which the author is a central point of reference vary quite considerably on the question of how far the authorial intentions which are assumed to govern a text are conscious, and how one might account for any lack of consciousness on the part of the author: traditional Marxists and classical Freudians will obviously give very different accounts of this issue.

(3) *Text and reader.* Not many of the theories discussed in this book devote much attention to the reader, and until recently the reader has been the most neglected element in the framework of literary communication. The premium placed by a number of theories of literature on their scientific status is no doubt a major reason why the reader has been given such a small role in so many of them; for the variable factor in subjective responses to literature would seem to be at odds with the systematic requirements of any rigorous theory. This was certainly what the Russian Formalists felt, and they specifically excluded subjective response from their theory because they regarded it as unscientific; by implication, therefore, the reader is left passively to observe features of a text whose presence can be otherwise established by 'objective' scientific analysis.

I. A. Richards is unusual in combining an interest in reader response with scientific aims. His was, however, a somewhat naively psychological view of the reader, and the recent recurrence of interest in the reader in literary theory has tended to account for his role in rather more sophisticated terms. In the Constance school of phenomenologically-inspired reader theory (not discussed in this book) the reader is no longer given a purely private and psychological definition, but is recognized to have a culturally and historically determined function: the way in which texts are read is determined by the historical and cultural situation of their readers. A similar insight is developed by Barthes in his *S/Z*, where he shows that the cultural and literary experience of readers affects the way in which texts are actually written—not in a vacuum, but either to endorse or to subvert cultural and literary norms of reading. In these theories the reader does not passively receive the impact that the

9

literary text may make upon him, but is involved in a more active, or rather, a more interactive process. Jacques Lacan makes this intersubjective basis of reading a central part of his theory, but takes it out of any historical context and places it back in a more psychological or psycholinguistic one. He contends that it is not just the author of a work (or indeed the sender of any linguistic message) who determines its meaning, but that the reader (or receiver of a message) plays a crucial part in the construction of that meaning.

It seems, then, that once fears about individual idiosyncrasy have been overcome, literary theory is perfectly capable of accommodating the role of the reader without losing any of its rigour, and, furthermore, that this role can be theorized in a variety of different ways.

(4) *Text and reality.* Reality here does not mean just the concrete world of material objects, but includes philosophical, psychological and social realities which exist independently of literature. The question for the literary theorist is how to formulate the relationship between the text and this reality. Is there a relationship in the first place? Is it direct or indirect, representational or genetic? What aspect of reality is evoked? Marxist theories will assume that by one means or another, literature is bound to social and political reality, whereas psychoanalytic theories will assume that literature represents primarily a psychological reality. One might ask further, does literature relate to reality referentially, by direct statement? or is reality indirectly represented through formal qualities, as the New Critics claimed for experiential reality, or as Lucien Goldmann claimed for social reality? or does literature have a negative, possibly even a subversive relation to reality? This last notion is what is implied in the Russian Formalists' concept of defamiliarization, whereby reality is presented in such a way as to 'make it strange'.

(5) *Text and language.* Theories of literature vary greatly in the importance they ascribe to the language component of literature. To the extent that literary theory can be separated from aesthetics, it seems fairly obvious that it needs to take some account of the main feature which distinguishes literature from the other arts—its linguistic medium. Certainly many of the theories concerned to establish the distinctiveness of literature as an independent category use language as a key element in their definition of that distinctiveness, usually by defining literature as a special use of language. In the case of the Russian Formalists as a deviation from ordinary language, and in the case of some New Critics as a shift from a logical and conventional to an imitative, 'iconic' use of language. In addition, literary theory has benefited from the enormous expansion in linguistic science that has taken place during the course of this century. Certain theorists like Roman Jakobson and his colleagues in

the Prague School developed their theories alongside and in relation to their work on linguistics. Other theorists, like those associated with Parisian structuralism, actually take linguistic theory as their starting point for literary theory, and indeed Saussurean linguistics in particular has been enormously influential in the development of a number of different kinds of literary theory.

These, then, are the major questions which one could ask of any theory, and which should help to pinpoint the particular issues that it is trying to account for. They also allow one to compare the theories with each other and with different kinds of critical practice. But most importantly, they allow one to make sense of a theory in literary theoretical terms, and not just as a symptom of historical or philosophical developments. To stress this as an advantage is to respond to the spirit of most of the theories discussed in this book which, to a greater or lesser extent, claim a quasi-scientific status for their own systems. In this they are, for the most part, profoundly opposed not only to positivist literary scholarship, but to most established forms of literary history; and they are equally at odds with the evaluative approach that characterizes a great deal of literary criticism. If literary theory, therefore, seems to be making both history and evaluation prime casualties of systematic thought, one might justifiably ask what place, if any, theory has found for history, and to what extent theories of literature might lead to or entail evaluative judgements.

Beginning, then, with history: ditching history seems for a number of theories to have been a necessary gesture in establishing the autonomy of literary studies. The argument is that literary theory and literary history are mutually incompatible, because of the risk that both literature and its theory will be seen as just part of an all-encompassing historical process, and that the idea of their specificity will thereby be lost. Marxist literary theory will, of course, be an exception to this rule, because Marxism itself is historical. One question, therefore, to ask of any given brand of Marxist theory is how far it allows for the independence of literature, and how far literature is subsumed into general history. Some theories, like Russian Formalism, have tried to fit a theory of literary history into a theory of the specifically literary, making sure that the theoretical terms of reference are firmly established before any notion of history is introduced. Others tend to evade the issue (one might cite New Criticism or psychoanalytic theories of literature). But since the differences between a work of Chaucer and a work of James Joyce, for example, must, in part at least, be regarded as historical, one may legitimately ask of *all* theories of literature how they will account for these historical differences, how they will define them, and what place they will give them in their overall system. Literary theory may have had good strategic reason for getting rid of history as an interpretative framework, but this does not simultaneously abolish the historical dimensions of literature itself. The question is how to theorize this historical dimension.

The problem of evaluation is a somewhat different one, since value is a far more elusive concept than history. It was traditionally expected of literary studies that its practitioners would tell society which were the good books and which the bad. This is still a common requirement of a newspaper critic, but with the increasing systematization of literary studies (much boosted, needless to say, by the development of literary theory) evaluation has become a rather peripheral aspect of the discipline. In particular, the objective and systematic rigour of literary theory is entirely at odds with the subjective response on which evaluation is thought to depend. However, a few of the theorists discussed in this book, do, none the less, make evaluation a central feature of their systems, and actually elaborate their systems in order to provide criteria for evaluation. For example, I. A. Richards's early work is designed to enable one to account for different degrees of poetic experience; Lukacs's concept of critical realism is explicitly evaluative and serves to justify his preference for Balzac over Zola, or for Thomas Mann over Kafka. But even the more objectively or scientifically formulated theories may imply a preference, if only for the sort of text which is most adequately described by their own analytic concepts. While Roland Barthes does actually specify that his distinction between the *lisible* and the *scriptible* is evaluative, the scientific pretensions of classical structuralism would deny any such purpose; nevertheless one could say that deviation and literary self-consciousness, for instance, are more highly valued in structuralist writing than convention and realism. Similarly, some New Critics' stress on analogy and iconicity inevitably means that poetry is more highly valued than prose in their scheme of things. Whether one regards evaluation as a necessary or desirable part of literary criticism, it seems that any literary theory has its own conscious or sub-conscious system of preferences. The inferences to be drawn from this are not that we could eventually dispense with the critic and submit new texts to some computerized evaluative process, but on the contrary, that we should question the possibility (or even the necessity) of total objectivity and scientificity in literary theory.

We have now sketched out the main questions asked by literary theory, questions which, as we have emphasized, are just as much a part of existing forms of critical and scholarly practice. They will also be very much to the fore in the chapters that follow, in the sense that we shall be keeping them firmly in mind as we expound the different theories we have decided to deal with and compare them with one another. Anyone who has looked at the contents page, however, will already have seen that we have followed a quite different scheme in dividing our material into chapters; that is, the sequence of our exposition does not correspond to the different kinds of question that literary theory asks, but rather follows the development of different schools or movements of thought within the subject. Although, as our title suggests, our constant concern has been to compare different theories with one another, and although we have tried constantly to hold in view the implications of each theory for critical and scholarly practice, there are a number of reasons why we have not adopted in the following chapters the systematic scheme of exposition sketched out in the last few pages.

The most important concerns our view of the nature of the subject. Modern literary theory is anything but monolithic; rather it consists of a multiplicity of competing theories which frequently contradict one another, as the preceding pages may already have shown. A number of recent books on the subject have been written from a single theoretical perspective; but although this obviously makes for clarity of presentation, it seems important that an introduction to literary theory as a whole should reflect the multiplicity of the subject, by adopting a relativistic position and emphasizing the range of possible alternatives that the subject offers (which in any case we have had to do in this particular book, since the four contributors have different views on a number of theoretical questions). Hence the word 'comparative' in our title; throughout the book it is the differences between leading literary theories that we have tried to bring out, without trying to impose our own evaluation of these theories on the reader, though also without avoiding evaluation altogether. Moreover our position is relativistic and not pluralistic; that is, we are not suggesting that the various theories we have dealt with are all compatible with one another, on the assumption which one sometimes meets, that different approaches to literature simply relate to different aspects of the subject, and can therefore all be added together to form a single comprehensive vision. The reader, we would stress, is faced with a choice between conflicting theories, and will not necessarily find the solution to that choice within the confines of literary theory alone.

Given this relativistic position, we could still, of course, have followed the systematic scheme of questions we have outlined, but the effect of this would have been to bewilder the reader with too great a variety of alternatives and open questions. For the sake of clarity and energy of presentation, therefore, we have presented our theories as self-contained systems of thought, and followed a partially chronological order of exposition. The added advantage of this is that it has enabled us to introduce the key concepts of literary theory in connection with the historical contexts in which they were first developed, a feature which, we hope, makes for greater precision. Nevertheless it must be said that as a survey of modern literary theory the book is far from comprehensive. This is due not only to practical considerations of space, but also to the fact that we have decided to focus firmly on what we believe to be the most important, and by that we mean ideas that do most to illuminate, either by clarification or by opposition, established critical and scholarly practice.

As a result we have given particular attention to the question of the specifically literary, and have dealt with a number of conflicting theories that place a high premium on defining literature as a distinct category. But, as our preceding discussion will already have shown, it would be to misrepresent the subject if we were to suggest that the different views it embraces consistently approached literature in this way. Thus after dealing with theories which are clearly strictly literary, in the greater part of our first three chapters, we move on, in the chapters on Parisian structuralism, psychoanalysis and Marxism, to theories whose scope is very considerably broader, and which in some cases make little or no distinction between literature and non-literature. This association of viewpoints of greatly varying scope is a striking feature of modern literary theory, the consequence of which is that one cannot draw a firm boundary between that part of it which is properly literary and that which is not. The subject has annexed a number of theories originally developed in non-literary contexts, and as a result on many sides it merges into other disciplines such as anthropology, psychoanalysis, linguistics or history. Literary theory, we must emphasize, can be thought in a number of different ways; and if, as we have already suggested, it cannot always defend the distinctiveness of its object, literature, this precariousness should be seen as a matter of intellectual adventure, not theoretical bankruptcy.

Finally, although throughout this introduction we have been stressing the connections between literary theory and critical practice, and although we shall keep this connection particularly in mind in the rest of the book, we must make it clear that it is not a matter we have pursued in great detail in our discussion of individual theories in the following chapters. We have preferred to present their practical implications in an open-ended way, without exploring extensively the critical methods which each theory may give rise to. One good reason for doing this is that in the end, even if it is sometimes hard to know exactly where to drawn the line, theory is not the same as method; had we wanted to discuss method in any detail we would have turned to different texts and written a different book. Although certain types of critical practice can be derived from theory, theory cannot determine the precise form and detail of that practice, and the same applies the other way round. Theory may have implications for practice, and practice may help to make sense of theory; but because of the inevitable limitations of abstract language, the two tend necessarily to remain different activities. The machinery of theory cannot be wheeled on as a substitute for criticism, which alone is capable of picking up the nuances and the particular idiom of the work of a given writer. With the current debate about the status and value of literary theory, it is perhaps worth stressing that we are not suggesting that theory should ever replace criticism.

Further Reading

On positivism as a philosopy see the excellent introduction by L. Kolakowski, *Positivist Philosophy from Hume to the Vienna Circle*, and J. S. Mill's *Auguste Comte and Positivism*. There is a substantial discussion of Taine's criticism in Wellek's *A History of Modern Criticism*, vol. IV, pp. 27-57 (where it is argued that Taine is not a positivist in the strict sense). Wellek's essay 'The revolt against positivism in recent European literary scholarship' in *Concepts of Criticism*, pp. 256-81, is a useful survey of the relationship between modern literary theory and the positivist approach. Some of Leavis's most important essays are collected together in *The Common Pursuit*; see also W. Walsh's recent *F. R. Leavis*.

The best-known introduction to literary theory in general is Wellek and Warren's *Theory of Literature*, which offers a systematic though not always very readable discussion of the different aspects of the subject within a general rather than a historical framework. An authoritative but dense and not very up-to-date history of literary theory is *Literary Criticism. A Short History* by Wimsatt and Brooks, and a reasonably comprehensive survey of modern literary theory is to be found in *Theories of Literature in the Twentieth Century* by Fokkema and Kunne-Ibsch. The following books are readable and stimulating inroductions to literary theory from either a structuralist or a Marxist position: Culler's *Structuralist Poetics*, Eagleton's *Marxism and Literary Criticism*, Bennet's *Formalism and Marxism*. On aesthetics see Wollheim, *Art and its Objects* and Osborne (ed.), *Aesthetics*.

1 Russian Formalism
Ann Jefferson

History and practitioners

The earliest beginnings of Russian Formalism can be dated from 1914 with the appearance of Viktor Shklovsky's essay on Futurist poetry, 'The resurrection of the word'. Its final ending, brought about by external political pressure, is marked by Shklovsky's recantation published in January 1930. But the movement had in fact been consistently under attack since 1923 when Trotsky devoted a chapter of his *Literature and Revolution* to a critique of Formalism.

Formalist theory emerged from the meetings, discussions and publications of two small groups of students—the *Opojaz* group based in Petersburg and the Moscow Linguistic Cirle. The Muscovites were primarily linguists who were interested in extending the field of linguistics to cover poetic language, and their best known member is the distinguished linguistic theorist, Roman Jakobson. The *Opojaz* group, as its full title implies (*The Society for the Study of Poetic Language*) consisted of students of literature who were united both by a dissatisfaction with existing forms of literary study and by a positive interest in the poetry of the Russian Futurists. Apart from its leader Viktor Shklovsky, the *Opojaz* group included Boris Eikhenbaum, Osip Brik and Yury Tynyanov. Although there are differences in emphasis in the contributions of individual Formalists, the theoretical value of their work is best understood and appreciated as a collective effort to establish a coherent theoretical basis for literary studies.

After 1930 when the concerted intellectual endeavour came to an end, the work of individual participants ceased to be of any theoretical interest. Most of them abandoned their former preoccupations and devoted themselves instead to less controversial types of literary study, such as text exegesis (Eikhenbaum and Boris Tomashevsky), or, like Shklovsky, actively put themselves at the service of the state-sanctioned literary orthodoxy of socialist realism. The ideas of Russian Formalism survived, however, in the work of the Prague Linguistic Circle, one of whose founders, Roman Jakobson, had left Moscow for Czechoslovakia in 1920. This group came into being in 1926 and disintegrated, also as a result of political events, in 1939. Two of its most important members were Jan Mukařovský and N. S. Troubetzkoy (whose *Principes de phonologie*, published in 1949, was to provide the model for Lévi-Strauss's structural anthropology).

The Czechs were, like the Muscovites before them, primarily linguists, and they did not significantly alter the basic groundwork of Formalist literary theory as it had been developed by the late 1920s. On the whole, their work can be read as a restatement of the late Formalist position. The importance of linguistics in Prague School literary theory will be discussed in the chapter on 'Modern linguistics and the language of literature'.

Although historical events have conspired to seal Russian Formalism off from other intellectual developments in the twentieth century and to give it the character of an isolated and localized phenomenon, it does nevertheless have connections with a variety of more recent theoretical movements. For example, Roman Jakobson and his Prague School colleague René Wellek have had considerable influence on literary studies through their teaching and work in the United States during the last three decades, and, although it carried no explicit theoretical creed, René Wellek's *Theory of Literature* (co-authored with Austin Warren and first published in 1949) was for many years the only widely available explicitly theoretical account of literary studies for Anglo-Saxon students of literature. Second, but perhaps not so much in the form of a survival as in that of a revival, Russian Formalism had a significant part to play in the development of Parisian structuralism during the 1960s (particularly in the work of Todorov and Genette). The structuralist desire to establish a poetics distinct from other academic disciplines, their scientific ideals, and, on a more detailed level, their work on narrative theory, all owe a considerable debt to Russian Formalism.

General theoretical principles
Russian Formalism represents one of the earliest systematic attempts to put literary studies on an independent footing, and to make the study of literature an autonomous and specific discipline. It is therefore of enormous interest to examine the means by which it did so; for it emerged not in order to correct or revise an existing literary theory, but in order to make possible the very notion of such a thing. One may hear echoes of this kind of project in I. A. Richards or the New Critics, but they none of them have the same degree of theoretical rigour and consistency, and they do not take the emphasis on the distinctively literary to the same degree. The Formalists would agree with T. S. Eliot that 'to divert interest from the poet to the poetry is a laudable aim' (1972: 22), but that agreement is expressed in their work as a theoretical system and not just as an intellectual preference. And although they shared I. A. Richards's impatience with the existing chaos of critical theories, and his desire for some scientific order in the study of literature, they would certainly not have endorsed his view that literary theory should be concerned with

experience or with value; nor would they have approved of his recourse to neuro-physiology or psychology as a means of making literary criticism more scientific. The Russian Formalist solution on all these issues is far more radical than the New Critical one. Formalist theory rigorously and systematically excludes the non-literary, so that where the Anglo-American tradition devotes much of its effort to exploring the different relations between life and art, the Russian Formalists see the two as mutual opposites.

The form that literary studies had taken during the second half of the nineteenth century, positivism, was, as we saw in the introduction, largely based on the genetic approach; critics, or rather scholars, concentrated their energies on uncovering the sources and genesis of particular works, and the role of biography, history and history of ideas in these genetic studies obviously reduced the importance of literature itself in literary scholarship. The study of literature had become little more than a loose aggregate of philosophy, history, psychology, aesthetics, ethnography, sociology, and so on, and the Formalists felt that any specificity it might have had had been swamped by its adjacent disciplines. As Jakobson put it, historians of literature had become practitioners of what he called 'homespun' disciplines based on psychology, politics and philosophy, where literature itself could only offer secondary and defective evidence; *Evgeny Onegin* is likely to prove a somewhat unreliable document for the people that Osip Brik called the 'maniacs . . . passionately seeking the answer to the question "did Pushkin smoke?"' (1977: 90).

The efforts of the Russian Formalists were directed towards justifying the independent existence of literary studies, and transforming students of literature into something more than second-rate ethnographers, historians or philosophers. This was not a simple task, for it was not just a question of choosing one approach in preference to another, but of defining the nature of the object to be studied. Formalism, as Eikhenbaum makes plain in his summary of its principles, was neither an aesthetic nor a methodology; it was 'characterized only by the attempt to create an independent science of literature which studies specifically literary material' (1965: 103). So that the first question for the Formalist 'is not *how* to study literature, but *what* the subject matter of literary study actually is' (p. 102, my italics). The way the theory construed its object would determine the nature of the theory itself.

If the Formalist definition of its object was going to allow for the specificity of literary studies, the Formalists regarded it as necessarily entailing the exclusion of all mimetic and expressive definitions of literature. The 'homespun' view of literature had tended to see literature either as an expression of an author's personality and world-vision, or as a mimetic (that is to say, realistic) representation of the world in which he lived; or, most typically, as the mixture of both which Catherine Belsey describes as 'expressive realism' (1980). In regarding the literary text as an instrument of expression or representation, the specificity of its literary qualities is likely to be overlooked. To see a literary work as an expression of the personality of the author leads inevitably to biography and psychology. To regard it as a picture of a given society leads in turn to history, politics or sociology. Even the Symbolist view (which held sway in Russia in the first years of the century) that 'art is thinking in images' cannot be admitted, because although it acknowledges that thought in art takes a different form from conventional philosophy, it will in the end lead the study of art beyond art itself to forms of knowing and feeling, to epistemology and psychology.

An alternative view might posit some quality peculiar to literature which would justify the independent existence of literary studies, but this would reduce the scope of the object of study to a considerable degree, and result in the repetitive sifting of works in search of the one magic ingredient. The Formalist strategy for dealing with the problem of definition not only had the virtue of ensuring that literature could not be reduced to anything else, but proved also to be immensely productive in the elaboration of every aspect of Formalist theory. The Formalist definition of literature is a differential or oppositional one: what constitutes literature is simply its difference from other orders of facts. Indeed the object of literary science turns out not to be an object at all, but a set of differences, and the science will consist in 'the study of those specifics which distinguish it [i.e. literature] from any other material' (Eikhenbaum 1965: 107).

The operative concept in this differential specification is *defamiliarization* or making strange (*ostranenie*). In his early essays on the subject, Shklovsky defines it in a very wide range of terms which, broadly speaking, add up to a view that art refreshes our sense of life and experience. In this he perhaps sounds like a member of a Leavisite 'reverent-openness-before-life' school, but his concept of *ostranenie* already has a certain edge through being defined in opposition to the habitual. According to Shklovsky, art defamiliarizes things that have become habitual or automatic. Walking, for example, is an activity which as we go about in everyday life we have ceased to be aware of; but when we dance the automatically performed gestures of walking are perceived anew. 'A dance is a walk which is felt,' says Shklovsky; 'even more accurately, it is a walk which is constructed to be felt' (1973a: 48). In the case of poetry (the first preoccupation in Formalist thinking) it is ordinary, or what the Formalists call *practical* language that constitutes the main automatized element made strange by art. In ordinary language a word is pronounced automatically, 'tossed out like a chocolate bar from an automatic machine', but the effect of poetry is to make language 'oblique', 'difficult', 'attenuated', 'tortuous'. Everyday language is made strange in poetry, and in particular the physical sounds of words themselves become unusually prominent. This defamiliarized perception of words which in ordinary circumstances we fail to notice is the result of the formal basis of poetry. 'Poetic speech is *formed speech*' because, claims Shklovsky, 'defamiliarization is found almost everywhere form is found' (1965a: 18). Poetic speech does not differ from ordinary speech just because it may include constructions or vocabulary not found in everyday language (the *lo!s thou*s and word-order inversions conventionally allowed in English poetry), but because its formal devices (such as rhyme and rhythm) act on ordinary words to renew our perception of them, and of their sound texture in particular.

In the end, the question of defamiliarization became focused primarily on the issue of language, and this is what gives Formalist theory both its power and its distinctiveness. The examples that Shklovksy's enthusiasm for the idea makes him choose in the early essays are extremely heterogeneous, and this heterogeneity makes him come close to spoiling the unique value of his case. For it is the importance that the Formalists give to language in their theory of literature that enables them to avoid the difficulties and the fuzziness that they had so disliked in their critical and scholarly predecessors. The later extension of the differential principle to non-linguistic issues is modelled on its original linguistic formulation.

For the Formalists, then, the business of literary studies is to analyze the differences implied in the opposition between practical and poetic language, relying on the concept of defamiliarization to bring those differences into focus. It is only by concentrating on the differential element that literary studies can maintain its specific object of study. For by remaining inside a given topic (in this case poetry) without setting it against what it differentiates itself from, the object of one's attention is likely to evaporate. It is impossible to define poetry from within. There are no inherently poetic themes: the poetic subjects of Romantic poetry (moonlight, lakes, nightingales, roses, castles, etc.) have given way in the modern era to the most prosaic and mundane of items. Similarly, poetry cannot be defined just in terms of is devices because these change over time. Poetry can be delineated as a specific area of analysis only by a comparison with what is not poetry.

With the object of literary studies circumscribed on the basis of differentiation and not on that of inherent qualities, it becomes possible both to establish the notion of *literariness*, and to give some kind of scientific status to the study of literature. These two features are central to Formalist theory. Literariness, and not this or that work by this or that author, is the object of literary studies. Or as Jakobson put it, 'The subject of literary science is not literature, but literariness, i.e. that which makes a given work a literary work' (O'Toole and Shukman 1977: 17). It was as a result of studying individual literary works that preceding types of literary study had been led astray into adjacent disciplines. The heterogeneous nature of its object had led to a heterogeneous discipline, and it was only by making literariness the object of its enquiry that literary science could exist as an independent and indeed as a coherent and systematic type of study.

It was the notion of literariness that made Russian Formalism scientific and systematic, and more than an eclectic set of insights into the workings of literature. And it was precisely the coherence of Russian Formalist theory that Tynyanov and Jakobson were still stressing in 1928 in their remarks on 'Problems of research in literature and language'. It was not simply that this or that particular topic might need revision or reassessment, but, they said, 'It is vital for us to turn our back on academic eclecticism . . ., and on the tendency to turn the study of literature and language from a systematic science back once more into a miscellany of episodic and anecdotal essays' (1977: 49). Although in actual practice the Formalists tended to concentrate on the formal qualities of literature, this was because formal devices were taken to be the means whereby defamiliarization was realized. When Jakobson asserted that 'If the science of literature wants to become a real science it will have to recognize "the device" as its sole "hero"' (O'Toole and Shukman 1977: 37), it was because he was concerned with the differential nature of literariness. 'Formalist' was in fact a misnomer for this theoretical enterprise and the term was actually coined not by the group but by their opponents. As Eikhenbaum says, they were 'not "formalists", but, if you like — specifiers' (O'Toole and Shukman 1977: 30). The Formalists' preoccupation with form derived from their preoccupation with the specificity of literariness and never constituted an end in itself.

It is important to appreciate this point when considering the way in which Formalist thinking subsequently developed. The synonymy of literariness and form is a feature of the first phase of Formalism. 'Art as technique' and 'device as sole hero' are principles which the development of the opposition between automatization and de-familiarization gradually altered and refined. Where the early view saw a work of art as the sum total of its devices, the later view took account of the fact that literary devices themselves were subject to the automatization of perception. This means that the habitual/made-strange opposition is now located within literature itself and is no longer co-extensive with the distinction between literature and non-literature. Literariness is a feature not just of form as *impeded speech*, but more importantly, of *impeded form*. As Shklovsky had already pointed out in his essay on 'Art as technique' (although the implications of his remarks were not fully drawn out until later) form and order can themselves act as powerful automatizing factors. The literariness of poetic rhythm, for example, cannot necessarily be ascribed to mere rhythm, but will more likely derive from disruption of the rhythm. 'There is "order" in art, yet not a single column of a Greek temple stands exactly in its proper order; poetic rhythm is similarly disordered rhythm,' explains Shklovsky. And furthermore, 'Should the disordering of rhythm become a convention, it would be ineffective as a device for the roughening of language' (1965a: 24).

It was because of the possibility of literary devices losing their defamiliarizing capacity that the distinction between *device* and *function* was introduced. The defamiliarizing effect of a device does not depend on its existence as a device, but on its function in the work in which it appears. The same device may be used for a variety of potential functions, just as different devices may share a single function. A given work will include passive or automatized elements which are subservient to the defamiliarizing or 'foregrounded' elements. The term 'foregrounding' was developed (chiefly by Tynyanov) as a necessary consequence of the view of the literary text as a system composed of interrelated and interacting elements, in order to distinguish between *dominant* and automatized factors. Whereas the earlier, Shklovskian view had been that form itself was a defamiliarizing agent, this subtler later development introduces a more dynamic and at the same time a more coherent notion of the literary work. As Tynyanov puts it, 'Since a system is not a free interplay of equal elements but presupposes the foregrounding of one group of elements ("a dominant") and the deformation of others, a work becomes literature and acquires its literary function through just this dominant' (O'Toole and Shukman 1977: 34). Both sets of elements are formal, but the work's interest for the Formalist (or rather, the specifier) will lie in the interrelation between the foregrounded and the subservient elements. In other words, the active components of a work are now differentiated not only from practical language but also from other formal components which have become automatized.

This shift of emphasis entails an alteration in the way in which individual works are conceived of. In the earlier view a work was regarded as a more or less arbitrarily agglomerated collection of defamiliarizing devices, but now it becomes important to see it as an entity, a structure or a system where it is the system which determines what the function of a given device will be, whether it will be foregrounded or automatized. (This view of the literary text as a system is developed in the work of the Prague School and is discussed in the next chapter.) This formulation also allows for a rather more subtle and flexible notion of the relationship between the literary and the non-literary. By locating the opposition between defamiliarization and automatization within the work itself, the Formalists were able to maintain the specifically literary nature of their concerns while at the same time avoiding an intransigent art-for-art's-sake position. Since the notion of literariness was not coterminous with the art object, it allowed for the inclusion of non-literary elements in a work without ditching the specificity of literariness. Indeed Jakobson went so far as to claim, 'Neither Tynyanov, nor Shklovsky, nor Mukařovský, nor I have declared that art is a closed sphere . . . What we emphasize is not the separatism of art, but the autonomy of the aesthetic function' (O'Toole and Shukman 1977: 19). It is this autonomy, the dominance of the aesthetic function over the other elements in a work, which justifies the existence of a literary science.

The notion of foregrounding within a literary work formed the basis of Formalist thinking in specific areas of literary studies, namely genre, and more particularly, literary history. I shall be returning to these topics below, but at this stage it should be stressed again that the rather more refined and flexible view of literariness that I have just outlined was derived from the founding principles of Formalism. Literary studies remain a specific and coherent science; literariness still remains its object, and is still constituted by the differential strategy which opposes defamiliarization and automatization.

Implications

Before going on to examine the more detailed contributions of Russian Formalism to specific areas of literary studies, it might be worth pausing to assess the Formalist position by comparing it with the assumptions which it had set out to replace, and which to a certain extent continue to inform (albeit implicitly) critical studies still being produced today. One could ask, therefore, what role is ascribed in Formalist theory to the author, on whom biographical criticism had been based; what had become of the reality which mimetic and historically orientated theories had placed at the centre of their concerns; and finally what function it gives to thought, which had been the focus of philosophically biased criticisms. As we said in the Introduction, the relations between text and author and between text and reality are key elements in any conception of literature. The question of ideas in literature could be regarded as one aspect of the question of reality, being part of literature's 'content', and it was an issue that the Formalists themselves were particuarly keen to confront. The distinctiveness of Formalist theory can, to a large extent, be appreciated by seeing what place these three factors are given in it.

First, then, the author. With literariness and not individual works of literature forming the object of literary studies, the status of the author underwent a radical change. As Osip Brik put it, *'Opojaz proposes that there are no poets or literary figures, there is poetry and literature'* (1977: 90). This stricture is one that has been variously repeated in a large number of literary and critical theories in this century. For example, T. S. Eliot's remarks about poetry being 'not the expression of a personality, but an escape from personality' seem to anticipate Brik's bold words. But the way in which the New Critics developed Eliot's axiom did not entirely do away with the author: instead, by shifting his position from the outside to the inside of the text, they merely justified a shift in methodology from the biographical to the words-on-the-page approach. The importance that the New Critics attribute to meaning and to vision necessitates the continued existence of the author. For the Formalists, by contrast, literature has nothing to do with vision or with authorial meaning. A given work of literature is related for them to literature in general, and not to the personality of its author. The author becomes nothing more than an expert at his job, a craftsman, and the means whereby literature develops in a more or less autonomous way. (This view closely anticipates that of Pierre Macherey whose work is discussed in the chapter on Marxism.) *Evgeny Onegin* would have been written even if Pushkin had never existed, claims Brik, just as America would have been discovered without Columbus. The poet is no longer regarded as a visionary or a genius; he becomes a skilled worker who arranges, or rather, rearranges the material that he happens to find at his disposal. The author's job is to know about literature; what he might or might not know about life is irrelevant to that job.

This view is more than a particularly extreme form of the New Critics' attack on the 'intentional fallacy.' But it is a logical consequence of the basic principles of Formalist theory, and in particular of the Formalist view of literary history and the distinction between practical and poetic language. Literary history will be discussed in greater detail below, but, briefly stated, a historical view of literature follows inevitably from the recognition of the fact that the perceptibility of given literary conventions or devices tends to decrease over time. New works have to revive the perceptibility of literature either by defamiliarizing over-familiar techniques (as in the case of parody) or else by foregrounding a previously non-functional device. In other words, changes in literature depend not on the personal circumstances or the psychological make-up of an author, but on the pre-existing forms of literature. For the Formalists originality is constituted only by a reworking of the available devices and not by a personal vision in the lived experience of writers. In this scheme of things there is obviously no place for the biographies and personalities of the producers of literary works.

It is ruled out equally by the Formalist opposition between practical and poetic language. They see the 'set' or emphasis in practical language as being on the referent, the reality referred to, and any potentially poetic features (such as rhyme or alliteration) as remaining subservient to the communicative aim. By contrast, in poetic language referentiality is irrelevant and the emphasis is on the means of expression itself. Because of this, a poetic utterance has no functional ties with the real context in which it is produced and cannot be assumed to refer to any aspect of its producer's existence. Although there are similarities between emotionally expressive utterances and poetic language, particularly in the importance of phonic elements, there remains a fundamental difference behind the superficial resemblance of the two: emotional speech is governed by its speaker's affect, whereas poetic language is governed by its own immanent laws. Language in poetry does not point to an object beyond itself, nor does it carry any emotional weight from its speaker; it is entirely self-sufficient, or, as the Formalists would say, 'self-valuable'. So the differential gesture which constitutes literature excludes the speaker from the very outset; the object of literary science is an authorless literariness.

All this rules out any causative connection between biography and literature, but there are cases where the Formalists allow biography a legitimate literary function. On the one hand it would be perfectly in order to write the biography of a poet as long as it is understood that it would be 'on a par with biographies of generals and inventors' (Tomashevsky 1978: 55) and was not mistaken for literary science. On the other hand, there are instances where biography can become a 'literary fact'. Although there are many periods in the history of literature where biography is quite irrelevant (Shakespeare is an exemplarily anonymous figure in literature), there are also periods where biography becomes an integral element of literary works. One has only to think of the Romantic period where poets became their own heroes, and their lives were seen as part of their poetic output. But in these cases the life was a product of the poetry, and not vice versa. Tomashevsky cites Pushkin as an example of someone who 'poetically fostered certain facts of his life' (1978: 50). He liked the idea of a hidden and unrequited love set against a backdrop of Crimean scenery, and he developed this theme both in his poetry and in his life. He began writing to his friends:

in an ambiguous and enigmatic tone about unrequited love. In conversation, he became prone to mysteriously incoherent outpourings. And behold, the poetic legend of a 'concealed love' was created with its ostentatious devices for concealing love, when it would have been much simpler to keep silent.

The life is as much a fiction as the poetry and becomes a kind of secondary creation against which the primary one may be read. Poets like Pushkin:

> used their lives to realize a literary purpose, and these literary biographies were necessary for the readers. The readers cried: 'Author! author!'—but they were actually calling for the slender youth in a cloak, with a lyre in his hands and an enigmatic expression on his face. This demand for a potentially existing author, whether real or not, gave rise to a special kind of anonymous literature: literature with an invented author, whose biography was appended to the work. (Tomashevsky 1978: 51).

Formalist literary science will use these legendary biographies as literary facts where relevant, but would never regard them as anything other than the by-products of a certain literary practice. The geneticists' error was to assume that the biographies were 'real' and were the primary cause and origin of the written literary text. Indeed, the biographers' determination to establish the identity of the woman Pushkin claimed to love so hopelessly has resulted in the destruction of its legendary status, and consequently of its constructive role in the reading of the poetry. On this question, then, the Formalists reverse the traditional relationship between biography and literature, making the author a product rather than the source of literary works.

Turning now to the question of the place assigned to reality in Formalist theory. Here again, the traditional priority of reality over literature is reversed; where it is an axiomatic principle that literature is derived from other literature and not from any non-literary source, reality becomes irrelevant to the writing and analysis of literature. In the Formalist view, a change in literary form is not determined by a changed reality, but by the need to refresh automatized forms of literature. The renewed perception of formal devices is an essential aspect of literariness, and the criterion of verisimilitude is irrelevant to the Formalist project. The Formalists evaluate literary form for its perceptibility and not for its mimetic capacity.

In his early discussion of defamiliarization Shklovsky chooses a number of examples which imply that the business of art is to restore our perception of the world outside art, 'to make one feel things, to make the stone *stony*' (1965a: 12). This restoration of the sense of life may well be an effect frequently produced by techniques of making strange, but Shklovsky makes it clear that in the end the object itself is not important, but merely a pretext for art. It is literariness and not mimesis which interests the Formalists. Ultimately defamiliarisation is a question of form and only of form. Most innovators in art invoke realism as a justification for a mode of writing which is primarily literary. But realism itself is just a matter of convention; for some people it is the defamiliarized codes which seem realistic, whereas for others it is the traditional devices which convey a sense of reality, and no one device is inherently more realistic than another. Like the legendary biographies of the Romantic poets, realism is at best a by-product of art and not its raison d'être.

The role played by reality in the construction of literature is only secondary and subservient. It enters into the work as one of the givens with which the artist begins. Reality is at his disposal in the same way that ordinary language and the current literary conventions and devices are. It is one of the components of the work and not a referent of it (literature has no referents). As Jakobson puts it in paraphrase of Mallarmé, 'la fleur poétique est l'absente de tous bouquets' (lit. 'the poetic flower is not the one to be found in any bouquet'). And where a work appears to refer to some external reality (where the flowers seem, as it were, to be present) the Formalists would regard this as a mere side-effect of the aesthetic function. Shklovsky calls this realistic side-effect 'motivation', which he contrasts to the laying bare of the device. In literature either a device is presented exclusively for its defamiliarizing effect, or else it may be motivated—that is to say its presence as a device is disguised by a veneer of realism. This makes all realism an incidental by-product of a certain kind of writing, and not the direct imitation of reality.

Much of the same reversal of priorities applies to the third question, ideas in literature. Meaning is not an issue that arises for the Russian Formalists, and it is here that they differ most fundamentally from the American New Critics with whom they otherwise have so many similarities. The American New Critics and I.A. Richards before them were as anxious as the Formalists to sever literature from its historical and biographical context, and their preoccupation with form and technique has many points of analogy with that of their Formalist counterparts. But for the New Critics art existed in order to convey a meaning, albeit a meaning that no logical discourse is capable of expressing, and attention to matters of form was regarded as the means whereby the non-rational meanings of literature could be uncovered. But for the Formalists meaning and ideas are neither here nor there; like reality, they enter into literature as part of the available material which is then put to literary use by the functional devices of the work. As Jakobson put it, 'we are dealing in essence not with thought but with verbal facts.'

It seems clear then that the Formalist position on all these issues (authors, reality and ideas) is not just an arbitrary preference, but that it stems from the concepts of defamiliarisation and literariness, whose differential basis will always serve to define literature in opposition to the things that it was traditionally viewed as expressing. The exclusion of authors, reality and thought from their central position in literature was part of a purification of the notion of literature which entails a radical alteration of one of the most deeply ingrained concepts in thinking about literature: the distinction between form and content.

Briefly put, Russian Formalism did away with the distinction between form and content, and in its interest in form succeeded in attributing a totally new function to it. In fact the terms 'form' and 'content' ceased to be operative and were replaced (in so far as it makes sense to speak of replacement) by the distinction between 'material' and 'device'. But the significance of what was at stake in this shift in terminology needs to be spelled out.

Traditionally form was considered to be a sort of 'decorative supplement' which provided the entertainment value while the business of instruction (associated with the content) went ahead. Or, to use another analogy, form was a vessel into which content could be poured, the same vessel being theoretically capable of receiving a variety of different contents. And if the form changed, it was as a response to the exigencies of content. All this put the emphasis on the content and was consequently responsible for the heterogeneous nature of literary studies. Formalist theory reversed the priority of content over form and devoted its attention exclusively to form. Content then becomes dependent on form (as the discussion of biography, reality and thought will have shown), and has no separate existence in literature. Literary analysis cannot extrapolate content from form, and form is determined not by content but by other forms. But the crucial factor that is obscured by continuing to use these terms is the dynamic and interactive relationship that exists between material and device. Devices act on their material and in putting raw materials to a certain use often transform their appearance. Jakobson uses a culinary example in his discussion of the question which nicely complements the vessel-liquid image which is so often implied in the form-content distinction. 'Poeticity', he says, is like oil in cooking; you cannot have it on its own but when it is used with other food it is more than a mere addition. It changes the taste of food to the extent that some dishes no longer appear to have any connection with their oil-less counterparts: a fresh sardine, for example, is quite different from one which has been transformed by being preserved in oil (a point implied by the existence in the Czech language of two quite different words for the fresh and the oil varieties: a sardine in oil is called *olejovka*, from *olej*=oil). The defamiliarizing principle in art has exactly the same effect on its material 'ingredients': it subordinates and transforms the way they are in non-literary circumstances. For example, the word *sardine* in a poem would cease to function as a substitute for the thing itself, and instead its linguistic features would be 'maximally foregrounded'. Like Mallarmé's poetic flower, the fish to which the word normally refers would be lost from sight.

The dynamic principle implied in the material/device distinction means that elements of form itself can be included in the concept of material. Outworn devices which are no longer functional in the defamiliarization process are as much a part of the work's material as ideas or aspects of real life. The opposition between automatism and making strange which underlies the one between material and device draws a line in a quite different place from the line that separates form from content. Indeed, it can draw the line in such a way as to make synonyms of the terms form and content. For example, when a work is constructed in order to lay bare all its devices form itself becomes the content. In Shklovsky's view, Sterne's *Tristram Shandy* consists of a series of violations of literary conventions which draw our attention to the forms of fiction; in so doing it transforms formal questions into content. In Shklovsky's words, 'awareness of form constitutes the subject-matter of the novel' (1965b: 35).

This radical redistribution of the terms form and content follows inevitably from the principle of defamiliarization and perceptible form. Once form is foregrounded it becomes impossible to speak of any other content except form itself.

Poetry, prose and literary history

Although the object of Formalist literary science was literariness and not individual works of literature, one of the principal consequences of the Formalists' interest in literariness was an increased awareness of genre. Literariness being defined as the difference between automatism and defamiliarization, it was soon perceived that it was not constructed in the same way in all works, and that the devices manifesting difference in prose narrative were not the same as the devices manifesting difference in lyric poetry. Poetry and narrative are constructed from quite different 'dominants' or 'genre-markers'. And in fact what marks the two genres off from each other is not so much the nature of the devices, but the nature of the opposition which constructs them as literature. The operative differentiation in poetry is between practical and poetic language, but this is obviously likely to be less pertinent to prose. Here the opposition isolated by the Formalists is between what they call *fabula* and *syuzhet,* and concerns the organization and the presentation of the narrative (more of this later). It was in these two areas (poetry and prose narrative) that Formalism made most of its practical contributions to the study of literature.

Poetry was the starting point for Formalist literary theory, and it lent itself in a very obvious way to the differential definition of literariness. Poetry, says Jakobson, is 'organized violence committed on ordinary speech' (Erlich 1980: 219), and Formalist work on poetry covers three main areas where this violence is carried out. The primary one is sound texture. The violence here consists in the foregrounding of the phonic aspect of ordinary speech, which in normal communication remains subservient to the referential 'set' of utterances. Poetry is 'speech organized in its entire phonic texture' (Erlich 1980: 212), and not just ordinary speech with added musical embellishment. The Formalists maintained that there are a variety of devices in poetry which have the effect of 'roughening' or 'impeding' pronunciation. An early contribution to Formalist analysis of poetry by Leo Jakubinsky reveals a marked presence in poetry of 'hard-to-pronounce conglomerations of similar sounds' (Shklovsky 1965: 19). However, it is not just that poetry may differ statistically from ordinary language, but, more significantly, that the devices of poetry foreground phonic elements that are usually ignored in practical speech. The adoption of a new metric form, for example, frequently has a roughening effect on the sounds of ordinary language: Pushkin reports that General Ermolov ended up with a stiff jaw after reading poetry by Griboyedov.

Second, the effect of the laws of rhythm in poetry is to set up a tension between two different principles of word combination: syntax, which determines it in ordinary language, and rhythm, which constitutes a second determining principle in poetry. A full understanding of poetry requires that both principles are seen to be at work, for to analyze the laws of poetry without taking account of those of ordinary language would be to overlook the specifically verbal nature of poetry and to transform it from the domain of language to that of music. Equally, to ignore the constraints of poetry would be to 'destroy the poetic line as a specific, verbal structure based on those facets of the word which retreat into the background in ordinary speech' (Brik 1978: 124). So once again the emphasis is not on poetry in itself, but on the *difference* between poetry and ordinary language.

The third aspect of ordinary language which is violated by poetry is semantics. Poetry differs from ordinary language in that it activates the secondary or collateral meanings of a word simultaneously, a strategy which would disrupt ordinary communication, which depends on the absence of ambiguity through there being only one functional meaning for a word. As Eikhenbaum puts it 'as words get into verse they are, as it were, taken out of ordinary speech. They are surrounded by a new aura of meaning' (1965: 129). This seems to be familiar Anglo-American territory, and to evoke New Critical or Empsonian ambiguity. But the Formalists did not share the New Critics' view of poetry as paradox or resolution of contradictions, since they were not interested in poetry's meaning. And, even more importantly, the Formalists differ radically from the Anglo-Americans on the way in which they relate poetic ambiguity to ordinary language, and it is this differential function and not any as one of conformity and intensification whereby poetry heightens and enriches ordinary communication. The Russian Formalists would, on the contrary, want to stress the differences between the two types of language, poetic language being defined at every level (including the semantic) in opposition to practical or ordinary language.

In every case, then, the devices of poetry are studied not for themselves, but for their defamiliarizing capacity. Image, hyperbole, parallelism, comparison, repetition or any other trope are all potentially equally effective in committing poetic violence on ordinary language, and it is this differential function and not any inherent quality that constitutes their interest for Russian Formalism.

The Formalists' approach to prose narrative was, to a certain extent, predetermined by their original interest in poetry. Shklovsky's ingenious attempts to draw parallels between poetic devices and devices of plot construction show how far Formalist literary theory did indeed have its roots in poetry. However, despite the ingenuity of Shklovsky's efforts, it became clear that the differential principle behind poetry could not be very extensively or very effectively applied to prose, and the functional opposition had to be constructed on rather different lines. In broad terms, the Formalist study of narrative was based on a distinction between the events on the one hand and the construction on the other, between the *fabula* and the *syuzhet*. *Fabula* (sometimes translated as plot) refers to the chronological sequence of events, and *syuzhet* to the order and manner in which they are actually presented in the narrative. Because of the difficulty of finding precise equivalents in English, I shall follow the common practice of sticking to the original Russian term.

The relation between the *fabula* and the *syuzhet* is roughly analogous to the one between practical and poetic language. The *syuzhet* creates a defamiliarizing effect on the *fabula;* the devices of the *syuzhet* are not designed as instruments for conveying the *fabula,* but are foregrounded at the expense of the *fabula.* These devices can vary enormously in nature and scope: from the overall presentation of narrative structure down to linguistic play. Eikhenbaum's essay on Gogol's *Overcoat* is a good example of the latter. He sets out to show that in Gogol's tale 'the centre of gravity is transferred from the theme...to the devices' (1963: 377). The dynamic principle in the construction of the tale is not in the events narrated but in their manner of presentation. And this manner itself is determined not so much by the putative character of its narrator, but by puns and other verbal sound effects which result in the breaking up and displacement of the reality which may appear to be their starting point. So that the *fabula,* such as it is in this tale, is the product of certain purely

31

linguistic devices.

A more quintessentially Formalist approach to narrative is contained in Shklovksy's essay on *Tristram Shandy*. This novel, with its chaotic narrative order and its prominent self-conscious authorial commentary, is an ideal example for the Formalists of the privileging of the *syuzhet* over the *fabula*. The Formalist principle whereby 'the forms of art are explainable by the laws of art; they are not justified by their realism' (Shklovsky 1965b: 57) is manifest in almost every aspect of Sterne's novel and does not have to be inferred from it by analysis (as perhaps it does in Gogol's *Overcoat*). The constructional devices are laid bare and not motivated by the events or situations in the story. The *fabula* is repeatedly disrupted by such *syuzhet* devices as the transposition of material (the preface does not appear until Volume III, Chapter 20), temporal displacements which reveal effects before causes, the inclusion of secondary anecdotes and the proclivity towards digressions of various kinds. But perhaps the most striking of all the devices are the frequent self-conscious comments made by the author, laying bare his devices precisely by pointing out the differences between *fabula* and *syuzhet*, as, for example, in the following:

> Is is not a shame to make two chapters of what passed in going down one pair of stairs? for we are got no farther yet than to the first landing, and there are fifteen more steps down to the bottom; and for aught I know, as my father and my uncle *Toby* are in a talking humour, there may be as many chapters as steps.

In *Tristram Shandy* (and in the O.Henry stories discussed in another essay by Eikhenbaum) the devices are laid bare to such an extent that there remains hardly any motivation for the much diminished *fabula*. This degree of self-consciousness is rare in literature, but it is nevertheless based on the opposition between *fabula* and *syuzhet*, and it is on this opposition that the literariness of all prose narrative rests.

This view of prose narrative is rather different from the one implied in the Anglo-American tradition which, in its reading of fiction has systematically subordinated questions of *syuzhet* to questions of realism. Where form has been an issue in this tradition, such as with narrative point of view in Henry James, it has been subsumed into more conventional questions such as theme and moral vision: form becomes a means of conveying these other questions. And where technical qualities are very obtrusive, as in Joyce's *Ulysses*, the novel is dismissed by this tradition as a 'dead-end, or at least as pointer to disintegration' (Leavis 1962: 36). Adopting a Formalist approach to the nineteenth-century realist novel would certainly involve a thorough-going change of mental habit, and the critic would have to work harder than he does when reading Joyce to see round the *fabula* and the realistic motivation; but this is not to say that it might not produce some interesting results. Its applicability to the eighteenth-century novel seems, on the other hand, to be less questionable, and one can equally well see its revelance to twentieth-century writers like John Fowles.

The third area of practical contributions made by the Russian Formalists — literary history — represents a third differential opposition for the specification of the literary. Where poetry involved the distinction between ordinary and poetic language, and narrative that between what one might call literary form and its non-literary content, literary history as conceived by the Formalists entails a distinction between automatized and perceptible form within literature itself. This differential element in literary history marks it off quite radically from previous accounts of the historical dimension in literature. The genetic view might at first sight appear to constitute a supremely historical way of thinking about literature, as the literary text was explained in terms of its causes and its origins. But the view it implied of literature as a whole was ultimately a non-historical one. By taking only 'the greats' and dealing with them as isolated phenomena, conventional literary critics and scholars failed to convey any sense of the overall historical development of literature.

The conventional notion of literary 'tradition' does, it is true, compensate for the lack of an historical overview, but because it implies a common pool of resources repeatedly drawn on by a succession of different writers, it is profoundly antithetical to Formalism and its key principle of defamiliarization. Indeed, for the Formalists, '"literary language"...and its development cannot be understood as a planned development of tradition, but rather as *colossal displacements of traditions'* (Tynyanov 1978c: p. 144, my italics). Literariness is a product of the deformation of the canonized or automatized elements, in other words of precisely those factors which constitute a tradition. Form is made perceptible against a background of existing literary form,and the function of a device is determined not just by the structural hierarchy of a particular work, but by its place in the literary system as a whole. The principle of defamiliarization simultaneously undoes the idea of tradition and reintroduces an historical dimension in the relationship between individual literary device and the overall system. Discontinuity replaces continuity as the basis of historical progression. The fact that the specificity of literary science is constituted by literariness means that an historical dimension is inevitably brought into play. In contrast both to the genetically based view of literary history which tends to ignore questions of form, and to other formally-biased approaches which tend to ignore history, the Russian Formalist view is that it is history itself which allows the specificity of literature to be established.

Roughly speaking, the Formalists see two complementary forces at work in the evolution of literature. The first concerns the dominant devices in a particular genre and/or period. As time goes by these devices become familiar and cease to be perceptible. When this stage has been reached a new work will pick them up and, usually by parodic means, make them perceptible again as devices. This is what happens in the O.Henry stories, for example. The conventionality of particular devices is made palpable by ironic comments from the author—such as: 'Thus, by the commonest article of the trade, having gained your interest, the action of the story will now be suspended, leaving you grumpily to consider a sort of doll biography beginning fifteen years before' (Eikhenbaum 1978: 255). This draws attention to the formal strategies behind the opening scenes in stories and to the conventional basis of the 'doll biographies' that accompany the presentation of the major characters. It is by making form perceptible through this parodic treatment of devices that a genre evolves.

The other evolutionary principle concerns the introduction of devices from marginal or popular genres into the mainline of literary development to replace outworn ones. Dostoyevsky, for instance, raises the devices of what Shklovsky calls the boulevard novel to the status of a literary norm, and Chekhov transfers features from comic magazines into Russian literary prose. This too is a profoundly discontinuous evolutionary mode. The succession passes 'not from father to son, but from uncle to nephew' (O'Toole and Shukman 1977: 42) in a series of defamiliarizing displacements. Literary history is no longer a causal explanation of masterpieces in world literature, nor a continuous tradition. It is a major enterprise in Russian Formalist poetics, because ultimately 'the task of literary history…is precisely to reveal form' (Tynyanov 1978b: 132).

In stressing the ubiquity of the differential principle in all aspects of Russian Formalist thought one runs the risk of implying that the coherence of the theory is the result of an intellectual *parti pris,* and that the intention on the part of the Formalists was to establish a fixed dogmatic system. However, the astonishing consistency of Formalist theory cannot in any way be attributed to the pressure of orthodoxy within the group. Individually they were always at pains to stress the provisional nature of the conceptual apparatus, and their flexibility can be seen in the way in which the theory evolved to include new topics such as narrative and literary history. As Eikhenbaum so firmly insists: '[they] were not advocates of a method, but students of an object' (1965: 131). It is in fact this object (literariness) and the way in which it was defined that guarantees the coherence of the science. The insistence on specificity (both of the science and of its object) and its basis in a differential strategy proved not only to be enormously productive and adaptable, but also remarkably consistent. Moreover, a number of the major aspects of Formalist theory prove to have anticipated, if not directly influenced, some of the most important ideas in twentieth-century literary theory. The central position of language, the devaluing of the biographical element, the notion of a science of literature, and the importance placed on the deviation from the norm constitute some of the main recurrent features of literary theory from Jakobson to Barthes.

These, then, are the strengths of the theory. As to its shortcomings, these derive, in the main, from its exclusive concern with the literary. The non-literary elements against which the literary is differentially defined are insufficiently theorized. The Formalists have no developed theory of language and no theory of culture and society, and this lack poses certain limitations on their theory of literature. The theoretical sophistication of the literary half of their equation is not matched in the non-literary part of it. In Formalist theory we are dealing with a very limited and pre-Saussurean view of language, and we shall see in the next chapter how much more subtlety and refinement a theoretically consistent view of language can bring to literary theory—as in the case of Roman Jakobson's six-function model. And we shall see, furthermore, in the chapter on structuralism how far a Saussurean or semiotic theory of language in particular opens up the scope of literary theory, because it provides a means of theorising non-literary reality as well as literature itself.

Marxist criticism of Russian Formalism has concentrated parti-cularly strongly on the absence of any social dimension in their conception of literature. The main thrust of the interesting critique of Formalism made by the Bakhtin school (discussed below in the chapter on Marxism) is based on the claim that all use of language, including a literary use, is both social and ideological. The advantage of this argument is that it allows one to define literature's relation to reality in a much more positive and coherent way: both literature and the reality which it represents are of the same order and, according to Bakhtin, this order is ideological. But although literature is necessarily ideological, its qualities as literature have a distancing effect on the ideologies that it represents, and so allow the reader to become aware of them as ideologies. The structuralist view of language also yields a much more flexible and wide-ranging view of the relationship between literature and reality. Both literature and social or cultural reality are defined by structuralist theory in semiotic terms, so that (as in the Bakhtinian theory) they are seen as belonging to the same order. At the same time for most structuralist theorists, literature still retains its distinctiveness through its peculiar linguistic awareness—a premise which, again, depends on a relatively complex theory of language.

In other words, although the Formalists took a very important step in making language central to their definition of literature, their theoretical shortcomings could largely be attributed to their failure to extend a theory of language to other spheres. Their idea of reality remains trapped in the cultural viewpoint which their theory of literature was trying to replace, and the difficulties which this led to can be most clearly seen in their theory of literary history: despite their innovatory definition of literary history as a discontinuous series, they were unable to explain how literary history related to other historical series. Had they had a more sophisticated social and cultural theory, they would have been in a much better position to address themselves to this problem.

The vulnerability of Russian Formalism on this score seems, therefore, to suggest two important things: first, that any theory of literature, however specifically literary, needs to develop an adequate theory of non-literary issues; and second, that an adequate theory of language is likely to be of enormous help in doing so.

Further Reading

This account has been based largely on the existing English translations of Russian Formalist writing: *Russian Formalist Criticism: Four Essays,* ed. Lee T. Lemon and Marion J. Reis, whose contents provide the best general introduction to the subject and whose own introductory essays offer useful background; *Readings in Russian Poetics: Formalist and Structuralist Views,* ed. Ladislav Matejka and Krystyna Pomorska, which contains essays illustrating the implications of the general theory in more detail; *Russian Formalism,* ed. Stephen Bann and John E. Bowlt, a mixture of Formalist texts in translation and articles on Formalist theory; and finally, *Russian Poetics in Translation,* vols 4 and 5, which are devoted to Formalism. Vol. 4 is an essential working tool for study of the subject as, apart from some useful texts, it contains an invaluable contextual glossary of Formalist terms and a bibliography of Formalist writing in translation.

These English translations may be supplemented by French and German ones, namely: *Théorie de la littérature: Textes des Formalistes russes,* ed. Tzvetan Todorov, and Roman Jakobson, *Questions de poétique,* in French; *Texte der russischen Formalisten,* Band I: *Texte zur allgemeinen Literaturtheorie und zur Theorie der Prosa,* ed. Jurij Striedter, and *Texte der russischen Formalisten,* Band II: *Texte zur Theorie des Verses und der poetischen Sprache,* ed. W.-D. Stempel, in German.

The discussion of Russian Formalism in this chapter has not included consideration of the work of Vladimir Propp on the folktale or (in any detail) of the Bakhtin school, all of whom appear in some of the collections of Formalist writing. This omission was made for reasons of coherence, since their work does not follow the theoretical principles of the Formalists proper. The Bakhtin school is discussed in Chapter 6 below. Propp's main work is *The Morphology of the Folktale.*

For examples of Prague School structuralism see the Further Reading section in Chapter 3.

The best introductory account of Russian Formalism is Victor Erlich, *Russian Formalism: History — Doctrine,* which when it was first published in 1955 was the only source of information about Russian Formalism for non-Russian speakers.

There are also two very lively and illuminating accounts of Russian Formalism, whose merit is due to the fact that they examine Formalist theory in the light of one or two specific issues and compare it in each case to another major literary theory. They are: Tony Bennett, *Formalism and Marxism,* which evaluates Russian Formalism on the question of the specificity of literature in relation to Marxism and ideological criticism; and Fredric Jameson, *The Prison-House of Language,* which analyzes the role of the linguistic model for Russian Formalism and for structuralism.

For more specialist and and more explicitly committed approaches of this kind, see P. N. Medvedev/M. M. Bakhtin, *The Formal Method in Literary Scholarship: An Introduction to Sociological Poetics,* for the Bakhtinian critique of Russian Formalism; and Hans Robert Jauss, 'Literary History as a Challenge to Literary Theory' in *New Directions in Literary History,* ed. Ralph Cohen, which elaborates a new view of literary history on the basis of the Russian Formalist approach.

For any further reading see the bibliography of translations and commentaries in *Russian Poetics in Translation,* vol. 4.

2 Modern Linguistics and the Language of Literature

David Robey

The relationship between linguistics and literature has been one of the most widely discussed issues in modern literary theory. Indeed of the many disciplines that have contributed to the growth of modern literary theory, linguistics is almost certainly the most important. This is a consequence of major developments in both literary practice and in the study of language. On the literary side, in the course of the century or so that has passed since the Symbolist movement in France, both poetry and, to a lesser extent, literary prose have been characterized by a degree of linguistic innovation unknown in most earlier periods. The language of 'modernist' writing is, typically, difficult and challenging; it makes considerable demands on the reader, and even greater demands on the critic. Since the late nineteenth century it has thus become increasingly difficult for critics interested in contemporary literature to ignore problems of linguistic form. At the same time linguistics has evolved in a direction that has increased enormously its explanatory potential for literary studies. Nineteenth-century linguistics was mainly interested in the ways in which languages change across the ages; modern 'structural' linguistics prefers, in contrast, to concentrate on the ways in which they function for purposes of communication. Since literature, whatever else it might be, is undoubtedly a form of communication, this development is obviously an extremely important one as far as literary studies are concerned.

The reason why linguistics has had such importance for literary theory, however, is not just that a change of direction has taken place in the development of the discipline. It is also to be found in the special character of the theory of language which more than any other was responsible for this development, that of the Swiss philologist and professor of linguistics Ferdinand de Saussure (1857—1913). The implications of this theory are so powerful that the impact of modern linguistics on literary studies has not been limited to problems of literary language alone, but has produced new theories of the nature and organization of literature as a whole and indeed of all social and cultural life. With his concept of the linguistic sign Saussure created the basis of structuralism, both in linguistics and as a more broadly based movement of thought, in which all forms of social and cultural life are seen to be governed by systems of signs which are either linguistic or analogous to those of language.

Saussure explained his concept of the sign in a series of lectures given in Geneva between 1906 and 1911 and published posthumously from his students' notes under the title *Cours de linguistique générale*. In view of the importance of this work for modern literary theory I shall deal with it in some detail in the pages that follow. I shall then discuss two theories of literary language and of the literary text as a whole, which were developed under the joint influence of Saussure and the Russian Formalists. In conclusion I shall consider four alternative approaches to problems of literary language in which the influence of Saussure and the Formalists is less strongly felt, though the impact of modern linguistics is still clear. My aim will be to illustrate different ways of approaching literature through its linguistic form, ways involving the direct application of linguistic theory and linguistic methods of analysis in order to illuminate the specifically literary character of texts. Later, in the chapter on modern French structuralism, we shall see how Saussure's concept of the linguistic sign can lead to theories of the *non*-linguistic aspects of literature as well as of its language. There we shall be dealing not so much with direct applications of linguistic theory as with extensions or analogies of it.

Saussure: the concept of the sign

Saussure's fundamental proposal is that languages are *systems*, constituted by *signs* that are *arbitrary* and *differential*. A linguistic sign consists in the union of two elements, a sound-image (or its written substitute) and a concept; for the first the term *signifier* is used, for the second *signified (signifiant* and *signifié)*. For instance, the sound 'tree' that I hear is the signifier, to which there corresponds a signified *tree* in the sense of the concept that the sound evokes in my mind. The sign made up of these two elements is arbitrary for two reasons: because, more obviously, the association of a signifier (the sound-image 'tree') with a signified (the concept *tree*) is, except in a very few cases, fundamentally the product of linguistic convention, not of any natural link; and, less obviously, because there is also no natural or necessary relationship between the sign as a whole and the reality to which it refers.

This second postulate, the most radical and fertile feature of Saussure's thought, rests on the idea of an essential disjunction between the world of reality and the world of language. Words articulate our experience of things, they do not just express or reflect it; they give form to what, without language and other sign-systems, would merely be a chaotic and undifferentiated jumble of ideas; instead of things determining the meaning of words, words determine the meaning of things. Thus the signified *tree* is not the expression or

39

reflection or product of the series of vegetable objects to which it is conventionally attached in English usage. Rather, it is entirely by virtue of the sign in question that we distinguish a class of objects *trees* from other objects such as bushes, etc. It follows from this that signifier and signified are effectively inseparable, like the two sides of a single sheet of paper. Not only can we not recognize sounds as linguistic units unless concepts are attached to them; we also cannot entertain concepts independently of their physical manifestations, without, that is, evoking in our minds the verbal forms to which they are attached.

Saussure illustrates these principles with a diagram (1974: 112), which may help to clarify his point:

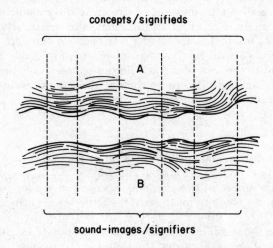

The two bands of wavy lines A and B stand for what in a pre-linguistic state would be two continua: respectively an 'indefinite plane of jumbled ideas' and 'the equally vague plane of sounds'. What language does, as represented by the dotted lines, is divide or articulate these continua, thereby creating the sound-images and concepts which, when bonded together, we recognize as words. To put Saussure's point in a different way, we can take as an illustration an area of language to which he did not pay particular attention, but which subsequent theorists have considered significant: that of colour terminology. Clearly the colour spectrum is a continuum which is divided up into distinct units by colour terms. If we did not have certain terms, for instance if we did not have a word 'orange' as well as a word 'yellow', it is easy to imagine that we would not have a concept of the corresponding colours; indeed the fact that there is nothing natural or necessary about colour terms is proved, as one of Saussure's successors argued (Hjelmslev 1961: 52ff.) by the fact that different languages divide up the colour spectrum differently. We can restate Saussure's argument by saying that he is taking colour terminology as paradigmatic for all language; just as colour terms impose arbitrary divisions on the continuous spectrum of light waves, so all other words impose arbitrary divisions on the 'indefinite plane of jumbled ideas' which, without language, would constitute our mental experience.

If the relationship between sign and reality is not natural but arbitrary, how are we to understand the sign's ability to signify, the capacity of language to generate meaning? Saussure's answer is that the function of the sign depends exclusively on its relationship with, or more exactly its difference from, other signs. 'Arbitrary and differential are two correlative qualities' (1974: 118). We identify words not by virtue of any intrinsic qualities in them, but by virtue of their difference from one another, and it is therefore their differences which allow words to give meaning to things by dividing up the continuum of experience. As Saussure says (1974: 120), 'in language there are only differences without positive terms'. We identify the sound-image 'tree' by differentiating it from 'free', 'try', and so forth; equally the meaning of the concept *tree* depends entirely on its difference from such related concepts as *bush, plant*, etc., that of the concept *orange* on its difference from *yellow* and *red*. From this theory (often called 'diacritical') of language and meaning it follows that to study how a language functions we must take as our object not individual signs in isolation, but the relationships that obtain between them. Language is not an agglomeration of separate facts but a closed system, in the sense that the function of each element depends entirely on its position within the whole. Saussure makes a crucial distinction, in the study of language, between *langue,* the language-system, and *parole,* the individual act of communication which the system produces and conditions. *Langue,* not *parole* must be the primary object of a science which aims to show how language functions.

In connection with these principles Saussure introduced two further oppositions, both of which have had the greatest importance for the development of modern linguistics: the opposition between *synchronic* and *diachronic* language study, and that between *syntagmatic* and *associative* relationships in the language-system. Language study before Saussure was predominantly diachronic, in the sense that it was predominantly interested in the way languages change through time. While accepting wholeheartedly the value of this sort of study—the discipline that goes by the name of philology in English-speaking countries—Saussure argued that it gave only a partial account of linguistic phenomena. In practice the analysis of linguistic change

41

meant tracing the history of individual linguistic facts across the centuries, and consequently a neglect of the properties of language as system. Synchronic study, on the other hand, considers how a language functions as a system at a given moment in time, analyzing the simultaneous relationships between its constituent parts; it examines how a language works, not how it develops. A tradition of language study which neglected this, as nineteenth-century philology did, failed to account for the real nature of its object. Saussure called for, not the abandonment of diachronic study, but the recognition that synchronic and diachronic study led to different kinds of knowledge, and that both were necessary for the true understanding of language.

The distinction between *syntagmatic* and *associative* relationships relates to this concept of the synchronic study of language as a system. In linguistic communication terms have to be arranged in sequences. The term syntagmatic was attached by Saussure to the sequential or combinatory relationships that a given language system permits: the relationship between the three sounds, for instance, that make up the word 'tree', or the syntactical relationship between the words 'the tree is green', and so on. But to understand a language sequence it is not enough to recognize the relationships between the elements present in it; we also have to refer to relationships of absence, and it is these that Saussure calls associative relationships. The concept of associative relationships is a necessary supplement to the idea of the differential nature of the linguistic sign, since difference in language can only be functional in conjunction with similarity. In Saussure's theory we identify and attach meaning to an individual word in a sequence by placing it mentally against the background of other words, not present in the sequence, which are both similar and different to it. The sound-image 'tree' is associated with 'free', 'try', etc., the signified *tree* with *bush, plant,* and the like, and the singular 'tree' with the plural 'trees'. Nowadays the term *paradigmatic* is normally used for this type of relationship, on the model of the grammatical notion of a paradigm, a tabular representation of the conjugation of a verb or the declension of a noun or adjective. However the term includes not only the different forms of a given verb, adjective or noun ('tree'/'trees'), but all types of association of form and meaning. A given word can be seen as the point of intersection of a bundle of different strings of associations, all of which contribute to its function as a sign.

As a number of alternatives to and criticisms of Saussure's theory will be discussed in the following chapters, I shall only mention here some of its positive implications for the study of literature. In the first place, as must already be evident, it shows some striking parallels with the Formalists' views on literature and literary studies — views which were developed for the greater part quite independently of it, for although later Formalist theory may have been influenced to some degree by Saussure, the beginnings of the movement predate the publication of his *Cours*. Both theories entail a shift of attention away from considerations of origin or cause to those of function or effect; neither is as much interested in the ways in which language reflects reality, as in the ways in which it shapes our perception of things; both attach central importance to the concepts of system and difference. But it will also be evident that Saussurean linguistics did much more than simply reinforce the Formalists' view of literature. Although it is worth stressing that Saussure's work is open to a variety of interpretations, and although he himself did not use the concepts *structure* and *structural*, it was his idea of the arbitrary and differential nature of the linguistic sign, and therefore of the essential disjunction between language and reality, that became the foundation of the structuralist movement. It was from this starting-point that the structuralists arrived at the radical view that all meaning in every sphere of human activity consists of closed systems wholly independent of the material world. The full implications of this view will emerge in the chapter on modern French structuralism. In the next two sections I shall concentrate on ways in which Saussurean linguistics enlarged and refined Formalist theories of literature, before considering other less ambitious approaches to literary language.

The Prague School: structure and function

It was the Prague School that unified Formalism and Saussurean linguistics in a single theoretical programme, or at least—as there has been some discussion as to the exact nature of the Prague School's debt to Saussure—reformulated Formalist literary theory within the framework of a linguistics which shared most of Saussure's fundamental principles, and to which they attached the label structuralism. It was observed in the last chapter that the Prague School's views on literature and literary study were substantially those of the Formalists, but the Formalists' influence has owed a great deal to the shape that the Prague School gave to their theory, in particular to the Prague School's use of the concepts of *structure* and *function*. Without considering Prague School theory in detail, I shall therefore look at its use of these two concepts, both of which have played a crucial role in modern thinking about literature.

The main texts of Prague literary theory are the collective *Thèses* which the Prague Linguistic Circle presented (in French) to a conference in the city in 1929; and the writings of one of the Circle's leading members, Jan Mukařovský. The terms *structure* and *structural* are crucial to the programme of research which the *Thèses* proposed on both literature and language. Linguistic science should study the 'structural laws of linguistic systems' (Vachek 1966: 34), that is, the reciprocal relations of the individual elements in them. The poetic work too should be viewed as a 'functional structure' (p.46), the different elements of which cannot be understood except in their connections with the whole. As far as language is concerned, therefore, 'structure' is simply an alternative to Saussure's concept of relationships; to be exact, a structure is a set or totality of relationships. In the study of literature 'structure' replaces the Formalist concepts of form and device. We have seen how the Formalists challenged the traditional form/content opposition, and proposed the pair devices and materials in its place. Devices in a work are those elements which are defamiliarized and therefore poetically functional, materials are those which are not. Structure, which can also be opposed to material, is a broader concept than both form, in its traditional sense, and device; it embraces all aspects of a literary text, from sound to subject matter, and it includes both those which are defamiliarized and those which are not. To define the literary text as a structure is to view it as a set of Saussurean signs (or as a single sign, as Mukařovský (1970: 69ff.) suggested), in which both signifiers and signifieds are governed by a single complex system of relationships. In contrast both to traditional views of form, and to some Formalist statements about the device, it calls attention to the organization of the text in its totality, the structure of the text being simply the totality of the relationships that obtain within it.

In itself this notion of structure does not necessarily distinguish literary texts from ordinary acts of communication, since these too evidently have a structure. The Prague School explained the difference between literary (or poetic) and non-literary structures through an extension of the Formalist concept of *function* — hence the definition of the poetic text as a 'functional structure'. Whereas the Formalist concept was related to the literary devices within a text, the Prague School theory applied it to all forms of language. The best known version of this theory of functions is Jakobson's 'Closing statement: linguistics and poetics' (Sebeok 1960: 350-77) delivered to a conference in America in 1958, which builds on a set of categories proposed by Mukařovský some years earlier (1938: 100-1). According to Jakobson, any message can have six different functions, corresponding to the six factors necessarily present in any act of communication: an *addresser*, an *addressee*, a *context*, a *code*, a means of *contact*, and the *message* itself. The function consists in the message's focus on, its orientation or 'set' towards one or another of these factors (1960:353-7). The focus on the *addresser*, for instance a speaker or an author, constitutes the *emotive* function, that of expressing the addresser's attitudes or feelings; the focus on the *addressee* or receiver, the *conative* function, that of influencing the feelings or attitudes of the addressee; the focus on the *context*, the real, external situation in which the message occurs, the *referential* function; the focus on the *code*, as when a message elucidates a point of grammar, the *metalingual* function; the focus on the means of *contact*, as in the case, say, of expressions inserted by one party into a telephone conversation simply in order to reassure the other party that they are both still on the line, the *phatic* function; the focus on the *message* itself, the *poetic* function.

The advantage of this concept of function is that it avoids absolute distinctions between one kind of text and another. All functions may be present, though sometimes to a minimal degree, in any set of signs, constituting a hierarchy according to the relative predominance of each. If the poetic function is *dominant*, then the message can be described as 'poetic', or 'aesthetic' or 'literary', or 'artistic'. This occurs, following the Formalist principle of defamiliarization, when existing linguistic or literary practice (a 'norm') is violated at one level or another of a text's structure, which then itself becomes dominant. The dominant level generates an enhanced attention to the relationship between that level and all the others, and therefore *foregrounds* or *actualizes* the text in its totality. But this does not prevent other functions from being present, lower down in the hierarchy, in texts in which the poetic function is dominant; equally, the poetic function may be present in texts which are mainly expressive or referential. Thus, like the later Formalists, the Prague School were able to insist on the specific properties of the 'poetic' text, and at the same time recognize its links with the author and the social context. For them the task of the critic was not to ignore literature's connections with the external world, but to take full account of its internal, poetic properties in his analysis. It must be stressed, in this connection, that the 'poetic' text in question is not necessarily a part of what is normally described as poetry, but can be any form of literature that possesses aesthetic or artistic properties.

From what I have said so far it may sound as if the Prague School did no more than restate the Russian Formalists' theories in more systematic language. But by integrating these theories with their version of structural linguistics, they developed them in a very important direction: they placed them within a semiotic or semiological framework, semiotics and semiology being to all intents and purposes interchangeable terms. Saussure speaks of semiology (1974: 16) as a 'science that studies the life of signs within society', a science of which we shall hear more in the chapter on modern French structuralism. When Mukařovský (1936 and 1970: 70ff.) wrote of art, literature, or poetry as semiological facts, he meant that artistic works constitute particular kinds of signs which can only be understood within the framework of a general sign-theory. The significance of this proposition is that it provides the basis for a theory of literary or poetic meaning which both distinguishes this meaning from the external world and relates it to it. It distinguishes it, because if the literary text is seen as a sign or set of signs in the Saussurean sense, then its meaning or content must be the product of a structure of relationships or differences whose connection with the 'real' world is purely arbitrary. Literary meaning must therefore be analyzed in its own terms, in the words of the *Thèses* (Vachek 1966: 49) as a 'semantic composition', and not as the reflection of external factors. At the same time this meaning is related to the 'real' world by virtue of the Formalist principle of defamiliarization. Our everyday perception of the world is enclosed within the conventional sign-systems that we use, what Fredric Jameson (1972) has called the 'prison-house' of language. Art helps us to break out of this prison-house by subverting conventional sign-systems and forcing us to focus our attention on signs themselves rather than taking them for granted. It is through this process that art leads, as Mukařovský puts it, to a 'renewed awareness of the manifold and multivalent nature of reality' (Garvin 1964: 33). So we return to Shklovsky's early principle that art refreshes our sense of life and experience; but the principle is now stated in the form of a far more coherent, complex and far-reaching theory.

This semiotic version of the Formalist position is therefore what the Prague School understood by 'structuralism' in the study of literature. It is worth emphasizing its major difference from the structuralism of the sixties and seventies: whereas this later structuralism is mainly interested in the structure of literature as a whole, to the extent that this too can be viewed as a system of signs, the Prague School version took as its main object the structure of the individual text and, like the later Formalists, viewed the individual text as a system. As Mukařovský wrote (Garvin 1964: 22):

> The mutual relationship of the components of the work of poetry, both foregrounded and unforegrounded, constitute its *structure*, a dynamic structure including both convergence and divergence, and one that constitutes an indissociable artistic whole, since each of its components has its value in terms of its relation to the totality.

The task of the structuralist analyst is therefore to identify deviations from existing linguistic and literary practice ('norms') occurring at one level of the text (say its syntax), and then relate the structure of this level to that of the other levels (rhythm, syllable-structure, aspects of subject matter, etc.), in order to define the structure of the text as a whole. The analysis thus involves the exact description not only of the language of the text, but also of its content. Prague School structuralism is a programme for the precise and systematic explanation of the aesthetic effect of a text in its totality.

There are a number of objections that can be made to this kind of structuralism, although some of them are equally applicable to other branches of literary theory. To begin with those relating mainly to the Prague School, there seems, first, to be no objective way of determining what limits can be imposed on the description of the text's structure. An element of focus is provided, it is true, by the concept of the *dominant*, in the sense of the level of the text showing the highest degree of deformation. According to Mukařovský, all components of the text and their interrelationships 'are evaluated from the standpoint of the dominant', which thus 'creates the unity of the work of poetry' (Garvin 1964: 20-1). But the fact remains that, even if the dominant is taken as the starting-point, a description of the relationships of all the components of a text would be potentially endless. Some further criterion of selection is required, which in practice must mean the analyst's own preconceptions, or his overall impression, as to what is important or interesting about the text he is dealing with. The constant impression given by the Prague School is that the sort of description and analysis they call for is essentially objective and scientific in character, but in practice it seems impossible to exclude a strong element of subjectivity from this kind of structural study. Moreover while the analysis of interrelationships at the verbal level can draw on a highly-developed set of tools, in the form of the concepts and categories supplied by linguistics, the same analysis is much more difficult at the levels of content. To maintain that the content of literature is part of a system of signs with a structure of its own, independent of the 'real' world, is clearly to maintain that it is in theory analyzable in the same way as its language; but in practice a ready-made set of conceptual tools is simply not available. As we shall see, though, it is precisely such a set of conceptual tools that more recent structuralism has attempted to supply.

As for the less specific objections to the Prague School, the weight one attaches to them will depend very much on one's own theoretical position. Clearly positivists, and, as we shall see, Marxists as well, will feel unhappy about any approach to literature which, like that of the Formalists and the Prague School, concentrates on the analysis of a text's structure rather than its genesis, and on the explanation of literary facts within a predominantly literary framework of reference. But a more general objection still relates to any theory that defines, as theirs does, such categories as poetry, literature or art in absolute terms. Flexible though the Formalist/Prague School approach may be in this respect, it still attaches overwhelming importance to the element of innovation in literature, thus reflecting the permanent revolution in poetic language, and in literary forms in general, brought about by the modernist movement from the later nineteenth century onwards. Clearly innovation is a characteristic of all

47

literature, but equally clearly it is far less prominent in, say, the classicist tradition that dominated European culture from the Renaissance to the beginning of the nineteenth century. In the end the Formalist/Prague School principle of defamiliarization must lead to the conclusion that modernist literature, with its greater element of innovation, is more 'poetic' than most literature of preceding periods—a conclusion explicitly stated, for instance, in a modern French version of Formalist analysis, Jean Cohen's *Structure du langage poétique*. A Formalist/Prague School approach thus necessarily projects back onto earlier literature the aesthetic standards peculiar to the modern age. This may seem perfectly acceptable so long as we are convinced of the absolute rightness of these standards; but the question must arise whether there is any point in seeking for single comprehensive definitions of such categories as poetry, literature, art, etc., or whether it is not better to regard the definitions that may be devised as applicable only to certain kinds of literature or certain aspects of texts. Since their different literary predilections are one of the major factors that distinguish literary theories from one another, this is a question that will arise frequently in the course of the rest of this book.

Roman Jakobson: linguistic poetics

Jakobson's name has already been mentioned under the headings of both Formalism and the Prague School. But while part of his famous 'Closing statement' is, as we have seen, a development of Prague School theory, it also puts forward a view of poetic language in some respects markedly different from that of the *Thèses* and Mukařovský. In speaking of the literary text as a functional structure, the Prague School stressed its effect as a totality, through the interaction of all its constituent parts including the subject-matter. In his 'Closing statement' Jakobson does not explicitly reject this view, which after all he played an important part in developing; but speaking as a linguist he insists that the difference between poetic and non-poetic texts can be explained in purely linguistic terms. Poetics, which 'deals primarily with the question, *What makes a verbal message a work of art?*', is an 'integral part of linguistics', because the answer to this question is to be found entirely in the message's verbal structure (Sebeok 1971: 350). Jakobson's essay thus constitutes as strong a claim as can possibly be made for the relevance of linguistics to literary study.

According to the Prague School 'poetic' texts distinguish themselves from others through the violation of a norm. Jakobson, however, proposes a different 'empirical linguistic criterion' for the definition of the poetic function: *'The poetic function projects the principle of equivalence from the axis of selection into the axis of combination.* Equivalence is promoted to the constitutive device of the sequence' (Sebeok 1971: 358). This distinction between the axis of selection and that of combination corresponds to Saussure's distinction between associative and syntagmatic relationships, between relationships of absence and presence in language. Reformulating Saussure, Jakobson had pointed out earlier (Jakobson 1956: 55ff) that every linguistic message is the product of a double process: (1) the act of selection among items not present in the message but associated in the code (i.e. in the *langue* or language system), and (2) the combination of the items selected into a sequence. While the relationship between the items present in the sequence (Saussure's syntagmatic relationships) is one of *contiguity*, the relationship between those not present in it (Saussure's associative relationships) is one of the *similarity* or *equivalence*, in the sense that the items perform an equivalent function and can therefore replace one another. For instance if I take the sentence 'I woke up late this morning' the items present in the sequence are obviously different from one another; but according to Saussurean theory we make sense of this sentence by implicitly relating it to items which are absent from the sequence but equivalent to those in it, for instance 'You went down early that afternoon'. (Jakobson associates relationships of contiguity with the figure *metonymy*, and those of equivalence with that of *metaphor*, a point which need not concern us for the moment, but which will become relevant in the discussion of Lacan later.)

The thesis of Jakobson's 'Closing statement' is that in poetic language relationships of equivalence or similarity not only concern absent items, but also become dominant *present* factors in the verbal sequence—that the two aspects of what he calls the 'bipolar structure of language' (1956: 78) in a sense merge. He explains what this means in practice as follows (1968: 602-3):

> Any unbiased, attentive, exhaustive, total description of the selection, distribution and interrelation of diverse morphological classes and syntactic constructions in a given poem surprises the examiner himself by unexpected, striking symmetries and anti-symmetries, balanced structures, efficient accumulation of equivalent forms and salient contrasts, finally by rigid restrictions in the repertory of morphological and syntactic constituents used in the poem, eliminations which, on the other hand, permit us to follow the masterly interplay of the actualized constituents.

This assertion, in another conference paper (of 1960) entitled 'Poetry of grammar and grammar of poetry', was subsequently corroborated by a series of studies of individual poems in six different European languages, ranging in date from the thirteenth to the twentieth century. To illustrate Jakobson's approach to these texts, let us take his analysis (with L. G. Jones) of Shakespeare's Sonnet cxxix, 'Th'Expence of Spirit' (1970):

I Th'expence of Spirit in a waste of shame
   Is lust in action, and till action, lust
   Is perjurd, murdrous, blouddy full of blame,
   Savage, extreame, rude, cruel, not to trust,

II Injoyd no sooner but dispised straight,
   Past reason hunted, and no sooner had
   Past reason hated as a swollowed bayt,
   On purpose layd to meke the taker mad.

III Mad[e] In pursut and in possession so,
   Had, having; and in quest, to have extreame,
   A blisse in proofe and provd a[nd] very wo,
   Before a joy proposd behind a dreame,

IV All this the world well knowes yet none knowes well,
   To shun the heaven that leads men to this hell.

The analysis considers in turn the following relationships of equivalence and contrast (which evidently depends on and emphasizes equivalence) in the poem (the spelling and punctuation follow the first edition): (1) those which oppose the first seven lines to the last seven; (2) those which are constant features of the text as a whole; (3) those which oppose strophes I and III to II and IV; (4) those which oppose strophes I and IV to II and III (the outer and the inner); (5) those which oppose strophes I and II to III and IV; (6) those which oppose the final couplet to the rest of the poem; and (7) those which oppose the middle couplet (lines 7 and 8) to the rest of the poem.

Without following Jakobson's analysis in detail—it does not make for easy reading—I shall simply give examples of the sort of relationship he identifies under each of these headings. (1) The first seven lines are each characterized by a break after an unstressed fifth syllable; the last seven by a break after a stressed fourth and/or sixth syllable. (2) Constant features: each strophe in the poem has an infinitive construction in the second or fourth line, and each line is characterized by the repetition of a sound sequence. (3) The odd strophes have far more nouns and adjectives than the even ones (17 nouns as opposed to 6, 10 adjectives as opposed to 1); the nouns in the odd strophes are all abstract, those in the even strophes all (more or less) concrete. (4) The inner strophes have 11 participles and no conjugated verb-forms, while the outer strophes each have a conjugated form repeated in the form of a chiasmus *(Is lust...lust/is; well knowes...knowes well)*; to this parallel between strophes I and IV there also corresponds a set of echoing pairs within strophes II and III *(Injoyd—joy; had—Had; mad—Mad; purpose—proposd)*. (5) The first two strophes have three rhymes ending in a plosive and nine occurrences in stressed position of the dipthong /ay/, whereas both of these elements are absent from the second two strophes; strophes I

50

and II have, respectively, one definite followed by one indefinite article, and one indefinite followed by one definite article, in contrast to the three indefinite articles in strophe III and the two definite articles in strophe IV. (6) The final couplet has no adjectives, participles, indefinite articles or 'relational' verbs (such as *is*); its nouns are all concrete and 'original' whereas those of the rest of the poem are abstract and/or derived from verbs (and it has only one plural noun). (7) The middle couplet of the poem abandons the grammatical or syntactical parallelism which characterizes all the other lines, and also contains the only comparative construction in the text.

One may quibble with some of Jakobson's distinctions and classifications, but it must be stressed that these are only a small selection of the multitude of relationships that he identifies in the space of this short poem. If one takes the not inconsiderable trouble of following his analysis right the way through, it is hard not to be impressed by the picture he draws of an intricate network of equivalences and contrasts, corresponding to the different possible metrical divisions in the poem, and layered one upon the other in a kind of elaborate verbal counterpoint. Since he has shown this sort of network to be discernible in a wide range of different kinds of poetry, and since it is hard to imagine that it could also be found in non-poetic language, there seems to be a strong *prima facie* case for accepting his argument that the principle of equivalence provides an objective criterion for identifying the poetic function. Yet this style of analysis must strike most readers as wholly alien to their experience of poetry. How are the two positions to be reconciled?

It should be apparent, first of all, that the relationships of equivalence described by Jakobson include at least two different types of structure (see Todorov 1977b: 346): similarities of linguistic form immediately evident to the ear or eye (in Saussurean terms, syntagmatic structures); and groupings, according to grammatical and other classifications, which depend on the reader's ability to categorize the different linguistic features of the text (in Saussurean terms, paradigmatic). Now while there is no reason to doubt that the first kind of structure contributes in one way or another to the effect of the poem, it can be and has been argued (Riffaterre 1966: 206ff.) that the second is in most cases irrelevant to the text's poetic status, since it tends to fall well below the ordinary reader's level of consciousness. Jakobson's answer to this argument is, however, a powerful one: all users of a language must necessarily know the system of categories into which its different elements are divided, even if only unconsciously; and his analysis of poetry does not claim to represent what goes on in the reader's mind, but to account for the special effect which the poetry, for reasons of which he may well be unaware, exercises on him. What he is offering is a technical explanation of the total impact of poetic language, not just a description or interpretation of the reader's conscious understanding.

It is of course possible that structures of the second kind, the equivalences of category, can be found in equal quantity in non-poetic language; all that may be required, it has been argued (Culler 1975: 62), is a sufficiently flexible system of categorization. But until this has actually proved to be possible—and Jakobson would strongly deny that it is—it seems reasonable to accept that both kinds of equivalence constitute a distinguishing feature, if not of all poetic language, at least of a great deal of it. The important question, though, is not so much whether such features are or are not objectively present, but what significance and function one should assign to them if they are. After all, rhyme and metre are forms of equivalence which distinguish a very great deal of poetry, yet nowadays few would maintain that the presence of either or both is a necessary and sufficient condition for defining a text as poetic. Equally the mere presence of further equivalences at other levels of the text, however intricate and profuse, may simply constitute one among many possible distinguishing features, and not necessarily the essential one, of poetry.

Jakobson's poetic analyses are mostly concerned with establishing the mere presence of relationships of equivalence, and only to a small degree with discussing their significance. But in his theoretical essays he gives some interesting indications of the ways in which they may contribute to a poem's effect. At a simple and obvious level, he argued fairly recently (1973: 491) that they served to satisfy our innate desire for regularity and symmetry, and also permitted effects of relief and surprise through contrast. More fundamentally, he suggested in the 'Closing statement' that they were the means whereby the poetic message focuses attention on itself and thus, in accordance with Prague School theory, 'by promoting the palpability of signs, deepens the fundamental dichotomy of signs and objects' (Sebeok 1971: 356). While Mukařovský and the *Thèses* proposed that the 'set' towards the message was brought about by deviation from or violation of a norm, Jakobson here in his later work is arguing that it is the consequence of the peculiar symmetry or convergence of the 'poetic' text. Both, however, suggest that the 'set' towards the message leads to a renewed perception of reality, by generating a renewed awareness of the forms of signification in which reality is articulated.

What this renewed awareness of signs means in more precise terms is put by Jakobson as follows (Sebeok 1960: 370, 372): 'In poetry not only the phonological sequence but in the same way any sequence of semantic units strives to build an equation. . . . In poetry, any conspicious similarity in sound is evaluated in respect to similarity and/or dissimilarity in meaning'. That is, the parallelisms and symmetries which poetry manifests at the level of verbal form automatically cause the reader to look for corresponding parallelisms and symmetries at the level of meaning. The consequence of this is ambiguity, since parallelisms and symmetries of meaning are imposed on sets of words not normally connected in this way in ordinary language. 'Similarity superimposed on contiguity imparts to poetry its throughgoing symbolic, multiplex, polysemantic essence. . . The supremacy of the poetic function over the referential function does not obliterate the message but makes it ambiguous. . .'(pp. 370-1). The example Jakobson gives of this process is the last stanza of Poe's 'Raven':

> And the Raven, never flitting, still is sitting, *still* is sitting
> On the pallid bust of Pallas just above my chamber door;
> And his eyes have all the seeming of a demon's that is dreaming,
> And the lamp-light o'er him streaming throws his shadow on the
> floor;
> And my soul from out that shadow that lies floating on the floor
> Shall be lifted — nevermore.

The marked sound repetitions in this verse suggest, Jakobson argues ('Words similar in sound are drawn together in meaning') such connections of meaning as these: *raven,* being contiguous to and similar in sound (/r/ — — /v/ — — /n/) to *never,* appears as the 'embodied mirror image of this "never"'; the parallelism in sound between *never flitting* and *lifted nevermore* underlines the Raven's significance as an image of 'everlasting despair', and so on (pp. 371-2).

Irrespective of the merit of these particular observations (and indeed of this particular poem), it is clear that once formal patterns of equivalence are connected to relations of meaning, as they are here, they become a good deal more interesting. But it needs to be borne in mind that such connections are not an automatic or necessary consequence of the formal structure of the poetry; they are the result of the reader's bringing his own sensibility and experience to bear on the text, and interpreting it in the light of his own conscious or unconscious idea of the nature and function of literature. There is no guarantee whatever that all formal equivalences can be given meaning, and there is no guarantee that such meaning as can be given to them will seem interesting or important from a poetic point of view. The interest of Jakobson's theory, then, is that — apart from the fact that it has had such wide circulation — it shows both the strengths and limitations of the linguistic approach to literature. It can point to structural features not evident to the non-linguistic critic, but which the critic must admit may well be an important source of effect. On the other hand the structural analysis of the language only tells part of the story; the question how structural features contribute to the text's overall effect still remains to be answered by the critic.

MODERN LINGUISTICS AND THE LANGUAGE OF LITERATURE

'Stylistics'

If we relate Prague School theory and Jakobson's poetics to the five questions about the literary text listed in our introduction, we will find, not surprisingly, that their position in almost every respect is substantially the same. Both, as we have already seen, propose definitions of the specifically literary or poetic properties of texts, definitions which assign a dominant role to language, and which treat the relationship between text and author and text and reality as only secondary considerations. What should be stressed here also is their shared conception of the role of the reader, as this involves an issue that will recur in this book. The Prague School's and Jakobson's assumption is that the structures they describe are all objectively present in literature, and can be perceived by anyone who reads with sufficient skill and attention. No allowance is made for the separate contribution that the reader himself might bring to the text, and that might help to determine its meaning and effect. In their 'objective' analysis both theories claim to give exhaustive accounts of literature's essential features.

Although neither theory claims to be such, both the Prague School's and Jakobson's are frequently treated nowadays as part of the subject of 'stylistics'. However most of the work that comes under this heading is a good deal less ambitious in its claims; it also approaches literary texts through their linguistic form, but on the whole does not pretend to define the essential properties of literature in purely linguistic terms, making greater allowance for other factors such as the role of the reader. The words 'style' and 'stylistics' have a great many meanings, and there is little point, especially here, in arguing about which meanings are the right ones. In accordance with the theme of this chapter, I shall simply use 'stylistics' as a convenient label (hence the inverted commas) for the branch of literary studies that concentrates on the linguistic form of texts, and I shall take four different examples of this kind of work as alternatives to the Prague School's and Jakobson's approach to the relationship between linguistics and literature. By the same token, I shall use the word 'style' only in connection with literary uses of language.

It needs to be said, however, that 'stylistics' is also developing as a branch of general linguistics that studies variations in *non*-literary language use, notably variations connected with the different contexts in which language is used (the style of journalism, official documents, radio commentaries, etc.). Stylistics as a branch of literary studies can draw on this kind of work, but its concerns must in general be very different, because from a literary point of view the linguistic form of texts is of interest only in certain respects. It is possible, roughly speaking, to sum up under four main headings the different ways in which literary stylistics views the language or style of literature: as *embellishment,* as *self-reference,* as *representation* and as *manner.* These four categories admittedly overlap in theory and in practice, but I use them since they correspond to real differences of approach in the study of literary language, and help to show in what way stylistic and linguistic studies differ. I shall be illustrating each of these four views of style with one of my four examples of modern stylistics, but let me first say exactly what my headings mean.

To view style as *embellishment* is the oldest way to view it. At its crudest this takes the form of the assumption that writing is automatically made beautiful through the addition of certain standardized linguistic ornaments (*ornatus* in Latin) of which the best known are the various poetic 'figures', metaphor, antithesis, hyperbole and the like. Classical and classicizing treatises on rhetoric and poetics are filled with descriptions of these linguistic ornaments, most of which have been codified to a very high degree. In justice to these treatises, however, it must be said that at least in antiquity they rarely assumed that style was automatically improved through the use of ornament. Rather, the use of ornament was viewed strictly in its relation to the tone or level of style required by different kinds of writing, in accordance with the principle of *decorum*. It is this principle that forms the central consideration in my example of the stylistics of embellishment, Auerbach's *Mimesis*, and I shall explain it further shortly. Style as *self-reference*, on the other hand, has already been dealt with in the preceding two sections of this chapter; linguistic deviation, according to the Prague School, and structures of equivalence, according to Jakobson, served the purpose of focusing attention on the linguistic message as a whole, of making it refer to itself. My further example of the stylistics of self-reference, from the writings of Michael Riffaterre, is a more recent instance of deviation-theory, but assigns to it a more restricted role than the Prague School did within the literary text.

These two views of style evidently concern the general properties of literary language more than the individual features of authors or texts, whereas it is to these features that the stylistics of representation and manner both give their attention. By *representation* I mean the use of language to reflect or reinforce the content of a text, following the much-quoted dictum of Pope, 'The sound must seem an echo to the sense' (*Essay on Criticism*, 1. 365). The most obvious form that this use of language takes is the device of onomatopoeia ('the murmur of innumerable bees'). A more widespread and less blatant kind of sound-symbolism is discussed by the many style studies that see, for instance, suggestions of gloom or obscurity in the 'dark' vowels *o* and *u*, feelings of speed or haste in certain rhythms, and so forth. Such studies tend to be impressionistic and are frequently questionable, but modern linguistics, by offering more exact and subtle methods of analysis, has opened up new possibilities for the study of sound-symbolism in literature. More importantly perhaps, it has encouraged literary criticism and stylistics to look for connections between other levels of language, such as syntax or vocabulary, and the content of literary texts. We shall meet an interesting example of this kind of approach shortly. To avoid confusion in this connection, it is worth stressing that while the stylistics of embellishment is also concerned with the relationship between the language and content of texts, the relationship there is confined to general questions of tone. What I mean by the stylistics of representation concerns the connection between individual features of the language of a text and individual features of its content, an interest which is much more characteristic of modern approaches to literature.

Finally, the view of style as *manner*: I mean by 'manner' the way in which a text, or an author's work as a whole, or the work of a group of writers, or even a period of literature, may be distinguished by typical patterns of language-use, a repeated preference, for instance, for a certain kind of construction or a certain class of word. In most cases the point of looking at style in this way is to connect it with something outside the text. It may be seen as expressing the personality of the author, in accordance with the famous formula of the French scholar Buffon (1978: xvii), that the style *is* the man ('le style est l'homme même'); or it may be related to a literary movement or period (e.g. futurist style, baroque style). But one can also think of style as manner irrespective of such external connections, by identifying distinctive patterns of language use in a text simply as a means of differentiating it from other texts, on the general assumption that such distinctive patterns must be a part of the text's overall effect. This last instance of the stylistics of manner begins to merge into the stylistics of embellishment, self-reference or representation. Even here, however, the separate heading is worth preserving, since modern style-studies can and do content themselves with the mere description of distinctive linguistic patterns, abstaining not only from relating them to external factors such as authors or literary movements, but also from attributing to them any specific literary function. My example of the stylistics of manner will belong to this last type. Whether or not it is properly a part of literary studies may be a matter for dispute, but it undoubtedly constitutes an important position concerning the relationship of linguistics and literature.

The example I have taken of the stylistics of *embellishment*, Erich Auerbach's *Mimesis* (written between 1942 and 1945), is a history of the representation of reality in Western literature, and in particular of the literary forms in which reality has been represented. I include it under the heading of embellishment because its framework of reference is the classical theory of the grand, elevated or sublime style. Following the principle of *decorum* (to be found, for instance, in Horace's *Ars Poetica*), the classical view was that the style which dealt with serious matters had to be non-realistic, in the sense of systematically eliminating references to everyday life and using a type of language much more elaborate and refined than that of everyday usage; non-serious subjects could be dealt with realistically, in ordinary language, but on no account could the different levels of style be mixed together. Starting with Homer and finishing with Virginia Woolf, Auerbach uses this framework to characterize the different ways in which a selection of writers represented reality across the centuries, and in so doing traces the gradual abandonment of the principle of *decorum* in favour of a more modern standard, according to which seriousness and realism are wholly compatible.

Mimesis has been one of the great seminal works for the study of literary style, and on that ground I am discussing it here; for a number of reasons, however, it now seems to stand on the margins of modern approaches to literature. Its classical framework of reference evidently limits its range of applicability, especially because the view of style as embellishment has not found much favour in modern literary studies. Apart from this, its description of linguistic structures is not as exact and analytical as modern style studies tend to be. Auerbach prefers the more sweeping, synthesizing statement that sums up stylistic tendencies in evocative, metaphorical language rather than in technical terminology; he draws much less on modern linguistics than on the older tradition of philological scholarship. Moreover as a history of realism the book is concerned with larger matters than the detailed description of style. The study of the individual text is only the starting-point for a more general discussion of literary and cultural developments; it is not the major focus of interest in itself.

It may already be evident that the stylistics of embellishment has much in common with the stylistics of *self-reference,* as both can involve the idea of deviation from some kind of standard. The reason why I think it important to distinguish between the two is that the principle of embellishment entails deviation in a single direction— that of elevation and elaboration—and for the purpose of achieving an emotive effect—that of dignity, sublimity and so forth. Deviation as a means of self-reference, on the other hand, can take any direction, and is not necessarily concerned with a particular kind of emotive effect, since self-reference is an end in itself. This difference is clearly illustrated in the work of Michael Riffaterre, my example of the stylistics of self-reference, which is interesting both for this reason, and because it contains a forceful criticism of and alternative to Jakobson's linguistic poetics.

Riffaterre's criticism of Jakobson is to be found principally in an article of 1966 on Jakobson's analysis (with Claude Lévi-Strauss) of Baudelaire's poem 'Les Chats', an analysis which follows the same model as that of the Shakespeare sonnet. In this article Riffaterre argues from a position already developed in a series of papers written in the late fifties and early sixties. His principal criticism is one to which we have already referred: that Jakobson does not differentiate linguistic features which are perceptible to the reader from those which are not, and which therefore remain 'alien to the poetic structure' (Riffaterre 1966: 207) of the text. Since the poetic structure includes only those elements which evoke a response in the reader, it is this response that must be taken as the analyst's starting point; the linguist as such cannot tell us what is interesting or important about a work ('No grammatical analysis of a poem can give us more than the grammar of the poem' (p. 213)). But this emphasis on the reader's response does not mean that Riffaterre accepts that literary analysis is subjective. He had earlier distinguished (1964) between the categories 'poetry' and 'literature' on the one hand, and 'style' on the other. The first two are necessarily variables, in that their meaning depends on the time and circumstance in which they are used; 'style', however, can be defined as possessing a constant and specific property. Like Jakobson, he believes that literary language can be analyzed objectively and exactly, though rather than speaking of its 'poetic' function, he opts for the term 'stylistic' function instead.

Like Jakobson's 'poetic' function, Riffaterre's 'stylistic' function consists in the 'set' towards the message. But this 'set' is the product not of equivalences, nor of violation of an external norm, but of the violation of norms which the *text itself* creates. Style consists in the establishment of a certain pattern of linguistic regularity which creates expectations in the reader that the 'stylistic device' then disrupts. Riffaterre stresses the theoretical and practical problems involved in defining (as the Prague School tried to do) external literary and linguistic norms, and suggests that in any case 'normal' language can itself be a source of stylistic effect in a text. By taking the 'contextual' norm as one of his defining factors, he avoids this difficulty and locates his framework of analysis firmly within the text itself (see Riffaterre 1959 and 1960).

But how does this allow a study of style that is objective and exact? Riffaterre's answer (1959) was first to propose taking a group of average cultivated readers as informants. These were to identify, but not describe or interpret, the stylistic devices present in a given text. All they had to do was indicate the points in the text at which the language created an effect of surprise; the task of the stylistician was then to analyze the contrast, between the linguistic structure of the device and that of its immediate context, that accounted for this effect of surprise. In the article on Jakobson this position was somewhat modified; Riffaterre proposed taking as his informants not average readers but the so-called 'Superreader', a figure representing the sum of reactions to the language of a text manifested in the published work of its interpreters, translators and so on. Once again, however, it was not their analysis or explanation that counted, but the mere fact that they found certain features stylistically striking. Why they found them striking was for the stylistician to explain.

In retrospect what Riffaterre and Jakobson have in common seems more striking than their disagreements. Riffaterre's recognition of the variable character of the 'poetic' and the importance of the reader's role may well mark a step forward from Jakobson's views. But his definition of style, like Jakobson's of poetry, fails to allow for its multiplicity and changeability, even if it points to an important possible source of literary effect; and in his claims concerning readers' responses he attributes to these a degree of regularity which to many must seem quite unrealistic. Both therefore share the same confidence, which now seems rather questionable, but is typical of the structuralism of the sixties, in the possibility of defining and analyzing scientifically the essential feature of literature.

When we pass to the treatment of style as *representation* we come to an approach to literature which is less likely to make such claims to scientific status; for rather than defining style in purely linguistic terms, its purpose is to relate it to interpretations of literary content, and these must inevitably be somewhat approximative. The best known example of this kind of stylistics, indeed the best-known example of stylistics in any sense, is the work of Leo Spitzer. Like Auerbach a scholar of Germanic origins who finished his career in the United States, Spitzer developed, in contrast to him, a method of stylistic analysis which concentrated firmly on the individual text. In a collection of essays published in 1948 under the title *Linguistics and Literary History,* Spitzer defined his method by the term 'philological circle'. The process of stylistic study should begin, he suggested, from any detail of the text that strikes the analyst first as deviant in relation to established modes of writing, second as potentially significant in relation to the work as a whole. The first step, the 'click', is mainly intuitive. Once it has occurred, the analyst connects the feature in question with his impression of or feeling for the whole work, and may be led to modify this as a result. He then returns in a circular movement, a 'to-and-fro voyage', to other details of the text's language, with a view to relating together both details and general impression in an organic whole. He thus arrives at the 'common spiritual etymon, the psychological root' of the multiplicity of linguistic features in the work, the 'creative center' from which everything in it emanates (Spitzer 1948: 1-39).

This talk of the 'common spiritual etymon [i.e. origin], the

pychological root' of stylistic forms sounds more like my definition of
the stylistics of manner than a view of style as representation. Much of
Spitzer's work, however, does not conform to this psychological view;
the 'to-and-fro voyage' takes place between a text's linguistic forms
and an interpretation of its content taken in itself, not in relation to its
author. His analysis of Yeats's 'Leda and the Swan' (Spitzer 1962: 3-13)
is a clear instance of this kind of approach, and therefore falls under
my heading of the stylistics of representation:

> A sudden blow: the great wings beating still
> Above the staggering girl, her thighs caressed
> By the dark webs, her nape caught in his bill,
> He holds her helpless breast upon his breast.
>
> How can those terrified vague fingers push
> The feathered glory from her loosening thighs?
> And now can body, laid in that white rush,
> But feel the strange heart beating where it lies?
>
> A shudder in the loins engenders there
> The broken wall, the burning roof and tower
> And Agamemnon dead.
>   Being so caught up
> So mastered by the brute blood of the air,
> Did she put on his knowledge with his power
> Before the indifferent beak could let her drop?

Starting from 'the most immediately striking, the most individual, the
least "cataloguable"' feature of the poem, Spitzer focuses his attention
on the 'rendering of the time-place sequence'. This conveys 'one of
the mysterious paradoxes of copulation and procreation...: the
overwhelming strength of a moment engenders events whose
meaning will become clear only in their result in time'. For instance,
the 'syntactically brusque beginning of the poem' (a nominal sentence
without any kind of introduction) corresponds to the violent,
irrational character of Jupiter's rape of Leda in the guise of a swan.
The rapid progress of the narrative to the bird's orgasm (the 'shudder
in the loins') and consequent loss of sexual desire (the last line)
mirrors the speed of the sexual act. The paradox is that this sudden,
violent, essentially mindless process (the *could* in the last line
underlines the 'demoniac compulsion to which the divine bird
himself is subject') is the cause of events of enormous, tragic
magnitude for the human race: the birth of Helen and the Trojan war.
The unusual constructions in lines 10-11 ('The broken wall', etc., in
the place of 'the breaking of the wall') enhance the impression that
these subsequent events are already a *fait accompli* at the time of the
rape. The poem, Spitzer suggests, is a 'protest against the gods who let

sex be the effect of power uncoupled with knowledge', and at the same time such a drastic force in human affairs.

Now this is not perhaps one of the best of Spitzer's analyses, and in any case it contains a great deal more than we have space to repeat here. But it should be evident that it is true to his professed method, in that it executes a constant back-and-forth movement between the specific description of linguistic structures and the interpretation of the meaning of the poem as a whole. In some respects this method has much in common with the structuralism of the Prague School; there is an apparently similar interest in elements of deviation, and an apparently similar view of the literary text as a closely knit set of interrelated features. It is the emphasis on interpretation, however, that sets Spitzer apart from the Formalists and their successors, and brings him closer, as we shall see, to the Anglo-American New Critics; the term 'philological circle' is modelled, in fact, on the 'hermeneutic circle' of nineteenth-century German theorists of interpretation such as Dilthey. Individual points about style are always made in the context of a discussion of the feelings, attitudes or ideas that the text as a whole expresses, a discussion which is inevitably to a large extent intuitive and impressionistic. As we have seen the Prague School were also interested in the content of texts as well as their language, but what concerned them was the structure of the content as a self-contained system of signs to be separated out into its different levels, not the overall impression that it conveys. Spitzer's approach may therefore seem less scientific than theirs, but it is also a great deal closer to most readers' experience, as the revelatory quality of his best studies shows.

As I have already suggested, the stylistics of representation may merge into the view of style as *manner*, and Spitzer's own work does move between the two categories. However the example I have chosen of the stylistics of manner should make clear the potential difference between the two approaches, and at the same time illustrate the use of a more technically advanced linguistics than that drawn on by Spitzer, who like Auerbach belonged to the European philological tradition more than to the modern tradition of linguistics. In an essay entitled 'Descriptive linguistics in literary studies', the distinguished British linguistician M. A. K. Halliday also offers a stylistic analysis of Yeats's 'Leda and the Swan', but one which makes points of a very different kind from Spitzer's. The most important of these points are three in number, and I have expressed them for the sake of clarity in less technical and exact terminology than Halliday uses. According to Halliday's analysis Yeats's repeated use of the definite article in combination with an adjective before a noun ('the great wings', etc.) is unusual to the extent that, in contrast with most English usage, the article in this combination does not define anything, but instead refers back to the title (it is 'anaphoric' rather than 'cataphoric'). Second, the verbal items in the poem are 'considerably deverbalized', in that the great majority are participles or infinitives, and only five (e.g. 'holds', 'put') are in finite groups in free clauses, the most 'verbish' use of verbs. Third, the less 'verbish' the verbs in the poem are, the greater their lexical power tends to be, lexical power being in inverse proportion to the number of different terms with which a given term is habitually associated ('the fewer the items with which a given item is likely to collocate... the more "powerful" it is said to be'); and the more powerful, and less 'verbish', words are 'items of violence', such as 'staggering'.

Halliday's analysis thus differs from Spitzer's not only in using a more modern and technically advanced linguistics, but more importantly because it makes no attempt, to speak of, at interpretation. What he has done is describe certain linguistic features of the text which distinguish it from other texts (he refers to Yeats's 'Phoenix' and Tennyson's 'Morte d'Arthur', as well as instances of non-literary usage), and which look as if they may be of some literary significance; but he leaves it to the literary specialist to determine what the nature of that literary significance is. This corresponds exactly to his views on the relationship between linguistics and the study of literature (Halliday 1967: 217-23). Linguistics cannot supply a key to the specific qualities of literature as such, or a guide to interpretation; all it can do is provide the means for describing a text on the basis of a general linguistic theory, and therefore relate the text to the language as a whole in which it is written. 'Stylistics' thus becomes an essentially comparative study of the patterns of preference shown by the writer in his selection from the linguistic resources available to him, a question of the relative frequencies of choice which distinguish the language of his text from that of others; it is an 'application rather than an extension of linguistics' (p.217).

This suggestion, that stylistics should characterize comparatively the language or style of texts and leave it at that, would seem to constitute a sort of minimal claim for the relevance of linguistics to the study of literature. I say minimal both because it is rather modest, in contrast say to Jakobson's, and because it seems to present a demand that it should be very difficult for modern literary studies to deny: that in describing the language of literary texts a degree of rigour is required such as has been notably absent from the work of a great many critics. As Halliday (1964: 37) says, 'if a text is to be described at all, then it should be described properly'. This certainly does not mean that there is only one way of describing a text. Modern linguistics is a field full of conflicting theories, and an external observer would be hard put to accept one as better than the rest. Yet most modern models of language, from Saussure's onwards, give a fuller and more coherent account of it than traditional grammar ever did, and therefore offer the possibility of describing the linguistic features of texts far more exactly than was possible with the rag-bag of grammatical and metaphorical terminology on which criticism has traditionally depended. If, as Halliday argues, linguistics must defer to literary criticism when the literary properties of a text are in question, literary criticism, so long as exactness remains an academic virtue, must also respect the claims of linguistics when aspects of language are discussed.

To say, however, that this is as far as the relevance of linguistics to literary studies goes, would seem to be playing excessively safe. I hope that this chapter has shown, and the chapter on modern French structuralism will show, that although further applications of linguistics to literature are open to all sorts of criticisms, they also provide new and fruitful ways of discussing the specifically literary properties of texts. Not only this aspect, but all aspects of modern literary theory are by their very nature subject to controversy. The more modest and easily defensible claims concerning the relevance of linguistics are not therefore necessarily the more promising ones.

Further Reading

For an historical survey of the subject of this chapter, see Uitti's *Linguistics and Literary Theory*. There is a good English translation of Saussure's *Cours (Course in General Linguistics)* with a useful introduction by Culler; see also Culler's compact *Saussure*. An excellent introduction to modern linguistics from Saussure onwards is Lepschy's *A Survey of Structural Linguistics;* Lyons's *Introduction to Theoretical Linguistics* is systematic, substantial, but not always easy to read.

The *Thèses* of the Prague School were originally published in the *Travaux du Cercle Linguistique de Prague*, 1 (1929), 5-29, and have been reprinted (in the original French) in Vachek's *A Prague School Reader in Linguistics*. There is an interesting selection of Prague School literary theory in Garvin's *A Prague School Reader on Esthetics, Literary Structure and Style,* and two of Mukařovský's works have appeared in English in book form: *Aesthetic Function, Norm and Value as Social Facts* and *On Poetic Language*. There is some discussion of the Prague School in Erlich's *Russian Formalism: History — Doctrine,* and a useful essay by Wellek, 'The literary theory and aesthetics of the Prague School', in his *Discriminations* (pp. 275-303); see also the periodical *Russian Poetics in Translation,* vol. 4. More suggestions for reading on structuralism can be found at the end of Chapter 4.

The articles by Jakobson referred to in the text are probably the best introduction available in English to his approach to poetry. The volume of his collected works containing his writings on literature has been expected for some time but has yet to appear. All his major writings on literature have been translated into French and collected together under the title *Questions de poétique,* and there is also a French anthology of his work on linguistics, *Essais de linguistique générale.* See also the forceful critical discussion of Jakobson's poetics in Culler's *Structuralist Poetics* (pp. 55-74), and a more sympathetic view (in French) in Todorov's *Théories du symbole* (pp. 339-52). An interesting American application and development of Jakobson's poetics is Levin's *Linguistic Structures in Poetry.*

Stylistics has become an enormous subject. Some convenient collections of contributions to it are Sebeok's *Style in Language,* Fowler's *Essays on Style and Language,* Chatman and Levin's *Essays on the Language of Literature,* Freeman's *Linguistics and Literary Style,* Chatman's *Literary Style: A Symposium.* Each of these collections contains an interesting range of approaches to the stylistic study of literature. The articles by Riffaterre discussed in the text of this chapter have been collected together, along with others, and translated into French under the title *Essais de stylistique structurale.* Spitzer's *Linguistics and Literary History* is the best introduction to his work, and further illustrations of his approach can be found in the volume *Essays on English and American Literature;* see also Wellek's commemorative essay, 'Leo Spitzer (1887-1960)', where the point is made that much of Spitzer's work cannot properly be called stylistic (a bibliography of Spitzer's writings is also included).

Some articles on the theory of stylistics: Bloomfield, 'Stylistics and the theory of literature'; Chatman, 'On the theory of literary style'; Fowler, 'Linguistics, stylistics; criticism?'; Ohmann, 'Generative grammars and the concept of style'; Wellek, 'Stylistics, poetics and criticism' in Wellek 1970: 327-43, and Chatman 1971: 65-76. Two useful introductory manuals are Epstein, *Language and Style,* and Turner, *Stylistics,* respectively on literary and non-literary stylistics.

3 Anglo-American New Criticism
David Robey

The term 'New Criticism' is usually used for the literary theory and criticism that began with the work of I. A. Richards and T. S. Eliot before the war in England, and was continued by figures such as John Crowe Ransom, W. K. Wimsatt, Cleanth Brooks and Allen Tate in the United States during the forties, fifties and sixties. Although it developed quite independently of the Russian Formalist/Prague School structuralist theory discussed in the last two chapters, there are some fundamental affinities between the two movements. Both rejected positivistic literary scholarship and called for a renewed attention to literature as literature; both insisted on the differences between literature and other kinds of writing, and tried to define these differences in theoretical terms; both gave a central role in their definitions to ideas of structure and interrelatedness, and treated the literary text as an object essentially independent of its author and its historical context. Considering that the New Critics seem to have known nothing at all about the work of the Formalists and their successors (it is not mentioned at all, for instance, in Wimsatt and Brooks's *Literary Criticism: A Short History* of 1957), these affinities are really very striking. It is the differences between the two movements, however, that will be of more interest to us here.

The New Criticism almost certainly constitutes the English-speaking world's major contribution to literary theory, and as such it has exercised until recently a dominant influence on the teaching of literature in the United States and, to a lesser extent, in Britain. In the last few years, however, with the entry of European literary theory into British and American academic life, its prestige has definitely been on the wane. Yet there are good reasons for continuing to read the New Critics' work. At the very least they are interesting because they formulated a number of assumptions about literature and literary study that still play a significant part in the academic world today. More importantly, their work still has considerable validity as a theoretical alternative to Formalism and structuralism, an alternative which may seem a great deal closer to many readers' and critics' feelings about literature and life. For while they always emphasized the special qualities of literature, and in particular the idea that the meaning or effect of literature cannot be explained by a process of reduction to ordinary modes of expression, the New Critics also insisted on its connections with the 'real' world, and on the contribution it can make to coping with the problems of everyday human existence. In contrast to Formalism and structuralism, the New Criticism was empiricist and humanistic. I shall try to explain further the significance of this distinction in the pages that follow.

I. A. Richards: value

The New Criticism began, as I said, with the work of Richards and Eliot; more exactly one can say that it began with the publication in 1924 of Richards's *Principles of Literary Criticism*, a radical, polemical programme for the study of literature that has had an enormous impact on British criticism and scholarship in the past fifty years. This work, together with *The Meaning of Meaning*, written with C. K. Ogden immediately before it, and *Science and Poetry* and *Practical Criticism*, which first appeared in 1926 and 1929 respectively, was published early in Richards's long career (he was born in 1893, and died in the United States in 1979), when he was teaching English literature at Cambridge. I shall limit my discussion of Richards's views to these four books, both for the sake of clarity and simplicity, and because they were the most influential of his writings. It must be said, however, that it is something of an injustice to him to do this, since his ideas and interests subsequently developed in a number of important ways.

Like Russian Formalism, Richards's early work turns its back on positivistic scholarship, and calls for a criticism that deals directly with the distinctive properties of literature; where he differs from the Formalists, however, is in defining these properties in terms of human experience and human value. While the Formalists had treated them as objective features inherent in literature itself, Richards's emphasis was on the reader's response to literature and on the evaluation of this response. The central question of criticism is 'What gives the experience of reading a certain poem its value? How is this experience better than another?' (Richards 1967: 1). As a result he has relatively little to say about questions of literary form. What he is interested in above all is analyzing the process of reading, and formulating criteria by which to evaluate the experience that reading produces.

According to Richards, therefore, critics need two things that they did not habitually possess at the time he was writing, and usually do not possess now: a theory of communication and a theory of valuation. Without these criticism lacks intellectual rigour, and is unable to justify itself adequately in a world in which the personal and social utility of the arts is increasingly called into question. As its title indicates, *Principles of Literary Criticism* sets out to remedy this deficiency, by developing a systematic theoretical framework within which criticism can be properly conducted.

The main point on which this framework rests is the distinction, already made in *The Meaning of Meaning*, between two different functions of language. The symbolic or *referential* function uses words to talk about the objective world, to point to things, as Richards puts it. The *emotive* function uses words to evoke subjective feelings or attitudes, by means of the associations that words carry with them. The clearest example of referential language is scientific prose, in which the evocation of feeling is as far as possible eliminated, and the writer's and reader's attention focused entirely on things. The clearest example of emotive language is poetry, which is entirely concerned with the evocation of feelings or attitudes, and in which the writer's and reader's attention is not, or should not be, directed at any of the objective relationships between words and things. Poetry is pseudo-statement, Richards argued; when we read it properly 'the question of belief or disbelief, in the intellectual sense, never arises...' (Richards 1970: 277). He thus comes close to Formalist/structuralist theory in denying the referential function of poetry, but differs significantly from it in his identification of the emotive with the poetic use of language; for Jakobson, it will be remembered, the emotive or what Jakobson calls the conative and the poetic are quite distinct. It is worth noting, however, that Richards's concept of poetry is similar to that which we have encountered in the previous two chapters, in that poetry for him is simply shorthand for literature that has aesthetic value; his belief was that the value of literature as a whole lay entirely in its use of the emotive function of language.

From this identification of the poetic and the emotive it follows that Richards is far less inclined than the Formalists to stress the difference between poetry and ordinary discourse. Or more exactly, while he does stress the difference between poetry and referential language, he also stresses that the experience which poetry produces differs only in degree, not in kind, from other types of emotive experience. Too many theorists have deluded the public by talking about one sort or another of 'Phantom Aesthetic State'; in reality value in literature is explainable in exactly the same terms as value in any other form of human activity. This proposition is more easily understood when one realizes that Richards's general theory of value is a materialist one. Man 'is not in any sense primarily an intelligence; he is a system of interests' (Richards 1926: 21). It follows that what is good is simply the 'exercise of impulses and the satisfaction of their appetencies' (1967: 44), an 'appetency' being defined as a conscious or unconscious desire in the broadest sense. Life being what it is, unfortunately, our desires inevitably conflict, especially since we are social beings as well as individuals (Richards invokes Bentham here), and thus have to consider the needs of others as well as our own. The problem of morality is therefore above all a problem of organization; we have to reconcile our conflicting impulses with one another, in such a way as to allow them collectively the greatest possible degree of satisfaction. 'States of mind,' Richards says (1967: 45), 'are valuable in the degree in which they tend to reduce waste and frustration.'

The difference between ordinary emotive experience and poetic experience, or any other form of artistic experience, is simply that poetry and art in general carry the reconciliation of conflicting impulses to an exceptionally high level. In this respect Richards's theory constitutes a materialist rewriting of the famous theory of the imagination in Chapter XIV of Coleridge's *Biographia Literaria* (Coleridge 1817: II, 12-13). For Richards the moment of poetic creation is characterized by an exceptional sensitivity or 'vigilance' towards the entire range of impulses relevant to the situation that is being expressed, and by the organization of these impulses into an ordered and harmonious whole. The conflict which characterizes our everyday feelings usually causes part of them to be inhibited or suppressed; in contrast poetry and the other arts 'spring from and perpetuate hours in the lives of exceptional people, when their control and command of experience is at its highest' (Richards 1967: 22). They renovate and enhance our reactions to life by disrupting established habits of response, and creating in us a state of equilibrium of a kind that other sorts of experience can rarely achieve. This leads Richards to a position which seems close to the Formalist principle of defamiliarization, when he says, for instance (1970: 254), 'Nearly all good poetry is disconcerting'. But in contrast with the Formalists his emphasis is all on experience, not on form, and on organization, not on difference. Unlike theirs, his position is an essentially humanist one, in that it stresses the relevance of art to life. The critic is 'as closely occupied with the health of the mind as the doctor with the health of the body' (Richards 1967: 25). Moreover, poetry can do for us what religion and philosophy no longer can, that is tell us 'what to feel' and 'what to do'; poetry, *Science and Poetry* concludes (p. 82), is 'capable of saving us'.

It is this view of the experience produced by literature that causes Richards to emphasize the role of the reader rather than the author or the text. The difference between the critic's activity and that of the good reader is not really all that great. The critic must study the text with the maximum degree of attention to all its parts (Richards suggests (1970: 317) that four poems may be too many for a week's reading), but his aim is to arrive at the 'relevant mental condition' (Richards 1970: 11) associated with it, and then to judge this mental condition according to the principles outlined above. It should be noted that in emphasizing the experience of reading Richards does not make the kind of distinctions between reader, author and text that have played an important part in a number of modern literary theories. That is to say, the 'relevant mental condition' which the critic/reader must recreate within himself is assumed also to be the mental condition of the author. The poem is defined, technically, as the 'experience the right kind of reader has when he peruses the verses' (Richards 1926: 10)), and the right kind of reader is the one who manages to recreate in himself more or less completely the collection of impulses which the poet expressed in the poem or, more exactly, the 'relevant experience of the poet when contemplating the completed composition' (Richards 1967: 178).

In contrast to those modern theorists discussed elsewhere in this book, who have insisted that the literary text is in a significant sense independent of its author, and that the author's and reader's experiences are not and should not be the same, Richards treats the text simply as a transparent medium, a mere vehicle for conveying the experience of the author to the reader. He never doubts that it is possible or desirable for the critic to recreate in himself the mental condition of the author; he only recognizes that it is difficult. *Practical Criticism* deals with the obstacles blocking the reader's approach to this 'mental condition'. Richards asked a sample audience in Cambridge to describe their responses to a set of thirteen poems supplied without titles or the authors' names. The book analyzes the different mistakes of interpretation and evaluation that Richards saw in these responses, and seeks to identify their causes. Some causes, he suggests, arise from the texts themselves: the difficulty of apprehending the full range of meaning, and the inevitable differences in readers' reactions to sound and imagery. The other causes lie in the readers alone: the habits of thought and feeling that they bring with them to the text, which distort or block their response to it. Richards emphasizes the low degree of critical competence which, as a result of these different factors, his highly educated audience in his opinion revealed. But the book is written in the faith that such errors in readers' responses can be corrected, and that when this is done their way will be open to the poet's mental condition, and therefore to the correct experience of the poem. Interpretation is not really a problem for Richards, but simply a matter of approaching the text with the right kind of attention.

This aspect of Richards's work is worth stressing, because it expresses a belief which is taken for granted by a great deal of literary scholarship and criticism, and which from a more modern point of view may well seem somewhat naive. But it needs to be said that it is not a belief that Richards himself takes for granted. Much of his early writing is concerned with the theory of communication as well as the theory of valuation, with the result that his view of the author-text-reader relationship is placed within an elaborate and sophisticated theoretical framework. The details of this framework need not concern us here, except in one important respect. In *The Meaning of Meaning* Richards's discussion of communication takes place under the heading of *symbolism* or the theory of signs. As we have seen in the previous chapter, the terms *semiotics or semiology* are now usually used for the general theory of signs, which in its European structuralist versions has played an enormously important role in modern literary theory. If we contrast Richards's symbolism with the semiotics of the European structuralists, we shall be able to clarify a fundamental difference of principle between his view of knowledge and experience and theirs. The difference turns on the fact that his view is empiricist, whereas theirs very definitely is not.

Like Saussure's *Cours, The Meaning of Meaning* starts from the proposition that there is an essential disjunction between language and reality, that it is a superstition to believe that 'words are in some way parts of things' (Ogden and Richards 1936: 14). Words, the authors argue, are really a barrier between us and the world; we cannot escape from the structure of our language, and the structure of our language and the structure of the world are far from being identical. From this common starting-point, however, Ogden and Richards move in a quite different direction from Saussure's. For Saussure the meaning of words does not depend in any way on their relationship with things; it is wholly determined by the arbitrary and conventional structure of language. Ogden and Richards, in contrast, stress that words are used to 'point to' things, and that their meaning does in the last analysis depend on the things they are used to point to, their referents; language may be different from reality, therefore, but it nonetheless reflects it. For this reason they specifically criticize Saussure for 'neglecting entirely the things for which signs stand' (p. 6). Their position is thus an empiricist one, in that it rests on the principle that knowledge is the product of experience. The structuralist position derived from Saussure is anti-empiricist, inasmuch as its emphasis on the arbitrary and conventional nature of language leads to the view that knowledge is not in any way the product of experience. This aspect of Richards's thought is not so important for understanding his literary theory, since, as we have seen, he associated poetry with the emotive, not the referential, use of language. But it illustrates a radical divergence between the Anglo-American tradition as a whole and a great deal of modern European literary theory. In particular it is a fundamental feature of the American New Critics' work, to which I will shortly turn.

Some features of Richards's theory may now seem rather out of date: his notion that poetic language is purely emotive, his materialistic conception of literary value, his view of the author-text-reader relationship. But other features have become established parts of the Anglo-American critical tradition, and have by no means necessarily been superseded. These are his empiricism and humanism, and what we can call his organicist insistence on close reading, on careful attention to every detail of a literary text, on the principle that the text, like a living organism, functions through the interaction of all its constituent parts. One other feature of Richards's work has had little impact in this country, but a much greater impact, as we shall see, in the United States: the demand that criticism be founded on theory. Until very recently the theoretical issues raised by literary study have been largely ignored in British academic teaching and research. Richards's influence in Britain is thus to be found more in the practice of literary study than in the theory, in the form of undiscussed assumptions rather than systematically developed ideas.

Most of all this influence is to be seen in the practice of close reading, which has become an established part of English literature courses in Britain. Richards's influence in this respect has been much reinforced by the work of his pupil William Empson, the author of *Seven Types of Ambiguity*, first published in 1930. This is not the place for a proper discussion of Empson's views, which like a great deal of British work are more concerned with critical method than with theory (he wrote (1950: 594) that 'a critic ought to trust his own nose, like the hunting dog, and if he lets any kind of theory or principle distract him from that, he is not doing his work'). But his practical, analytical development of Richards's theory has been an important model for British criticism during the last few decades, and I will therefore conclude this section with a very brief indication of the difference between his and Richards's approach. In his early works Richards outlined in a general way the different textual factors contributing to the effect of poetry; he distinguished, for instance, between the sense, feeling, tone and intention of a text in *Practical Criticism* (pp. 180-3), and in *Principles of Literary Criticism* (pp. 103-12) he offered some discussion of rhythm and metre. But since his principal concern was with the psychological effect of poetry on the reader, he did not carry this sort of analysis very far. His interest was to ensure that poetry was read with the right kind of attention, not to analyze or explain the textual means by which its effect is achieved. *Seven Types of Ambiguity*, on the other hand, is entirely occupied with this sort of explanation, through the 'verbal analysis' of ambiguity in poetry, ambiguity being defined (in the second edition) as 'any verbal nuance, however slight, which gives room for alternative reactions to the same piece of language' (Empson 1965: 1). Empson's work thus comes close to the theories discussed in the last chapter, which approach the literary text through its linguistic form; it differs from most of these, however, in being less systematic and theoretical, and in particular in being less influenced by developments in modern linguistics.

American New Criticism: the text in itself

The American New Critics remained true to the spirit of Richards's
work by emphasizing the distinctive properties of literature or poetry,
and by dealing with them in a way which was not only empiricist,
humanistic and organicist, but also theoretical as well. Their
conception of literature differed from his, however, on at least one
fundamental point: they were much less interested in the experience
of reading than in the objective features of the medium, the literary
text itself; and they therefore spent much less time on evaluation than
on description and analysis. In this respect, clearly, they were a great
deal closer than Richards to the Russian Formalists and their
successors. But this shift of emphasis was not due to any direct
influence from the Formalists whom, as I have said, the New Critics
did not know; it was due to the influence of a figure much closer to
home, the poet T. S. Eliot. The point is frequently made, quite rightly,
that the American New Criticism is a development of Richards's and
Eliot's work fused together.

Eliot's writings on poetry do not contain a systematic theory, but on
two matters of principle he adopted a stance strongly opposed to that
of Richards: he refused to accept either that poetry consisted in the
use of emotive language, or that it was simply a vehicle for
communicating the author's experience to the reader. 'Poetry,' he
argued (1920: 52-3), 'is not a turning loose of emotion but an escape
from emotion; it is not the expression of personality, but an escape
from personality.' Good poetry objectifies feeling, expressing it
indirectly through the description of things—through the 'objective
correlative' (Eliot, 1972: 145). Good poetry is also equally concerned
with thought; Eliot admired particularly the English Metaphysical
Poets who, he suggested (1972: 286), 'incorporated their erudition into
their sensibility'. On such grounds as these he argued that the
experience of the author and that of the reader must necessarily be
different, that 'what a poem means is as much what it means to others
as what it means to the author' (Eliot 1955: 130). From these rather
brief suggestions the New Critics built up a much more definite and
systematic theory of the literary text, and of the relationship between
text, author and reader.

The term 'New Criticism' seems to have come into circulation with
the publication in 1941 of a book of that title by the American poet
and critic John Crowe Ransom. Like many terms of the sort, it does
not have a very precise definition. The British and American critics
for whom the label is commonly used, however, can be distinguished
by a common rejection of established modes of criticism and
scholarship (Empson and Leavis are sometimes included among
them), and in the case of the Americans by the fact that they proposed
alternative methods of criticism supported by well-developed literary

theories. I shall limit myself in the rest of this chapter to the most interesting and influential of these theories, those of Ransom and the other Southern critics Cleanth Brooks and Allen Tate, and those of W. K. Wimsatt and his collaborator the philosopher Monroe Beardsley; all of these writers were active mainly in the forties and fifties. More exactly, since these five writers differ not only from other New Critics but also among themselves, I shall for the sake of clarity and simplicity concentrate on two texts, Wimsatt's *The Verbal Icon* and Brooks's *The Well-Wrought Urn*, referring to the work of the others only insofar as it corroborates or develops what is said there.

One further point that is often made to explain the nature of the New Criticism is that it developed outside the ambit of the main university graduate schools, in small colleges mainly in the South. This is particularly evident in the work of Allen Tate, who like Ransom was a poet as well as a critic, and was certainly not a scholar of the traditional type. Tate was a fierce critic of the 'cloistered historical scholarship of the graduate school', with its positivistic assumption that the literary text 'expresses its place and time, or the author's personality' and nothing more (Tate 1959: 7 & 54). Criticism, he argued, should be opposed to this kind of scholarship, and concern itself with the specifically literary properties of texts. The same opposition of criticism and scholarship and the same demand that criticism should concern itself with specifically literary properties are the inspiration of two of the best-known theoretical products of the New Criticism, the essays on 'The intentional fallacy' and 'The affective fallacy' written jointly by Wimsatt and Beardsley and published in the *Sewanee Review* in 1946 and 1949 respectively (now in Wimsatt 1958: 1-39). Together these two essays are an attempt to construct the theoretical basis for an alternative to positivistic scholarship, an alternative that will deal with the specifically literary properties of texts, and deal with them with the same degree of objectivity and rigour as scholarship has traditionally claimed.

Wimsatt and Beardsley argue that a poem (short-hand, as usual, for a literary work of art) is, and therefore should be treated as, an object in the public domain, not the private creation of an individual. The N. C. author's experience and intentions at the time of writing are matters of purely historical interest, that do not—contrary to the 'intentional fallacy'—in any way determine the meaning, effect or function of his creation. As far as the author's experience is concerned, what counts from the viewpoint of criticism is only what is embodied in the text, and that is wholly accessible to anyone with a knowledge of the language and culture to which the text belongs. As for the author's intentions, what counts is only whether or not he has succeeded in writing poetry, and that too can be discerned by reference to the text alone. Thus most of what passes for literary scholarship is excluded from the sphere of criticism: studies of authors' lives, of their immediate environment, of their ideas about writing and of the genesis of their works. The only history that the critic must master is the history of words; he must grasp the full historical meaning of the language used in the text, including all its associations, and of the names to which reference may be made, but only to the extent that their meaning is a matter of public record about the culture in which the text was produced.

Wimsatt and Beardsley's approach is thus not a-historical, but it severely restricts the role of history in literary study, relegating questions about 'how the poem came to be' to a different, and by implication inferior, branch of enquiry. In this respect their position is not far removed from Richards's, since he too ignored the external history of texts, on the assumption that the 'relevant experience' of the author is entirely accessible from his work alone. But in another respect they take issue directly with Richards, following the guidance of Eliot. The 'affective fallacy', they maintain, is the fallacy of arguing, as Richards does, that poetry consists in the emotive use of language, and that the primary consideration of the critic must therefore be the effect that the poem has on the reader. Wimsatt and Beardsley's view is that a poem is not just a vehicle for conveying feelings, but an independent object with distinctive features of its own. To study the effect of the object rather than the object itself is to put the cart before the horse, since the cause of the effect is to be found in the object, and besides the effects of literary objects vary notoriously from one reading and from one reader to another. It is therefore essential to distinguish between effect on the one hand, and meaning or 'cognitive structure' on the other. It is with meaning, as the publicly accessible and thus objective constituent of texts, that literary criticism must be concerned; effect, being both variable and private, is much better left outside the field of enquiry. It is on this basis that the New Critics argued that criticism was capable of the same degree of objectivity and rigour as traditional scholarship could achieve.

If we follow Wimsatt and Beardsley this far, we arrive at a position that has had a great deal of attraction for literary critics, that the object of criticism must be the literary text itself. Moreover along with much modern literary theory, the New Critics also held that literary texts are texts of a special kind, and that the task of criticism is to give an account of this special character. The theory developed for this purpose by Wimsatt and Brooks (and in a rather different way by Ransom and Tate) takes as its starting-point Richards's (and Coleridge's) principle of the reconciliation of opposites, though the view it arrives at differs from Richards's in a number of important respects. From their views on the intentional and affective fallacies (Brooks seems to have agreed entirely with Wimsatt and Beardsley about these) it follows that this reconciliation of opposites must be seen not as an event in the mind of the author or reader, but as an objective fact about the text's meaning or structure. As Brooks put it, the New Criticism 'is concerned with the structure of the poem as poem' (Brooks 1962: 108). By 'structure' Brooks meant the organization of meaning in the text, which in the case of good literature ('poetry') possessed a different character from that of ordinary discourse. The chief property of poetry is coherence, not of a logical kind, but consisting in the harmonization of conflicting meanings or attitudes; poetry is objectively characterized, Wimsatt suggested (1958: 236), by a 'wholeness of meaning established through internally differentiated form', the reconciliation of diverse parts'. Coherence is thus associated with complexity; the meaning of the text is the product of the interaction of its parts, but this interaction depends as much on their difference from one another as on their similarity. For Brooks, Wimsatt and Beardsley complexity and coherence together constitute the key considerations in the analysis of literary texts.

Before illustrating the practical consequences of these principles, it will be useful to clarify further the American Critics' relationship with Richards on the one hand, and with the Russian Formalists and their successors on the other. To take the latter first, the New Critics clearly come very close to the Formalists and the Prague School in the importance they attach to the ideas of structure and interrelatedness (they even occasionally called themselves formalists), and in their insistence on the objective character of criticism and the distinction of the author and the reader from the text. But their notion of structure is a good deal narrower than that of the Prague School, which included all the different levels of the text and not just its meaning; and they were not much interested in the ideas of difference, defamiliarization or deviance to which the Formalists and their successors attached so much weight. What the New Critics emphasized was convergence within the text rather than deviation from an external standard. As a result they were far less interested in literary innovation than the Formalists tended to be.

A further important difference between the New Critics and the Formalists and structuralists emerges if we return to the question of the New Critics' relationship with Richards. This difference concerns their conception of meaning, a conception which is crucial to their insistence on the objective character of criticism. For the materialist Richards meaning was to be explained as the use of words either to point to things or to evoke feelings—in terms of behaviour, in the last analysis. If, as he argued, poetry could not be seen as pointing directly to things, then to explain it as relating purely to feelings seemed to be the only alternative. Wimsatt and Brooks, on the other hand, approached the question of meaning from a more mentalistic point of view, and for this reason were able to argue that poetry related to knowledge rather than emotions, while still accepting that its function was not, like that of ordinary discourse, to point directly to things. Meaning for them was not to be defined in terms of use or behaviour, but as a mental entity independent in an essential sense (as 'intension') of the material world, although in another sense (as 'extension') related to it. At the same time, we have seen, they stressed that meaning was not a purely subjective phenomenon; as Wimsatt put it (1958: 10 and 24) one can distinguish between what is public and what is private or idiosyncratic about a poem, or between its meaning, which is an objective fact about it, and its 'import', the reader's subjective response. The specific property of poetry consists in the organization of the public, objective meanings of words, that is of the concepts and associations which a culture as a whole, rather than an individual, attaches to them.

Although they do not seem to have been familiar with the work of Saussure, Wimsatt and Brooks here might appear to be approaching his principle that the meaning of words is purely conventional and arbitrary. But in fact they stopped well short of this principle, because they believed that the peculiar organization of meaning in poetry led back in the end to the 'real' world. According to Wimsatt, for instance (1958: 241), 'Poetry is a complex kind of verbal construction in which the dimension of coherence is by various techniques of implication greatly enhanced and thus generates an extra dimension of correspondence to reality, the symbolic or analogical'. The interrelations of the meanings and associations of words within a text ('the dimension of coherence') is in the first place, one might say, a purely mental event, but its effect is to modify, enrich or enlarge the reader's experience of the realities to which these meanings and associations refer. Art, Wimsatt and Brooks wrote in their joint history of literary criticism (1957: 743), 'ought to have the concreteness which comes from recognizing reality and including it'. They did not believe, therefore, as the structuralists do, that structure in literature is a wholly closed system, and that language is a prison-house that shuts us away from reality. Their position keeps much of Richards's humanism, and is in the end an empiricist one, midway between Saussure's and Richards's views of meaning, or, as some might nowadays feel, an uncomfortable mixture of the two.

To sum up what I have outlined so far, the view of Wimsatt and Brooks is that the essential property of poetry consists in the reconciliation or harmonization of opposites; that this takes the form of an objective organization of the objective meanings of words; and that although the same organization generally cannot be found in other kinds of discourse, it nonetheless contributes to our knowledge and experience of ourselves and of the world. What specific forms, one must ask, does this organization take? According to Wimsatt it commonly consists in the use of analogy, especially through metaphor. In a really good metaphor, according to Wimsatt (1958: 149), 'two clearly and substantially named objects... are brought into such a context that they face each other with fullest relevance and illumination...' This means that one brings to bear on the other the full range of mental associations that the culture attaches to it; it is important to note that the objective meaning of words includes, for the New Critics, not only their dictionary definition (sometimes called their 'denotation'), but also their associations (or 'connotations'). An example of Wimsatt's (1958: 147-8) is what he calls the metaphor, and many would call the simile, in the last line of this passage from Donne's 'A Valediction: forbidding mourning' (like Eliot, the New Critics were particularly attached to the Metaphysical Poets):

Our two soules therefore, which are one,
Though I must goe, endure not yet
A breach, but an expansion,
Like gold to ayery thinnesse beate.

The comparison between the lovers' separation and the hammering of gold into leaf-form brings together two terms which are clearly quite different and therefore might justifiably be described as opposites; and the conjunction of meanings thus established creates a series of connections (the relationship between the separated lovers is like gold leaf in that it is ethereal ('ayery'), delicate, easily damaged, but at the same time precious, pure, bright, etc.), which when related to real experience possesses considerable illuminating force. This is the sort of procedure that Wimsatt had in mind when he said (1958: 149) that 'poetry is that type of verbal structure where truth of reference or correspondence reaches a maximum degree of fusion with truth of coherence—or where external and internal relation are intimately mutual reflections'.

The New Critics did not believe, of course, that the value of poetry lay in isolated metaphors or similes; on the contrary, they insisted that in good literature all the components of the text contributed to the reconciliation of opposites that constitutes its poetic function. Clearly there may well be more than an element of exaggeration in this insistence, but it makes more sense if we accept their view that a great many features of literature that might not normally be recognized, at least at first sight, as terms of a comparison, nonetheless have a metaphorical or analogical function. For instance events or situations in narrative poetry or prose can act as metaphors for a state of mind; an obvious example would be descriptions of houses in Dickens or Balzac. A narrative theme can be a metaphorical image of a psychological process; Wimsatt suggests that the relationship between the knight and the lady in Keats's 'La Belle Dame Sans Merci' can be read as an expression of the 'loss of self in the mysterious lure of beauty' (Wimsatt 1958: 80-1). In fact all good poetry, according to Wimsatt, is characterized by an intricate network of analogical relationships created by what he calls the 'iconic' properties of the verbal medium. What does he mean by 'iconic'?

It is noteworthy that Wimsatt, like Richards, connects his view of literature to a semiotic theory. In Wimsatt's case the theory is that of the American behaviourist C. W. Morris, whose work follows in the empirical tradition established by Ogden and Richards. Wimsatt's use of the term 'iconic' (and the title of *The Verbal Icon*) derives from Morris's distinction (1971: 37) between the 'iconic' and the 'symbolic' sign; the former is that which 'characterizes... by exhibiting in itself the properties of an object', the latter that which does not do so, but has instead a purely conventional relationship with the object that it designates. Pictures are obvious examples of iconic signs; individual words, on the other hand, are generally symbolic signs, except for a limited number of cases such as those of onomatopoeia. Following Morris (1939), however, Wimsatt argued that one of the distinguishing characteristics of poetry was to exploit the 'iconic or directly imitative' powers of language (Wimsatt 1958: 115). This might seem at first sight to express the naive view that onomatopoeia and other kinds of sound symbolism constitute essential features of poetry, but Wimsatt's conception of the iconic function of language embraces a great deal more than this. 'Iconicity' in poetry was to be found, he argued, in metrical structures, in various figures of speech such as antithesis, and in general in the way in which words are arranged in sequence. Thus a disordered sequence of clauses or sentences can act as an iconic representation of material or emotional disorder. More importantly, the different types of phonetic, metrical, syntactic and semantic parallelism in poetic language indicate iconically a connection of meaning between the terms involved, and thus point to or reinforce the analogies between disparate elements from which, in his opinion, so much of the effect of poetry derives.

A random example of this process can be seen in two lines from Wordsworth's 'Intimations of Immortality':

Whither is fled the visionary gleam?

Where is it now, the glory and the dream?

Here the verse structure, especially the rhyme, together with the syntactic parallelism and the inverted semantic parallelism (*visionary gleam/glory...dream*), creates an exchange of effect between the two lines, whereby each illuminates the other. Because of the force of analogy, the meaning of the couplet as a whole is greater than the sum of the separate meanings of its two halves. This sort of analysis is substantially similar to Jakobson's discussion of Poe's 'Raven' (Sebeok

1971: 371-2), which I referred to in the last chapter, and it may well be that the New Critics' influence lay behind Jakobson's arguments there. It should be said, however, that Wimsatt's treatment of the iconic properties of language is as far as the New Critics went in the direction of stylistic analysis as I have defined it; in general they were much more interested in meaning than in forms of expression, and would have undoubtedly had scarce sympathy for Jakobson's attempt to define the properties of poetry in purely linguistic terms.

Finally, for both Wimsatt and Brooks a defining characteristic of poetry was *irony*. Here too they follow Richards, who used the same term to characterize the 'bringing in of the opposite, the complementary impulse' (Richards 1967: 197), which he held to be characteristic of all great poetry. In Wimsatt's definition irony is a 'cognitive principle which shades off through paradox into the general principle of metaphor' (Wimsatt and Brooks 1957: 747); according to Brooks, it is the 'most general term that we have for the kind of qualification which the various elements in a context receive from the context' (Brooks 1949: 191). 'Irony' here is clearly being used in a very broad sense to include the types of analogical or metaphorical relationship that we have so far considered. It might therefore seem a rather odd choice as a label, but Wimsatt and Brooks's reason for using it is that they view these analogical or metaphorical relationships as producing effects essentially similar to those for which the word irony is more commonly used, and which they also see as an important part of poetry. In all these cases a kind of reconciliation of opposites can be seen.

It is not easy to find a general definition of the normal meaning of irony, but it usually stands for a process by which the content of a statement is qualified either by the reader's attribution of a contrary intention to the author, or by the reader's awareness of factors that are in conflict in one way or another with what is being said. In this sense irony is closely related to paradox, which involves the association of conflicting elements within the same statement. Thus the term irony is used in something approaching its usual acceptance when Brooks associates it with Yeats's appeal to the Greek sages in 'Sailing to Byzantium':

Consume my heart away; sick with desire
And fastened to a dying animal
It knows not what it is; and gather me
Into the artifice of eternity.

That Yeats should speak of the 'artifice of eternity' evidently undermines in a sense the appearance of passion and sincerity with which he invokes the Greek sages, and thus can be said to bring about a kind of ironic reconciliation between his aspiration to a life free from Nature, and his rational awareness of his human limitations

(Brooks 1949: 173).

What is achieved by devices such as this is not a relationship of analogy, as in the preceding examples, but, in Brooks's words (1949: 189), a 'unification of attitudes into a hierarchy subordinated to a total and governing attitude'. This is also what Brooks sees in Keats's poetry in his analysis of 'Ode to a Grecian Urn', though here the notion of paradox rather than irony is invoked (1949: 139-52). Brooks emphasizes the internal contradictions of the poem: the fact that the urn is silent, but also speaks; that it is motionless, yet the scenes depicted on it seem to be alive; that unheard melodies are sweeter than those which one hears, and so on. What these contradictions add up to is the paradoxical point that the 'frozen moment of loveliness is more dynamic than the fluid world of reality *only* because it is frozen', that art is more vivid than life only because it is not alive. It is this paradox, according to Brooks, that is the main point of the poem.

It is interesting to compare Brooks's analysis with Spitzer's treatment of the same poem (Spitzer 1962: 67-97). Brooks's may not necessarily be much better, but Spitzer's undoubtedly attributes a more prosaic kind of meaning to the text, which he sees as expressing an (unreconciled) opposition between the 'archaeological message' and the 'aesthetic message' of the urn. The contrast may therefore serve to illustrate one major merit of Brooks's criticism and of the New Criticism in general: their use of ideas such as irony may seem exaggerated and confusing, but it makes the important point that the meaning of poetry, though possibly analyzable, cannot be expressed properly in the form of a conventional prosaic statement. 'Irony' is a strategic term that indicates the capacity of poetry to resist or elude our attempts to reduce it to conventional modes of expression. This capacity is the main theme of Brooks's important essay, 'The heresy of paraphrase' (Brooks 1949: 176-96). At the very most, Brooks argues, all that the practice of paraphrase can do is offer a crudely approximative outline of the poetic content of a text. The error of so many critics and scholars is to write as if the paraphrasable elements in literature constituted its substance, whereas the value of literature is to be found not in propositions, but in relationships, and these relationships are not logical, but imaginative.

I hope that I have made the merits of the New Criticism sufficiently clear in the preceding pages. As to their possible limitations, one's view of these depends, as it does in the case of most literary theories, on one's own theoretical position. Stylistic analysts are likely to hold that the New Critics paid insufficient attention to the linguistic form of texts since, apart from Wimsatt's discussion of the 'iconic' properties of poetry, they were really only interested in certain kinds of structure of meaning, and made no use of the tools offered by modern linguistics for the analysis of poetic effect. Structuralist critics are bound to disagree with the New Critics' insistence on the referential function of literature, with their view of literature's connection with the 'real' world. Post-structuralist critics will deny that literature possesses the organic unity to which the New Critics attached so much weight. An objection that can more usefully be discussed here, however, is the general principle formulated by Wimsatt, Beardsley and Brooks, and to some extent shared by Ransom and Tate, that literary criticism can and should be both evaluative and objective. That is to say, although the New Critics were less interested in evaluation than Richards, and more interested in description and analysis, they nonetheless assumed that their principles constituted criteria for distinguishing good literature from bad, and that good literature had an important part to play in human affairs. Since this is an assumption taken for granted by a good deal of modern criticism, we should consider some of the objections that can be made against the New Critics' arguments in its favour. These arguments in its favour concern, as we have seen, both the meaning and the structure of texts, and difficulties arise in connection with both of these factors.

The thesis of 'The intentional fallacy', that the meaning of the words in a text is, and should be treated as, a matter of public knowledge, seems wholly unexceptionable as far as the dictionary-definition (the 'denotation') of words is concerned; but it seems much more problematic when one takes account of the broader associations that words carry with them ('connotations'). The New Critics argued both that these broader associations were an essential part of the meaning of literature, and that a high degree of consensus existed, at least among experienced readers, as to which associations were attached to which words. Yet while it seems conceivable that a group of critics, given an adequate degree of historical or philological knowledge, might agree as to which associations are *possible* in the case of a given word, there is considerable room for disagreement, since every word possesses a very wide range of associations, as to which of these are relevant for the purposes of interpretation. Moreover the interpreter of a text has to make a decision on the relative importance of the different elements in a work, and he has to find a way of relating these elements to one another. Interpreting the meaning of a text is not just a matter of adding together cumulatively the individual meanings of the words of which it is composed. How can an objective solution to these problems be found?

Positivistic literary scholarship solves these problems by looking outside the text for information about the author's intentions in writing, but as we have seen, the New Critics rejected this solution. For them the answer to the question of interpretation, and at the same time to the question of evaluation, is provided by the concept of structure; good literature or poetry is distinguished from bad literature or non-literature by an objective structure of meaning, the balancing or reconciliation of opposing attitudes or terms. If we accept this, then we might have an objective principle for distinguishing between the relevant and irrelevant associations of words in a text, for ordering its parts according to their relative importance, and for connecting these parts with one another. But is such a structure of opposing factors really an *objective* property of poetry, and can we therefore as a matter of principle allow our interpretation and evaluation to be guided by it?

There is more than one reason why we might not. First, we can question whether the concept is an adequate one for distinguishing poetry from non-poetry. It is easy enough to identify opposing terms or attitudes in a text, but how does one decide whether or not they are balanced or reconciled? For Richards the reconciliation occurred in the reader's mind, and therefore could be identified introspectively. For the New Critics it was an objective structural feature of the text, but they offered no precise structural criteria for identifying it. In practice, like Richards, they had to rely on intuition rather than analysis, or at best on the consensus of experienced readers, a consensus which, the recent history of criticism seems to suggest, is not all that often achieved. Secondly, we may well doubt that the reconciliation of opposites is really a sound principle for defining poetry, whether it is truly applicable to all the texts one would wish to include under the heading of poetry or good literature. For like a great many theories, it seems much more easily applicable to some kinds of text than to others; one can see quite clearly its possible relevance to the sort of literature that the New Critics generally preferred to discuss, the lyric tradition from Shakespeare, roughly speaking, to Yeats (Wimsatt and Brooks described their movement (1957: 742) as 'neo-classic'); but it is much less easy to see its relevance to the novel, or to much modern *avant-garde* writing. This last objection can be put in a form applicable to many of the theories discussed in this book: that it may be a mistake to try to define the essential features of literature in absolute and objective terms; that such definitions as one may devise are likely to be relevant only to certain kinds or certain features of literature, or merely constitute one among a number of possible ways of approaching the subject.

As far as the New Critics are concerned, the best conclusion might be, not that their view of poetry was necessarily wrong, but that what was wrong was the claims they made concerning it. One may well agree with their rejection of positivistic historical scholarship, and their insistence on a combination of interpretation and evaluation in the study of literary texts. One may even agree that the best key to interpretation and evaluation is their principle of the reconciliation of opposites. One should also accept, however, that interpretation and evaluation are not objective statements about literary works, but statements about the interaction between works and their readers, because critics cannot avoid imposing their own views and their own preferences on the texts with which they deal. This is not to say that the best alternative to positivistic scholarship is the exclusive study of the reader's response, such as Richards advocated in his early works. Much more promising avenues are opened up by those schools of thought that combine a description of the structure of texts with an account of the knowledge and attitudes that readers bring with them and of the processes to which they subject them: phenomenological theory, which studies the process by which readers create meaning in a text with much more attention to the text itself than Richards was inclined to allow—but for which, regrettably, there is no space in this book; and some versions of structuralist theory, which will be discussed in the following chapter.

Further Reading

Of the four books by I. A. Richards mentioned in the text *Principles of Literary Criticism* is the best introduction to his work. A fifth book, *Coleridge on Imagination*, is of particular interest in view of the extent to which Coleridge's theory of the imagination influenced Richards's thinking. On Richards see Schiller's *I. A. Richards's Theory of Literature* and the more recent and brief essay by Butler, 'I. A. Richards and the fortunes of critical theory'. The celebration volume edited by Brower *et al.*, *I. A. Richards: Essays in His Honor* contains useful information about Richards's early work in Cambridge, and some interesting tributes from other New Critics. The most important collections of T. S. Eliot's writings are the *Selected Essays* and *On Poetry and Poets.*

The most important writings by Wimsatt and Brooks are collected in *The Verbal Icon* and *The Well Wrought Urn* respectively. Five further essays by Brooks are forceful statements of the New Critics' position: 'Literary criticism', 'The quick and the dead', 'The critic and his text', 'The formalist critics', 'Literary criticism: poet, poem and reader'. Tate's theoretical writings are collected in *Collected Essays* and *Essays of Four Decades.* Monroe Beardsley's *Aesthetics* translates the New Critics' views into more technical philosophical language and puts them in the framework of a general theory of art. Ransom's *The New Criticism* has interesting critical discussions of Richards and Eliot, but proposes a theory of literature considerably less sound than that of Wimsatt and Brooks, though he has strong affinities with them. An important critical discussion of the New Critics in general is Krieger's *The New Apologists for Poetry.*

Morris's semiotics is most easily accessible in his *Foundation of the Theory of Signs* and *Signs, Language and Behavior.* For phenomenological approaches to literature, see Poulet's 'Phenomenology of reading' and Iser's *The Act of Reading.* Hirsch's *Validity in Interpretation* also draws on phenomenology and offers a theoretical account of the interaction between reader and text, though its conclusions constitute a defence—an exceptionally intelligent and powerful one—of traditional literary scholarship.

4 Structuralism and Post-Structuralism

Ann Jefferson

The title of a recent book on structuralism describes it as a revolution—*La révolution structurale* (Benoist 1976)—and it is in this perspective that the phenomenon is best approached. Its revolution-ariness is, however, only incidentally political: in that it evolved outside the universities in marginal academic institutions, and in that its development during the 1960s reached a kind of peak in the years 1967-8, thus coinciding with the *événements* of 1968. But its aims and intentions, for all their revolutionariness, are not primarily political. Structuralism is revolutionary because it can be adopted only as an alternative and not as an addition to traditional academic habits. It cannot be incorporated as a handy extra methodological tool to be resorted to when all else fails. It is revolutionary too in its scope, for it has implications for a whole range of academic subjects in the arts and the social sciences. But what must finally be regarded as its most revolutionary feature is the importance that it attributes to language: not only is language a major preoccupation of structuralist thinking, but language itself is used as a model for all sorts of non-linguistic institutions.

Although literary theory is only one aspect of structuralism, the question of language is obviously peculiarly relevant to it, and it is the conceptual rigour and the range of possibilities provided by the linguistic component of structuralism that give structuralist literary theory its distinctive qualities. For although many aspects of structuralist theory may seem to be familiar from other literary theories, structuralist theory is developed to a point where issues previously unconsidered by linguistic approaches to literature have to be confronted. The exclusion of the author from critical analysis, the attention to form, the claims for scientificity are themes which have all been voiced before, but not in the same theoretical context, and so they acquire a different significance. Most important of all, however, is the way that structuralist principles lead eventually to a questioning of the nature of critical discourse itself. In structuralist theory the language of criticism ends up posing as many problems as the language of literature. As far as literary theory is concerned, it is perhaps this more than anything else which constitutes the structuralist revolution.

84

The linguistic model

French structuralism, applied as it has been to a wide range of intellectual disciplines, is a realization of Saussure's dream of a general science of signs — semiology. Although he saw language as the most complex and most characteristic of all systems of expression, it was, in his view, nevertheless analogous in structure and organization to any form of social behaviour. Because of its exemplary status, language was to be 'the master pattern for all branches of semiology'. What was involved in this extension of structural linguistics was a profound alteration of perspective in most of the human sciences; it was no longer a question of gathering empirically verifiable data, of turning a positivist gaze onto a world of objects, but it meant seeing forms of expression as signs whose meanings depend on conventions, relations and systems, rather than on any inherent features.

The earliest response to this proposed change of perspective was made by Lévi-Strauss, the founder of what he called 'structural anthropology'. Anthropology is potentially a positivist's paradise, inviting an endless recording of observable facts and data. But in his analyses of kinship relations or of cooking, for example, Lévi-Strauss's approach is based entirely on the assumption that they are systems which are structured like a language; that is to say, that their individual elements have meaning only in so far as they are part of an overall system. The anthropologist's task is to map out this system, and, by using the tools of linguistic analysis, to draw up what one might call the grammar of the various cultures he encounters.

This principle is not the special prerogative of anthropology, and it transcends all the boundaries of traditional academic disciplines. The axiom that 'culture, in all its aspects, is a language' (Barthes 1972) will affect any discipline that touches on cultural questions. At whatever level of detail or generality, culture consists of signs which are structured and organized like those of language itself. Barthes's *Système de la mode* exemplifies this linguistic principle in its attempt to read the grammar of fashion. Saussure himself uses the example of polite formulas many of which, as he says, do seem to be 'imbued with a certain natural expressiveness', but which are nevertheless entirely based on convention. He cites the Chinese gesture of bowing down to the ground nine times before an emperor. Although this might seem in one sense to be an unequivocal expression of deference, it becomes clear that it is purely conventional as soon as one imagines an Englishman acting in this way in the presence of his Queen. Whereas in a Chinese context the meaning of the gesture would seem perfectly transparent, in an English context this behaviour would be totally bewildering because it is not part of the English conventions of politesse. And for an Englishman observing Chinese manners, the exact significance of this gesture would be lost on him unless he was acquainted with the system as a whole. Only then would he know whether the Chinaman's gesture expressed the utmost in humility, and if so, whether this is marked in the depth or in the number of the bows. The structuralist brief, then, is to map out the conventions and rules governing all aspects of social behaviour.

Not all the people who have been called structuralists have been happy to accept the label, but this suggests not so much that it has been over-enthusiastically applied, but that far from being a school or a doctrine, structuralism is indeed a generalized revolution in ways of thinking. The definition of the term structuralism is best kept to this sort of generality, and the formula proposed by Barthes perhaps provides the best one. Structuralism, he says, is 'a certain mode of analysis of cultural artefacts, in so far as this mode originates in the methods of contemporary linguistics' (1970: 412). So, any systematic extension of Saussurean concepts may, broadly speaking, be regarded as structuralist. This at once opens up a huge field of enquiry, but since our concern here is with literary theory, I shall restrict my discussion to structuralism's contribution to the study of literature and, in doing so, unfortunately run the risk of understating the effects of the new pluridisciplinarity on the approach to literature. Anthropology, psychoanalysis, philosophy, history, cybernetics, information theory, semiotics and, of course, linguistics have all left their mark on structuralist discourse about literature.

The hegemony of the linguistic model (the premise of all structuralist thought) acquires a special significance in the sphere of literature. In one sense, literature is like any other form of social or cultural activity, so that it may be analyzed in semiological terms; this would involve discovering what the nature of its component signs are, and how the system governing their use and combination operates. To this extent literature is not so different from fashion or from the myths whose analysis is part of Lévi-Strauss's structural anthropology. But, unlike fashion or kinship systems, literature is not only organized like language; it is actually made of language. And in a third sense, literature is thought by many structuralists to have a special relationship to language, in that it involves a unique awareness of the nature of language itself. At one level, literature is always *about* language, so that, in the words of Tzvetan Todorov, 'the writer does nothing more than read language' (1969:84). Literature is regarded as distinct from all other uses of language, since only literature (by being non-referential) makes us aware of the true (i.e. Saussurean) nature of language. Thus, the linguistic model is triply pertinent to literature: to its material (verbal), to its formal organization (semiological) and to its themes (linguistic).

As we saw in Chapter 2, Saussure's view of language excludes the referential dimension with his concept of the sign as the combination of signifier (written or spoken) and signified (concept). He emphasizes that words do not depend on reality for their meaning. Similarly, since language is a self-sufficient system, meaning is not determined by the subjective intentions and wishes of its speakers: it is not the speaker who directly imparts meaning to his utterances, but the linguistic system as a whole which produces it. Transposed onto literature, this at once excludes both the author and reality as points of departure for interpretation. A structuralist approach will dispense with these linchpins of traditional literary history and criticism in order to reveal the signifying systems at work in literature. Taking its cue from structural linguistics, it will concentrate on the signifiers at the expense of the signifieds. It will be concerned with the way in which meaning is produced rather than with meaning itself. Genette speaks of this change in emphasis as a restoration of equilibrium in literary studies: 'Literature had been regarded as a message without a code for such a long time, that it became necessary to regard it momentarily as a code without a message' (1966:150). The 'structuralist method' consists in an analysis of the 'immanent structures' of a work in contrast with what Wellek and Warren call the 'extrinsic approach' (1963).

The value placed on this internal approach is reminiscent of American New Criticism, and also of Russian Formalism and the work of Roman Jakobson—all of whom Genette approvingly cites in this essay on structuralism and literary criticism. However, structuralist criticism differs from all of them on some important issues. It does not share the New Critics' preoccupation with meaning, and its attention to the signifiers of literature is never subordinated to any signified. Furthermore, the relationship between literature and language in the structuralist view is not primarily a negative or oppositional one, as it is in Formalist theory; in accordance with the basic principles of structuralist theory, the relationship between the two is one of parallelism, or, to use a structuralist term, homology. Literature (in the same way as kinship systems) is organized at every level *like* language, and it is a central part of structuralist purpose to reveal the similarity.

When the logic of the linguistic homology is taken a step further, the special status of language that literature is uniquely capable of revealing becomes apparent. By concentrating on the signifying structures of literature, the structuralist approach sets aside all questions of content. This means that the language of literature is no longer regarded as subordinated to the message supposedly carried by the text, and this emptiness of content illustrates far more powerfully than could anything else the primacy of language itself. Most human discourses behave as if language were transparent to a meaning or a reality beyond it, but, if we carry the lessons of Saussure right though to their logical conclusion, we see that this cannot be so. The organization of language precedes any message or reality, and indeed these are products constructed by the language system and not vice versa. Although for practical purposes in ordinary situations we use language *as if* it were transparent and as if meanings and intentions existed prior to it, literature, in its freedom from any referential obligation, demonstrates the supremacy of language over all other activities.

This is what Barthes means when he speaks of literature representing the sovereignty of language. 'Language,' says Barthes, 'is literature's Being, its very world; the whole of literature is contained in the act of writing, and no longer in those of "thinking", "portraying", "telling" or "feeling"' (1970:411). Language is not just the means of communication in literature, but, in so far as one can say literature has a content, language in all its opacity is also the content of literature. So that for the structuralists literature becomes 'a kind of extension and application of certain properties of language' (Todorov 1977:19). 'The writer does nothing more than read language' (Todorov 1969:84), he is 'someone for whom language is a problem' (Barthes 1966:46), and the literary work itself becomes 'a question put to language' (p.55).

The language foregrounded (so to speak) by literature in the structuralist view is not some supposed ordinary or scientific language: it is a Saussurean image of language, an image based on a coherent linguistic theory. In this the structural approach to literature has huge advantages over many other linguistically inspired theories. And it is this recourse to the Saussurean model which gives rise to the most innovative of structuralism's extensions of the linguistic analogy: poetics.

Poetics and narratology

The real originality of the structuralist application of Saussure to literary studies is not in the analysis of particular works, but in its elaboration of poetics as a general science of literature. As well as using the linguistic concepts of sign and system to analyze structures at various levels of a text, the structuralists returned to Saussure's distinction between *langue* and *parole* in order to outline a whole new approach to literature. Just as linguistics is not primarily concerned with individual utterances *(parole)* but with the language system as a whole *(langue)*, the structuralist proposal is that individual works should be regarded as instances of *parole* informed by rules which belong to a general literary *langue*. As Todorov repeatedly insists in his programmatic outline, *Poétique*, 'the individual text is simply the means by which one can describe the properties of literature in general' (1973a:20). Poetics is concerned with a general grammar of literature which will be only partially visible in any individual work. And just as linguistics ought to be able to account for the structure and organization of as yet unspoken sentences, so poetics ought to be able to account for the rules governing as yet unwritten works of literature: 'In this case each work is regarded only as the manifestation of a far more general abstract structure, of which it is only one of the many possible incarnations. To that extent this science does not deal with actual literature, but with possible literature.' (pp.19-20).

Todorov goes on to suggest that these properties of literary discourse are specific to literature itself, and invokes the Russian Formalist concept of 'literariness'. But in practice structuralist poetics have never been particularly interested in establishing the specificity of literature. This is partly because structuralist poetics are part of a wider semiological venture, and partly because any distinctiveness ascribed to literature in structuralist thinking takes it right back to linguistics; for the element that constitutes 'literature's Being' and its 'very world' (Barthes 1970) is simply language itself.

The shift of focus from the individual text to literature in general brought with it a new awareness of the different nature of different types of discourse about literature, and of the different ways of treating literature implied by them. Broadly speaking, these discourses can be divided into reading, criticism and poetics, and in the structuralist view these divisions are radical. Although the nineteenth-century literary historian would have acknowledged a distinction between literary scholarship and reading, the implication of much twentieth-century critical practice is that criticism is an extension of the reading process, and that the critic is simply an exemplary and particularly articulate reader. This view informs every page of a book like I.A. Richards's *Principles of Literary Criticism*, where the critic is seen as making explicit the states of mind produced in him as a reader by the literary work.

In his *Critique et vérité* Barthes outlines the nature of the distinctions that exist between poetics, criticism and reading. *Critique et vérité* was written as a defence of the structuralist position after the attack on Barthes's study of Racine *(Sur Racine)* by Raymond Picard (a Sorbonne academic) in a pamphlet entitled *Nouvelle critique ou nouvelle imposture* (1965). By uncovering the presuppositions of the sort of criticism typified by Picard's approach, Barthes shows that they are both arbitrary and ideologically motivated. The values of 'objectivity', 'taste' and French *'clarté',* which Picard claims to uphold, and in the name of which he defends traditional academic criticism, are ultimately political. This demonstrates that criticism can no longer be regarded as a straightforward and unproblematic response to a given work of art.

Criticism is quite different, in Barthes's view, from reading. Reading is a process of identification with a work and a faithful reading will be nothing more than a word for word repetition of the text. Criticism, on the other hand, places the critic at a certain distance from the work. For Barthes criticism consists in actively constructing a meaning for a text and not in passively deciphering *the* meaning; for in the structuralist view there is no single meaning in literary works. This insistence on the plurality of meanings in a text is the logical consequence of the absence of any authorial intention in literature. In structuralist theory this absence is far more radical than it is in the case of the New Critics. Doing away with authorial intention opens the way to doing away with the notion of unitary meaning in the text, since without some evidence about intentions it is usually impossible to reduce even everyday linguistic ambiguities. The New Critics did, of course, make room for ambiguity in their theory, but their stress on the organic coherence of the literary text prevented ambiguity from being genuinely open-ended. Being defined in terms of tension or paradox, ambiguity's potential diversity was restored to some sort of unitary wholeness. In other words, the New Critical concept of coherence took over the task of unifying meaning which could no longer be attributed to the author. In structuralist theory there is nothing to take over this task, so that ambiguity becomes fully polysemic, in the sense of consisting of an unreconcilable multiplicity of meanings. In a view which sees meaning as the product of the rules and conventions of different signifying systems, there is no role given to private meanings or intentions on the part of individuals. This is what is meant by the 'decentering of the subject' in structuralist theory. (The consequences of this decentering of the subject are most fully and interestingly developed in the post-structuralist work of Lacan and Derrida.)

So without any authorial guarantee concerning meaning, the critic's job is no longer to retrieve *the* meaning of a text, but rather, in the full knowledge that the meanings of the text are plural, to produce an interpretation which realizes just one of the possibilities contained in the text. Structuralist theory builds on connotation instead of trying to sweep the question under the carpet (as the New Critics might be said to have done). As Barthes says, if words only had one (dictionary) meaning, there would be no literature. Literature is based on 'the very plurality of meanings' (1966:50); or, put in a slightly different way which nicely reverses an old critical saw, 'a work is "eternal", not because it imposes one meaning on different men, but because it suggests different meanings to one man' (p.51).

It is the third category, poetics or the science of literature, which is most fully conscious of this plurality, because it is concerned only with the different ways in which meaning is produced in literature and not with its content. It is this emphasis on the signifier at the expense of the signified which makes poetics the type of discourse most favoured and fostered by structuralism. Structuralist contributions to narrative theory are probably the best instances of the nature of structuralist poetics. The first two examples discussed below illustrate different ways in which the linguistic model is used to develop a narrative model, and the third, Genette's *Narrative Discourse* (which does not use strictly linguistic analytical categories), illustrates somewhat differently the structuralist preoccupation with abstract models rather than with individual texts.

Todorov's *Grammaire du Décaméron,* despite the reference to a particular text in the title, deals primarily with 'the structure of narrative in general and not with that of one book' (1969:10). Its aim is to establish 'the science of narrative' which Todorov baptizes 'narratology'. The *Decameron* stories are used merely as test material and were chosen because they seemed intuitively to be constructed primarily in narrative terms, as opposed to psychological, philosophical or descriptive ones. The assumption is that each tale makes manifest a greater or smaller part of an 'abstract structure' and the task Todorov sets himself is the delineation of that abstract structure.

His starting point is that this structure will have the form of a grammar. The linguistic model will provide the basis of the narrative model, and Todorov justifies this procedure by making claims that go far beyond the usual assumptions of structuralism. He suggests that language is the 'master pattern' for all signifying systems not just because of the nature of the sign and the system, but because the human mind and the universe as well share a common structure which is that of language itself. This claim would need an enormous amount of evidence to substantiate it, but it does illustrate very clearly a particular view about the structures that a certain type of structuralism deals with: namely, that they actually exist, and that the task of structuralist sciences is to uncover them. This attitude is rather different from other instances of structuralist thinking which do not claim any intrinsic reality for their structures. What matters is not whether the human psyche is in itself constructed in grammatical terms (as Noam Chomsky has suggested), but that social behaviour lends itself to analysis in broadly linguistic terms. The real question in structuralist theory is how literally the linguistic model should be applied. The three examples discussed in this section suggest that the most fertile and productive uses of the linguistic model are the most analogical and metaphorical ones.

Todorov's analysis of the *Decameron* tales is based on a very rigorous and literal use of linguistic categories. He begins by dividing narrative up into *semantic, syntactic* and *verbal* aspects. The semantic aspect is what we would otherwise call its content, and the verbal aspect is Todorov's term for the language in which the stories are told. The syntax of narrative is the relation between the events and is the main concern of Todorov's study. As in a linguistic analysis, he begins by finding out what the basic units of combination are (by analogy with the phonemes, morphemes, etc. which constitute the basic units of language). In the case of narrative syntax this basic unit is taken to be the *clause* which is in turn composed of a *subject* and a *predicate*. Todorov then goes on to establish the primary categories of his narrative grammar, and they are *proper noun, adjective* and *verb.* The so-called secondary categories consist of almost equally linguistic concepts: negation and opposition, comparatives, modes, and so on. The detailed application of these categories to actual instances of narrative is, on the whole, tedious and not particularly illuminating. The most that can be claimed for it is that it is ingenious. Nevertheless Todorov's study is interesting for the principle which guides his whole enterprise, and which he sums up in his conclusion.

Here he accepts that his own grammatical categories may be questionable, but insists that his study confirms the belief that there exists a grammar of narrative, and moreover that there is a fundamental similarity between language and narrative which is mutually illuminating. He claims that one can 'understand narrative better if one knows that a character is a noun, and the action a verb'. And furthermore, 'one will understand nouns and verbs better if one thinks of the role that they adopt in narrative'. Indeed, to combine a noun with a verb, he says, 'is to take the first step towards narrative' (1969:84). This seems to be pushing the linguistic analogy too far, and to be taking too literally the structuralist tenet that literature is 'the essential manifestation' of language, and that 'the writer does nothing more than read language' (p.84). In practice, most work in structuralist poetics is not restricted to this direct transposition of linguistic concepts onto the structures of literature.

In his 'Introduction to the structural analysis of narrative' Barthes makes claims very similar to those of Todorov about the homology between language and narrative, with particular reference to the sentence: 'a narrative is a large sentence, just as any declarative sentence is, in a certain way, the outline of a little narrative' (1975b:241). But the model he constructs (and whose principles he expounds so clearly in his opening pages) is not based on such rigorously maintained categories. For instance, the basic units of narrative which he picks out are defined and differentiated principally in terms of their narrative effect and not of any prior linguistic analogies that he may have found for them. His distinction between *function* and *index* (two of his basic narrative units) is determined by whether the units link with others to form a chain of actions (the functions), or whether their role is a more diffuse contribution to the meaning of the story, such as information about characters (the indices). It is only when this distinction has been made in terms that comply with the workings of narrative that the linguistic analogy is introduced: the functions, Barthes suggests, are based on metonymic relations, the indices on metaphoric relations. And even here in his recourse to Jakobson's use of the two terms, Barthes is referring to two very broad principles of combination in language and not (as Todorov does) to specific grammatical categories. In other words, this approach treats narrative language as a second-order language which is therefore not susceptible to analysis in strict linguistic categories.

The same approach is evident in Barthes's use of the distinction made by the French linguist Emile Benveniste between *personal* and *apersonal* aspects of language. In a series of articles published under the title *Problems in General Linguistics,* Benveniste demonstrates with particular reference to the temporal and pronominal systems of the French language that linguistic items can be distinguished according to whether they include a reference to the moment or position of the utterance of a statement. Any tense which includes a component of the present tense such as the *passé composé (il a écrit)* is personal in so far as it acknowledges the present moment of the utterance. Similarly the pronouns *I* and *you (je* and *tu)* are personal because they can be defined only by the utterance in which they appear. They differ from the pronoun *he* whose referent can be identified without consideration of the linguistic utterance. What is important about this contribution to linguistic theory is that it allows one to analyze the personal or 'subjective' elements of language without having to resort to any real correlative outside language. They simply point to the fact that language is being produced and do not involve any questions of psychological reality. Rather than expressing the individual reality of the speaker who happens to utter them, these 'personal' aspects of language testify to a certain self-consciousness or reflexivity within language itself.

Barthes draws on Benveniste's distinction in order to analyze a level of narrative which Todorov ignores in his study: the 'narration', that is to say, the manner in which the story is told. His particular application of Benveniste's terms is actually rather bizarre and unproductive. However, the broad principle which informs Benveniste's category of the personal is most pertinently extrapolated onto a narrative model by Barthes when he points out that traditional critical practice has tended to attribute all apparently subjective (or personal) elements to a psychological reality placed outside the language of the text itself: the mind or personality of the author, the narrator or a character in the story. In other words, the subjective elements were read referentially and so it was implied that the logic of narrative derived from a reality outside itself. By including so-called subjective elements within the language system and associating them with a degree of linguistic self-consciousness, Benveniste is providing structuralist narratology with a very attractive analogy. Narrative, which at the level of narration is most threatened by referential interpretations, can now be regarded as a self-contained system with its own internal rules governing every aspect of its operation; the signs of the narrator are embedded in the narrative, hence perfectly detectable by a semiological analysis (1975b:261). Moreover, the principle of linguistic self-consciousness or reflexivity seems to be made even more explicit when transposed to the narrative model. Reference is emphatically excluded and reflexivity reinforced: 'What goes on in narrative is, from the referential (real) point of view, strictly *nothing*. What does "happen" is language per se, the adventure of language whose advent never ceases to be celebrated.' (p.271). The construction of models independent of any external reality seems to encourage an emphasis on this sort of linguistic reflexivity and it will be encountered again in other structuralist writings.

Genette's largest contribution to structuralist narrative theory is his *Narrative Discourse*. This is a remarkable study for a number of reasons, but chief amongst these must be its comprehensiveness. Most other structuralist theories of narrative take only one aspect, and usually this is the events of the narrative, as in Todorov's *Grammaire du Décaméron* or Greimas's *Sémantique structurale*. Barthes's 'Introduction to the structural analysis of narrative' deals with more than one level of narrative, but presumes that they are hierarchically arranged and that, therefore, to a certain extent, they can be discussed separately. The principle behind Genette's study is that narrative is a product of the interaction of its different component levels, and that the science of narrative consists in an analysis of the relations between them. This is why he calls the object of his study 'narrative discourse', which he defines as 'the oral or written discourse which undertakes to tell of an event or a series of events', and which he distinguishes from narrative as series of events (story), and narrative as the act of narrating. In fact, Genette's relational approach means that none of these aspects of narrative can be conceived of as independent units:

> Story and narrating...exist for me only by means of the intermediary of the narrative. But reciprocally, the narrative (the narrated discourse) can only be such to the extent that it tells a story, without which it would not be narrative (like, let us say, Spinoza's *Ethics*), and to the extent that it is uttered by someone, without which (like, for example, a collection of archaeological documents) it would not in itself be a discourse. As narrative, it lives by its relationship to the story that it recounts; as discourse, it lives by its relationship to the narrating that utters it (1980:29).

Consequently 'analysis of narrative will thus be for [him] essentially a study of the *relationships* between narrative and story, between narrative and narrating, and (to the extent that they are inscribed in the narrative discourse) between story and narrating' (my italics). This approach is reminiscent of the Formalist distinction between *fabula* and *syuzhet*, but despite the absence of any direct linguistic analogy it is supremely structuralist in its desire to construct a universal model of narrative discourse.

The linguistic model is, on the whole, used here in a very general and metaphorical sense, and not in a literal and detailed one. The introduction makes a perfunctory bow to linguistics when Genette puts forward the hypothesis that narrative may be regarded as 'the development — monstrous, if you will — given to a *verbal* form, in the grammatical sense of the term: the expansion of a verb... The *Odyssey* or the *Recherche* is only, in a certain way, an amplification (in the rhetorical sense) of statements such as *Ulysses comes home to Ithaca* or *Marcel becomes a writer*' (1980:30). Genette goes on to suggest that this authorizes the use of linguistic categories in the analysis of narrative discourse. In fact, however, he adapts the few terms he does borrow to fit his case, rather than forcing his view of narrative to comply strictly with linguistic principles. For instance, although he borrows the concept of *mood* from linguistics, he recognizes from the outset that, in contrast to ordinary language, narrative only knows the indicative mood (there are no imperative or subjunctive forms of narrative), and that if his use of the term is to have any value at all it must be 'stretched' and given a metaphorical function.

The adaptation of linguistic terms like *mood* and of rhetorical terms like *ellipsis* is not so much designed to construct rigid parallels either with language or with rhetoric, but rather is itself a rhetorical device for freeing narrative from any referential interpretation. Genette systematically coins new terms for aspects of narrative which have already been named but which imply a psychological or realist element: *flashback* becomes *analepsis, point of view* becomes *focalization,* the opposition between *telling* and *showing* is translated back into Plato's terms *diegesis* and *mimesis,* and so on. This 'jargon' serves not only to highlight distinctions which looser, more commonsensical terms might obscure, but they imply most emphatically that narrative is governed not by any relation to reality, but by its own internal laws and logic.

This logic is set out in a manner that illustrates in an exemplary way structuralist intention to map out all the possibilities of literature as distinct from its actual manifestations. Genette's relational strategy leads him to construct purely abstract combinations without any real existence in literature. For example, in discussing 'duration' he compares the relative speeds of the narrating and the story, and in order to draw up his table he needs to begin with a non-existent form, a 'hypothetical reference zero' where the duration of the narrative exactly matches the duration of the events narrated—an 'isochronous narrative' which, as he says, does not exist. But even though the category is entirely hypothetical, it is nevertheless part of the 'table of literature's possibilities' which it is the business of poetics to construct.

The poetic purpose of Genette's *Narrative Discourse* is curiously complemented by his study of Proust's *À la recherche du temps perdu* which takes up a good portion of the book. This procedure is unusual in that Genette devotes far more attention to Proust than other narratological studies have to actual texts, and it is also unusual in that Proust's novel is an infinitely more complex work than those which narrative theories have commonly analyzed: with Boccaccio's *Decameron*, Todorov was taking relatively simple specimens as points of reference for his narratological analyses. Genette's discussion of Proust is so far reaching that his book can be regarded as much as a reading of *À la recherche* as a contribution to narrative theory, and to this extent it represents a challenge to the generic distinctions normally made in structuralist thinking between poetics and criticism. At the same time it also illustrates the practical purpose narrative theory may have for the reading of individual works of literature.

In a limited sense Proust's novel is used as a testing ground for the analytic concepts; and in another equally limited sense, the novel is treated as a concrete manifestation of the abstract narrative model. But the most important and interesting aspect of its role in the book is the way in which Proust's narrative is shown to deviate from the model: Genette shows that in a number of ways *À la recherche* breaks and challenges the laws of narrative proposed by the abstract model but without undercutting their general validity. For example, one of the most far-reaching subversions of narrative logic comes in Proust's confusion of the *singulative* and the *iterative* modes. These are the terms Genette coins to describe different categories of frequency (a previously overlooked aspect of narrative). In the singulative mode there is a balance between the number of times an event occurs and the number of times it is narrated (an event occurring once is narrated once and an event occuring *x* times is narrated *x* times). In the iterative mode there is an imbalance whereby an event occurring only once is narrated several times or, much more frequently in literature, an event occurring frequently or repeatedly is narrated only once. Proust's narrative undercuts these distinctions in a way that defies logic as well as narrative models by narrating single events as if they had happened repeatedly. This apparent contradiction of the model by Proust's text is not a sign of the model's inadequacy but the reverse.

STRUCTURALISM AND POST-STRUCTURALISM

The existence of the category *frequency* in Genette's model alerts readers to a highly significant aspect of Proust's narrative which previous critical readings have failed to notice. At the same time, by not forcing the text to fit the categories of the model, the text can be seen as a transformation of it, or at least of a part of it. The model serves to illuminate literature without reducing individual literary texts to being miniature reproductions of it.

These three examples of structuralist narratology show varying degrees of success and interest in their use of the linguistic analogy. Todorov's *Grammaire du Décaméron* is the least successful (and perhaps the least interesting) because his topic (the events of narrative) remains too narrow, and the application of linguistics too literal. Genette's *Narrative Discourse,* by contrast, is able to include a much wider range of narrative elements and to use the linguistic analogy in the most flexible way. More importantly, his idea that narrative grammar may be transformed or subverted by individual texts gives his grammar far greater analytical power, since elements which might fall outside the scope of a more rigid model may now be read as transformations of it. But the chief advantage of the linguistic analogy in any narrative theory is that it allows literature in general and narrative in particular to be read as a self-contained system independent of any realist function. Finally, the variety of ways in which linguistic terms have been applied to literary narrative suggests that even in the most linguistically conscious theories of literature, the role of linguistics remains subservient: it can never supply literary analysis with prescriptive procedures when it is operating at this level of the literary text. In short, linguistics may provide literary theory with the broad outlines of a model, but it cannot determine either its detail or the manner in which it is applied to literature.

Structuralist criticism

Although structuralist writing on literature is predominantly in the field of poetics, there are some interesting instances of what Todorov calls a contradiction in terms: structuralist criticism (1973b:73). For, as he says in the introduction to his essay on the tales of Henry James, 'criticism seeks to interpret a particular work, while structuralism, for its part, is a scientific method implying an interest in impersonal laws and forms, of which existing objects are only the realizations' (1973b:73). Nevertheless, he goes on to justify his pursuit of the contradiction by claiming that the instruments provided by literary theory may be refined and transformed through their application to particular texts.

In practice, however, the experiment in structuralist criticism reveals something far more interesting: Todorov's reading of James's tales shows them to have much in common with the discourse of poetics itself. Their 'content' (as articulated by Todorov) both mirrors their form and implies a commentary on the nature of literary works in general. Literature is being read here as an allegory of poetics. Todorov begins by taking his cue from one of James's tales, 'The Figure in the Carpet'. The situation is an exemplary one for a structuralist: a young critic is chided by a writer for having failed to identify the motive principle of his work, the 'figure in the carpet' which governs every aspect of it. The critic never finds it, but Todorov sees in the tale both a set of instructions for any critic of literature and an outline of the figure to be read in the carpet of James's own work. The figure is, precisely, that of the existence of a secret or an absent essence, and he traces it in various forms through a number of different tales. In other words, the critical key to James's tales is provided by the tales themselves. At the same time, the critic will learn from this figure that, since the secrets are never disclosed, and since the absent essence only operates when it is absent, he should not force his text to produce a single interpretative meaning. The meaning will always be secret, absent. He should be content instead with outlining the motive principle and not try to predicate any content to it.

Todorov finds a variety of different manifestations of the absent essence in James's stories. It exists either as a secret, as unknowable information ('Sir Dominick Ferrand', 'In the Cage'), or in the form of ghosts, a 'form of absence *par excellence*' ('Sir Edmund Orme', 'The Turn of the Screw'), or in the form of death ('The Friends of the Friends', 'Maud-Evelyn'), or in the form of a work of art. This last variant of the figure of absence is regarded by Todorov as the key one, since the tales about art both incarnate the basic principle and amount to 'veritable aesthetic treatises'. In 'The Real Thing' a painter is offered the services of an extremely genteel couple who have fallen on hard times and are willing to act as models for his illustrations of aristocratic life. To his surprise his paintings become worse and worse. When he changes his models for a vulgar Cockney girl and a vagabond Italian his illustrations of lords and ladies immediately come to life. The moral of this tale is that 'the absence of "real" qualities in Miss Churm and Oronte is precisely what gives them their essential value, so necessary to the work of art'. And this in turn suggests its own moral, which is a constant theme of structuralist poetics:

Art therefore is not the reproduction of a given 'reality', nor is it created through the imitation of such a reality. It demands quite different qualities; to be 'real' can even, as in the present case, be harmful. In the realms of art there is nothing preliminary to the work, nothing which constitutes its origin. It is the work of art itself that is original; the secondary becomes primary (p.93).

The primacy of the system over what it represents is a conclusion that poetics derives from the extension of the Saussurean model to the sphere of the grammar of literature; and now we find literature itself endorsing these conclusions.

The exclusion of the author from literature is similarly represented by a number of James's tales. 'The Death of the Lion', 'The Private Life' and 'The Birthplace' all illustrate that the creation and reading of literature have nothing to do with the author as a real person, and that literature exists quite independently of the author's particular circumstances and personality.

Todorov makes the work of art in James's stories the supreme and exemplary form of absence: it is more essential than the hidden secrets, more accessible than the ghosts, more material than death. In short, 'it offers the only way of experiencing essence'. The implication behind this hierarchy of the forms of absence in James is that secrets, ghosts and death are merely pale prefigurations of art as absent essence, and therefore that any significance they might have in the functioning of the tales derives from their status as anticipatory metaphors of art itself. To a large extent, then, all the stories can be read as semi-allegorical or thematic explorations of topics in poetics. They are reflexive representations of their own form and construction, 'metaliterary stories, stories devoted to the constructive principle of the story', and by extension, representations of literature in general.

What all this shows is that a distinctively structuralist kind of criticism is possible, and moreover, that it is more than the simple application and refinement of the tools of poetics. It differs from traditional criticism by not pretending to retrieve a single, definitive meaning from the literary text, but on the other hand, it does ascribe a special kind of content to literature: form itself. Structuralist criticism is characterized primarily by this kind of reflexivity.

But although Todorov's analysis of James seems to conform to distinctions between reading, criticism and poetics in its attempt to prove that structuralist criticism is possible, it also undermines them. Literature's self-consciousness serves to blur the traditional opposition between literature and criticism. In his introduction to Part II of *Critique et vérité* Barthes argues that the degree of critical self-consciousness in literature means that it is not possible to draw a clear distinction between criticism and literature. And he claims specifically that this is because writing itself has a dual, a poetic *and* a critical function. The importance that structuralism in general and Barthes in particular place on the notion of writing both supports structuralism's challenge to traditional ways of talking about literature, and questions a number of presuppositions of the discourse of structuralism itself. This process is begun more explicitly in Barthes's *S/Z* which in its change of direction opens what is now called the post-structuralist era and marks the end of the so-called classical or scientific period of structuralism.

Lisible and scriptible

S/Z represents a break both with poetics and with criticism. Poetics is replaced by a basic evaluative typology of texts, and criticism by commentary (in this case of a short story by Balzac called 'Sarrasine'). The relation between literature in general and individual texts is seen by Barthes in a rather different way from that implied by poetics. He questions the structuralist practice of reducing individual texts to a microcosm of a general poetics, of using 'the indifferent gaze of science' to force them to 'rejoin, inductively, the Copy from which we will then make them derive' (1975a: 3). The alternative approach of the evaluative typology that Barthes sets out in *S/Z* privileges the writing of the text, and sees it not as a structure or as a copy of a structure (poetics), but as a practice. The static, closed image of the literary text that goes with the concept of structure is replaced by a dynamic, open one which is expressed in concepts like play and practice. All that remains of the Saussurean model is the primacy of language and an emphasis on the signifier, both of which are even more strongly asserted here than in poetics. The notions of system and homology are gone; neither literature in general nor individual texts are thought of as systems, and consequently analogies with linguistic structures do not apply. Literature does not copy language any more than it copies reality.

Barthes's typology is based on his distinction between the *lisible* (the readerly) and the *scriptible* (the writerly). The positive term is the *scriptible* because value is now attributed to production rather than reproduction or representation. The *lisible* is what we recognize and already know. The readerly text is the one that as readers we passively consume, whereas the writerly text demands the reader's active cooperation, and requires him to contribute in the production and writing of the text. It would in fact be more accurate to speak of readerly and writerly qualities in a text, since no text is purely readerly nor purely writerly. The *scriptible/lisible* distinction represents a scale of values by which individual texts may be evaluated. Broadly speaking 'classical' texts such as Balzac's 'Sarrasine' are predominantly readerly, whereas modern texts are predominantly writerly. Or, to use another of Barthes's terms, the modern text is more 'plural' than the classical one.

The *scriptible* is not a thing but a process, and is therefore not assimilable to the structures of poetics. There is structuration but no structure, production but no product. Although Barthes gives meaning a role in the text, the emphasis is on its production. Indeed, the production of meaning is seen as an essential part of the activity of the text, and it is not subordinated to an ultimate signified. Meaning itself is part of a process, always on the move. But the primary values are those of the signifier, and the writerly allows the reader to 'function himself, to gain access to the magic of the signifier, to the pleasure of writing' (p. 4). This conception of the signifier bears only a vestige of its Saussurean ancestry, for there is nothing formalist about it and it is not part of a structural attempt to outline the basic grammar of any system. In fact, Barthes's treatment of the signified is designed to maintain dynamism and break the stasis of structure and system. A reading which is faithful to the writerly will avoid the closure of static structures; reading a text in Barthesian terms does not lead to the construction of 'a Model' or a 'legal structure of norms or infractions', a narrative or poetic law, but opens 'a perspective (of fragments, of voices from other texts, other codes), whose vanishing point is nonetheless carelessly pushed back, mysteriously opened' (p. 12).

While the typology sets up these principles, only a commentary can be faithful to them and maintain the text's plurality. Criticism and poetics both constrict the text by making it conform to a meaning or to a model. Barthes's commentary represents what he calls the step-by-step approach which affirms the text's plurality by the attempt to 'star [*étoiler*] the text instead of assembling it' (p. 13), to fragment and disperse it, instead of unifying it. The commentary is based on totally arbitrary 'units of reading' which Barthes calls 'lexies'. These do not correspond to any pattern or structure inherent in the text, but consist of what the reader judges to be an identifiable unit, (a phrase, a sentence, a couple of sentences). The purely linear progression through the text based on the successive identification of *lexies* is a major contribution to the maintaining of the text's plurality.

So, to sum up the main points so far: the *scriptible* as a value and the commentary as a form of reading both imply an approach which is profoundly incompatible with the chief principles of classical structuralism. The third main way in which the idea of structure is undermined can be seen in Barthes's use of the idea of codes. Barthes identifies five major codes by which literature is constituted. They are the hermeneutic code through which an enigma is posed and eventually solved in a text; the semic code which determines themes; the symbolic code which is the sphere where meanings become multivalent and reversible; the proairetic code which determines action and behaviour; and finally, the cultural code which provides social and 'scientific' information. The important thing here is not so much the nature of the codes, nor whether they have been properly identified, nor even whether they are comprehensive enough, but the idea of codes structuring literary texts. These codes are shared by author and reader and their role in the text is what makes it a text. 'The five codes create a kind of network, a *topos* through which the entire text passes (or rather, in passing becomes text)' (p. 20).

These codes are rather different from the grammars of structuralist poetics because they do not have the status of a model, but are instances of *parole* which have no ultimate *langue*. In *S/Z* Barthes is not suggesting that literary texts implicitly refer to some transcendent model: literary texts can only cross-refer to each other. Moreover, there is nothing inherently literary about these codes, since they function as a part of culture in general. Reality therefore is not defined either concretely or semiotically. Instead reality becomes a kind of text itself, constituted by codes. In this case, then, to write about reality is not to relate word to thing, but text to text. A code is no more than a 'perspective of quotations' (p. 20), and 'its only logic is that of the *already-done* or the *already-read*' (p. 19). These codes are quite different from the models of poetics because they cannot be reduced to a structure, and consequently the text itself cannot in turn be reduced to a structural homology of a code. The codes participate in the structuring process of the text and cannot be rounded off or completed.

This intertextual model of what lies beyond it—reality, truth, author or reader—removes literature even further from any representational function. Representation is redefined as a kind of quotation:

> The 'realistic' artist never places 'reality' as the origin of his discourse, but only and always, as far back as can be traced, an already written real, a prospective code, along which we discern, as far as the eye can see, only a succession of copies (p. 167).

When a text turns its attention to giving a physical description of a character it resorts to various strategies which give its presumed object the status of a representation. Most typically, the apparent reality of the object is an effect of its being treated like a painting; the text frames its object and then refers to it in terms that suggest that it is already represented on a canvas. Realism, then, consists 'not in copying the real, but in copying a "painted" copy of the real' (p. 55). If the text represents anything 'real' at all, it is only the difficulty of representation. This is because, although on one level Balzac's story is 'about' castration (one of the characters is a castrato singer), in Barthes's reading the theme of castration is seen as a pretext for a kind of reflexive anxiety on the part of the text itself concerning the very possibility of representation. Since the hero takes the castrato to be a woman and makes a sculpture of him/her in female form, castration is linked to problems of representation. And it is because of this that Barthes treats the theme of castration as a metaphorical comment on the absence of the full reality which a naive view of literature might imagine it to derive from. '*Sarrasine* represents the very confusion [*le trouble même*] of representation' (p. 216), and precisely because of this, representation is replaced by reflexivity.

Truth is similarly found to have no real status in the literary text. Far from ordering and creating literature from without, Barthes shows truth to be a mirage produced by one of his five codes. By posing an enigma and deferring its solution, the hermeneutic code pulls off a sleight of hand which makes delayed information synonymous with truth. Truth is not something fixed and solid beyond and behind the literary text, and to which the text can be reduced: it is simply what comes last in the text.

Human subjects are also dissolved into codes or into the illusory products of those codes. Characters, for example, are not 'real' people but effects produced by the semic code through its naming of qualities, which are then given an appearance of individuality and reality through the attribution of a proper name. The character Sarrasine in Balzac's story is just a collection of traits which is arbitrarily unified through being called 'Sarrasine'. Nor has the author any more substance. Like the characters and indeed the reader himself he is simply a collection of codes: 'The "I" which approaches the text is already itself a plurality of other texts, of codes which are infinite, or more precisely, lost (whose origin is lost)' (p. 10). Any sense of individuality or substantiality is just another illusory effect of the codes. Subjectivity acquires 'the generality of stereotypes'. The plural text will undo the classical image of a tangible author sending a tangible message to a tangible reader; and the more plural a text is, the more it will make it impossible for the reader to find any origin for it, whether it be in the form of an authorial voice, a representational content or a philosophical truth.

Classical structuralism had already ruled out the possibility of explaining texts in terms of an author or a reality external to them, but its use of the linguistic analogy and its construction of a poetics had the effect of turning language and poetics into origins for literature. Even if literary texts were not seen as copies of reality, they were nevertheless regarded as copies of structuralist models. Barthes's approach to *S/Z* has the merit of respecting the individual play of a given text while at the same time relying on the general concept of the *scriptible* and the *lisible* to do so. Indeed, the *scriptible* is paradoxically what makes possible the respect for the individuality of each text. This combined with the format of the commentary allows structuralist discourse to exhibit many more of the qualities of the language of literature itself. There is a kind of contradiction in classical structuralist writing which attributes to literature a non-referential self-sufficiency supposed to incarnate language's very being, and yet which continues itself to employ a language whose referential scientificity ignores the very qualities that it speaks of.

It had in fact been an early aim of Barthes's to make structuralist discourse 'homogeneous with its object' (literature). And he suggested that Saussure's view of language meant that the 'logical continuation of structuralism can only be to rejoin literature, no longer as an "object" of analysis, but as the activity of writing' (1970: 413). *S/Z* comes very close to meeting that requirement, but as one continuation of Saussurean logic it seriously undermines the classical structuralist continuation of this same logic.

Derrida and post-structuralism

Like the later work of Barthes, the writing of Jacques Derrida is both a continuation and a critique of structuralism. We are, says Derrida, still inside structuralism in so far as structuralism constitutes 'an adventure of vision, a conversion in the way of putting questions to any object' (Derrida 1978: 3). Any critique, then, must necessarily be made from inside the structuralist system. Indeed, Derrida's quarrel with classical structuralism does not concern its Saussurean inspiration, but rather the way in which it has unwittingly betrayed the very principles on which the Saussurean revolution was founded. Broadly speaking, Derrida's rigorous and far-reaching exploration of the implications of Saussure's claim, that 'in language there are only differences without positive terms', leads him to question the key concepts of structuralism (in particular, sign and structure) and its methodology (as represented by poetics and semiology). But in order to appreciate Derrida's critique of these issues, it is necessary to know something of the position from which he makes it.

Of the various concepts that Derrida uses in conducting his argument, those of 'logocentrism' and *'différance'* are perhaps the most effective as a means of introducing his ideas. Logocentrism is the term he uses to describe all forms of thought which base themselves on some external point of reference, such as the notion of truth. Western philosophy, with Plato as an exemplary first instance, has generally acted on the presupposition that language is subservient to some idea, intention or referent that lies outside it. This idea is at odds with the Saussurean principle that it is language which is primary, and that far from preceding language, meaning is an effect produced by language. However, the conceptual oppositions which structure Western philosophical thought, such as *sensible* v. *intelligible, form* v. *content* all imply that ideas, and indeed content of any kind, exist independently of the medium in which they are formulated: the word 'medium' itself conveys the secondary status that language is given in these conceptual oppositions, always defined as a vehicle or an instrument of something separate from it which governs it from without. The privileged terms in all the oppositions which underpin

Western metaphysical thought are the idea, the content, and the subservient terms are the medium, the form, the vehicle. Language has always been regarded as belonging among these secondary categories.

For anyone who is not involved with philosophy and who has read and understood Saussure, the charge of logocentrism may not seem pertinent. But Derrida's subtle analyses show that logocentrism tends to manifest itself in extremely indirect ways. Notable examples occur in instances of what Derrida calls 'phonocentrism', and even Saussure was unable to avoid moments of phonocentricity. Phonocentricism consists in a privileging of speech over writing. This preference for speech tends to be based on a logocentric assumption that speech directly expresses a meaning or intention that its speaker 'has in mind'. Speech is somehow seen as being transparent to that meaning in a way that writing never can be, because writing is conventionally thought to copy speech rather than the ideas themselves. Any view which gives speech precedence over writing must be basing its preference on this sort of hierarchical model, which implicitly places ideas in a commanding position at the top, and writing as a degraded form of representation at the bottom. A truly Saussurean approach would give speech and writing equal status, since it regards language as a system of differences, and not as a collection of terms for conveying information existing independently of it. Derrida counters the temptation of phonocentrist thought by describing language in general as a kind of writing, as an 'archi-écriture'. The reversal of the conventional speech/writing hierarchy which is implied in the term archi-écriture makes it impossible to see any use of language, written or spoken, as being determined by presence, intention or representation.

The concept that Derrida uses in opposition to logocentrism of any kind is différance. The word is of Derrida's own coinage and is deliberately ambiguous (and therefore not translatable), being derived from the French différer which means both 'to defer, postpone, delay' and 'to differ, be different from'. The two senses of différance are needed to explain both the fact that any element of language relates to other elements in a text, and the fact that it is distinct from them. The function or meaning of an element is never fully present because it depends on its association with other elements to which it harks back and refers forward. At the same time, its existence as an element depends on its being distinct from other elements. The term différance could be seen as a conflation of Jakobson's distinction between the paradigmatic and the syntagmatic, but in Derrida's argument these are inseparable and the conflation is given great importance and power. Différance is the force behind, or rather in language; it produces the effects of difference which make up language. It is not a thing that determines language from without, and it therefore has a quite different status and function from that of truth in logocentric modes of thought. It is not an entity or an origin, although the language we use may predispose us to thinking of it in those terms. *Différance* is, says Derrida, 'the non-full non-unitary "origin"; it is the structured and differing/deferring [*différante*] origin of differences' (1973: 141). The word itself also nicely illustrates Derrida's point that writing does not copy speech, for it is only in the written form that one can see the difference between the word *'différance'* and the usual French *'différence'*. The distinction between the two written forms does not correspond to any distinction in their spoken form.

In a huge variety of ways and from a multitude of different perspectives Derrida shows that nothing escapes *différance*, that there are no inviolate entities, that everything becomes part of what he calls the play of differences. He also demonstrates how hard it is to maintain this view, and how easy it is to lapse into logocentric assumptions. These dangers can be seen both in structuralism and in other approaches to literature which all thought they were avoiding them.

Although Derrida adopts the Saussurean principle of the differential nature of language, he is nevertheless extremely wary of the concept of the sign which in Saussure is an integral part of the differential principle. Saussure's starting point is, as we have seen, that signs in language are arbitrary and differential. Derrida, of course, endorses this formulation, but stresses the *principle* of arbitrariness and difference as against the notion of the sign itself, since it risks degenerating into an entity and thus reverting to a metaphysical concept. Traditionally (that is to say, before Saussure) the sign was regarded as a substitute for something; signs were, by definition, signs for things. This view, quite obviously, does not involve any principle of difference. What Derrida points out is that this view can creep back into the definition of the sign itself once it has been broken down into a signifier and a signified. Saussure does say that the two are as inseparable as the two sides of a single sheet of paper, but the very existence of the terms themselves implies the possibility of an independent signified existing prior to its signifier, and therefore capable of being represented by more than one signifier. In other words the traditional concept of the sign as a vehicle or substitute for an idea or a thing can fairly easily be transposed to the structure of the sign itself, with the signifier being regarded as a substitute for the signified. The danger lies in the very distinction between signifier and signified, and for this reason Derrida prefers to use a concept like *différance* which, while preserving the Saussurean principle of the differential, is completely non-substantive and non-hierarchical.

The concept of structure also has its risks and its dangers, even though it appears to be based on the idea of relations as opposed to entities or determining origins (as we saw above in the discussion of the Prague School). First, the essential feature of the Prague School definition of structure is its totality. This encourages a teleological or hierarchical view of the relation between the elements of the structure on the one hand, and its existence as a closed totality on the other: the parts are subordinated to the whole in a manner that conflicts with the principle of *différance*. Similarly, being closed and self-contained, the structure implies a concentric form of organization with the centre as the organizing agent which would then be exempt from the play of differences which, instead, it appears to control. Third, the structural emphasis on form, which was originally designed to dispose of the objects of content, leads to the possibility of treating form itself as an object, so ignoring any differential value. And finally, the structuralist view of structures is supported by the Saussurean distinction between synchrony and diachrony which itself has a certain logocentric resonance. Structures are presumed to be synchronically organized, and this implies that their elements are all simultaneously present. This contrasts with Derrida's view of *différance* which cuts across the distinction between diachrony and synchrony by including a temporal as well as a spatial dimension: elements are seen as part of a chain of relationships which cannot be defined as either diachronic or synchronic and so cannot be reduced to the status of an object in the way that synchronically defined structures can. The concept of structure is replaced in Derrida's writing by the concept of a chain of signification which avoids the dangers implicit in the notion of structure: by being open-ended and non-teleological it does away with any idea of a commanding entity within the system, and by having a temporal as well as a spatial dimension it cannot itself be reduced to the status of entity or object.

All this may seem rather general and abstract, so at this point we might ask where literature fits into Derrida's scheme and how Derrida might be relevant to literature. Derrida himself writes with as much ease and penetration about literary texts as about philosophical ones. But it is perhaps primarily in his assertion that 'Il n'y a pas de hors texte' ('There is nothing outside the text/There is no outside text') that he may seem most relevant to literary theory, for in this claim one hears echoes of the principles of a number of the major theories of literature that have emerged in this century. Derrida's assertion is, of course, a summary of his thinking on language in general applied to individual texts. If language in general is not governed by anything outside it, no more are individual texts. This seems to have obvious parallels with the Russian Formalist attempt to found an approach to literature that would exclude all factors external to the texts—history, psychology, and so on. Similarly, it appears to evoke the principles behind the New Critics' 'words on the page' axiom. Indeed Derrida acknowledges the value of the Formalists' attempt to wrest literature from its secondary role as instrument in the logocentric sciences of history and philosophy. And in fact, some of the values that have often been associated with literature would seem to conform to Derrida's anti-logocentric approach, in so far as the so-called medium in literature (the form, the language) has been presumed to exceed to a greater or lesser extent any content or message it may have. In other words, the medium is not entirely transparent to its object. It is as if literature were perhaps necessarily less susceptible to the temptations of logocentrism than other forms of discourse. And Derrida certainly sees in a number of literary works (particularly those of Mallarmé and Georges Bataille) a keener sense of the principle of *différance* than can be found in any work of linguistics or philosophy.

Furthermore, there are certain aspects of Derrida's own strategies of writing which are likely to be familiar to anyone with any experience of literature. First, there is his attitude towards the texts he is writing about: because writing can never be governed by the intention and avowed aims of its authors, Derrida finds himself saying of Rousseau, for example, that what he actually writes is quite different from what he means to say: that he is bound, as we all are, to say 'more, less or something quite other than what he *would mean/would like to say* [*voudrait dire*]' (1976: 158). Literary criticism has often taken precisely this assumption as its starting point, and has presumed that a literary text is not necessarily saying what it intends to say or even what it appears to say—hence the need for critical interpretation. In a sense, the very institution of literary criticism is concrete testimony of this assumption. And this is what distinguishes the reading of literature from the reading of philosophy which requires that one understands as fully as possible what is meant, and where it is assumed that the writing will illustrate the meaning in a direct and immediate way. So that although the theoretical presuppositions of traditional literary criticism are very different from Derrida's, the student of literature is likely to recognize his strategy of not taking texts at face value.

Second, he will also be familiar with the elements of ambiguity and word-play which are so characteristic of Derrida's own writing. He will, of course, have encountered them in literary rather than in critical texts, but he will nevertheless appreciate the polysemy of a term like *différance* and not feel uncomfortable without a definition of its proper or primary meaning (there is none). Many of the key words of Derrida's arguments are similarly polysemic and their polysemy is essential to his argument: his reading of Rousseau in *Of Grammatology*, for example, turns on the ambiguity of the word *supplément* which can mean both an addition and a substitute. Ambiguity of this kind and degree demonstrates very forcibly that words are not determined on a one-to-one basis by the idea or thing which they supposedly represent.

However, although literature in general and certain works in particular would seem to support Derrida's claims about the principle of *différance* in language, the very nature of those claims means that we cannot regard literature as being a special kind or use of language. *All* language and not just literary language, is informed by the play of *différance*. If we take literary to mean something more than merely 'decorative', then, in a sense, all language may be seen as literary. This claim is directly opposed to the principle underlying the Formalist approach, according to which practical language is, so to speak, regarded as logocentric, and literary language as deviant, and therefore subsidiary use of language. Jakobson and Riffaterre base their poetics on a similar sort of assumption, when they define literary uses of language as both distinctive and measurable. Derrida reverses this priority by making all apparently logocentric forms of discourse secondary and indeed illusory. The discourses of science and philosophy, for example, which appear to be entirely directed towards some external referent and whose intelligibility would seem to depend on their transparency, are simply an effect produced by language itself. 'Philosophy is, within writing, nothing but the movement of writing as effacement of the signifier and the desire of presence restored' (1976: 287). In other words, philosophy is just a certain type of writing in which the signifying element of language has been illusorily repressed in favour of the signified. Because philosophy and science now occupy the secondary position that was previously ascribed to literature, it makes no sense to speak of literature as a special kind of language. This only worked as long as the 'primary' use of language was regarded as logocentric. In Derrida's thinking there is no special category for literature.

This challenge to the concept of literature combined with the questioning of the concepts of structuralist theory seriously undermine the apparent advances made by all those theories of literature which draw on linguistics in general and Saussure in particular. These threats are significantly extended in Derrida's discussion of the status of the discourse of the human sciences. As we have seen, most of the principal theories of literature discussed in this book have included as part of their purpose the creation of a scientific basis for the study of literature. It was, for instance, the Formalists' avowed aim and intention to create a scientific alternative to subjective chit-chat about literature. Structuralism, guided by the founding discipline of semiology, had equally firm scientific pretensions. And, to the extent that it comprises a certain body of knowledge and a certain set of principles for systematic enquiry, any theory of literature is likely to establish the study of literature as a science. What Derrida argues is that any discourse which conceives of itself as scientific is bound to be logocentric: it will assume that it is transparent to its object and that that object is a stable entity. But according to Derrida, neither language nor literature is a stable object, because neither the language of the texts we read, nor the language of the discourse in which we discuss them, is exempt from *différance*.

We have seen how structuralism showed increasing signs of unease concerning the nature of discourse about literature, and we noted the solution proposed by Barthes, namely that discourse *about* literature should take the form of the discourse *of* literature. But since Derrida has no special category for literature, this solution would clearly be of no use to him. His own solutions go by the names of 'grammatology' and 'deconstruction'. In Derrida's writing the science of semiology is replaced by grammatology which, as he says, takes the form of a question rather than of a new science. Similarly, structural analysis is replaced by deconstruction which also questions its objects rather than reflecting them. Grammatology is the 'science' of writing in so far as writing is regarded as a generalized phenomenon, as *archi-écriture*. Deconstruction is the form it takes when it turns its attention to specific texts. A deconstructive reading tries to bring out the logic of the text's language as opposed to the logic of its author's claims. It will tease out the text's implied presuppositions and point out the (inevitable) contradictions in them.

To take an example: in his reading of Rousseau's essay on the origin of language, Derrida shows that Rousseau saw music as consisting of two contradictory components, melody and harmony. Rousseau regards melody as authentic, springing directly from the passions. Harmony, by contrast, he sees as a corrupt and mediated construct because it is the product of articulation (i.e. of differentiation). However, when Rousseau's text is submitted to the questioning scrutiny of the grammatologist, it emerges that, although Rousseau clearly wants to say that melody originates in the passions, he actually has to formulate a definition of it that includes a notion of articulation and differentiation. A deconstructive reading of this kind, then, will take the metaphysical, logocentric oppositions at work in a text, reverse them, and then question them in such a way as to 'neutralize' them. As none of us can ever get outside logocentrism (its power over our habits of thought and over our language is so pervasive), the most that one can do is work against them from within in this sort of way.

The inevitability of logocentrism is perhaps best demonstrated by the format and the assumptions of this account of Derrida itself. The name of 'Derrida' has been used in such a way as to imply that it refers to a real person who has certain ideas and theories which he has

expressed in various books and essays, and which this introduction
has tried to repeat, treating them as signifieds that can be represented
in a number of different forms. What I have tried to say—namely that
writing is not governed by the subjective intentions of its author, that
ideas do not exist independently of the language which 'expresses'
them—has (inevitably) been partially contradicted by the manner in
which it has been said. To obey the rules of the genre of the
'introductory account', to use the rhetoric of exposition is, in a sense,
necessarily to betray the most interesting insights of 'Derrida'.

Further Reading

For an impression of the diversity of thought and work that come under a
structuralist heading, a glance at some of the collections of structuralist
writing might be instructive; for example, Michael Lane (ed.), *Structuralism: A
Reader,* Richard Macksey and Eugenio Donato (eds.), *The Structuralist
Controversy* and David Robey (ed.), *Structuralism: An Introduction.* See also the
essays on five major structuralist figures in *Structuralism and Since* (ed. John
Sturrock).

There are a number of books on structuralism, some of which are more
useful than others. Terence Hawkes's *Structuralism and Semiotics* offers a good
survey of the field (and includes a very useful annotated bibliography) but is
encyclopedic rather than coherent. A more rigorous and consistent account is
given in Jonathan Culler's *Structuralist Poetics* which explores the role of
linguistics in structuralism, and then goes on to develop a new theory of
literary competence. Philip Pettit, *The Concept of Structuralism* represents a
different kind of unifying account by examining the philosophical
implications of structuralism.

On the specific question of Saussurean linguistics and semiology, the most
representative texts are Barthes's *Elements of Semiology,* which could be
complemented by his (as yet untranslated) *Système de la mode,* and Julia
Kristeva, *Semeiotikè: Recherches pour une sémanalyse.* Useful introductory
accounts can be found in the chapter on semiology in Jonathan Culler, *Saussure*
and in Pierre Guiraud, *Semiology.* Fredric Jameson offers a critical account of
the role of linguistics in structuralist theory in his *Prison-House of Language.*

The two major texts of structuralist literary theory, Barthes's *Critique et
vérité* and Todorov's *Poétique,* have, unfortunately, not been translated into
English. Barthes's essay entitled 'Science versus literature' in *Structuralism: A
Reader* (ed. Lane) and some of Todorov's essays in *The Poetics of Prose* will give
some sense of the arguments contained in the larger works.

Narratology is a huge field and the works discussed in this chapter were
chosen primarily as *examples* of different kinds of approach. No serious
student of structuralist narratology should fail to read A.-J. Greimas's
Sémantique structurale (also not translated into English). Genette's *Narrative
Discourse* has a good bibliography of the major contributions to narrative
theory.

There are, by now, many examples of structuralist criticism, but two of the
best structuralist critics are probably Genette and Todorov. Genette's essays in
the three volumes of *Figures* (with the exception of *Narrative Discourse* which

comes from *Figures III* these books have not been translated) are fine examples of the genre, as are the essays by Todorov in his *Poetics of Prose*. (It contains two essays on Henry James, including a version of the one published in *Structuralism: An Introduction* (ed. Robey) which is discussed in this chapter.)

The later works of Barthes which introduce the post-structuralist phase are not representative of any wider group or movement—there is no other book remotely like *S/Z*. But for a sense of the impact that structuralism has left on an important writer, see Barthes's *The Pleasure of the Text*, which elaborates an unconventional (and erotic) view of the reader's experience of literature, and *Roland Barthes by Roland Barthes* which is an experiment in autobiography based on the largely anti-autobiographical assumptions of structuralism.

Derrida is a difficult writer and I have chosen for discussion those essays that have a direct bearing on major issues in structuralist theory: these are Part I of *Grammatology*, the first and last essays in *Writing and Difference* and the interview with Julia Kristeva in *Positions*. Having got the hang of Derrida from these, the essay entitled 'Différance' (in *Speech and Phenomena)* and the remainder of *Of Grammatology* should help the reader to get into his stride. Jonathan Culler's chapter on Derrida in *Structuralism and Since* is an extremely useful introductory aid. Paul de Man's essay on Derrida, 'The rhetoric of blindness', in his *Blindness and Insight* avoids the contradictions of the expository introduction by offering a deconstructive account of Derrida himself. It is extremely clear and readable. For a sense of what deconstruction might mean in terms of critical practice, see Bloom *et al, Deconstruction and Criticism,* which contains essays on English and American poets, including Shelley and Wordsworth.

5 Modern Psychoanalytic Criticism

Elizabeth Wright

The relationship of psychoanalytic theory to literary criticism has undergone many vicissitudes as developments in both domains have brought about changes in critical practice. As a result the critical focus has shifted from the psychology of the author—or his stand-in, the character—to that of the reader, and further to the relations between author, reader, text and language. Psychoanalysis, the name first coined by Freud in 1896 when he changed his method of treatment, began as a therapy which aimed at uncovering repression and verbalizing what had been repudiated. The reason why it is appropriate for psychoanalysis to speak about literature is that it has something to say about language. It is first and foremost the 'talking cure', for it is out of the dialogue between patient and analyst that the therapy proceeds, the diagnostic material being largely linguistic. Freud's original insight centred upon the determining force of the unconscious aspect of utterance which revealed that mechanisms working in dreams, puns and slips of the tongue can be shown to be analogous to certain mental and linguistic processes. Though these effects can be seen in other forms of discourse, this insight applies particularly to literature, a chosen canon of works valued for one reason or another, whose rhetoric depends much on figurative devices, involving multiple meaning: unlike most other discourses, which may try to escape from ambiguity, literature consciously cultivates it.

At first literature was used very much as a slave to the master-discourse of psychoanalysis, which used literature to validate its clinical findings. From 1912 to 1937 the chief organ for the publication of writings concerned with the relation of psychoanalysis to the arts and all aspects of culture was a periodical called *Imago*, published in Leipzig, Vienna and Zürich; one of its founding editors was Otto Rank, a psychoanalyst with wide interests in myth and fairy-tale. Freud's essay, 'The Uncanny', first appeared in the 1919 issue of this journal and is a good example of an attempt first to apply psychoanalysis to a general aesthetic problem and then to a literary text in the light of that investigation.

MODERN PSYCHOANALYTIC CRITICISM

Classical psychoanalysis and the author

Traditional applied psychoanalysis worked with a body of certain well-known presuppositions, which have become the hallmark of the classic psychoanalytic reading. Firstly, the work of literature was seen as analogous to fantasy and treated as a symptom of a particular writer. This led to the psychoanalysis of the author, which I will be discussing in some detail below. Secondly, the literary character was treated as if he were a living being within the fantasy, with a complex of his own. Freud's analysis of E.T.A. Hoffmann's *The Sandman*, in his essay 'The Uncanny' already mentioned, is a case in point. Although Freud briefly elaborates Hoffmann's biography in a footnote, his concern is to analyze the uncanny effect to the story via the central character's infantile complex. Thirdly, Freud's interpretation of symbols is applied to language wholesale, as if it were a given and rigid code. This code is often referred to as 'vulgar' Freudian symbolism: all things vertical are the male sexual organ and all things horizontal are the mother's body. Both the second and third presupposition implicitly relate back to the author's psyche, for they rest on the assumption that the purpose of the work of art is the same as that which psychoanalysis had taken to be the purpose of the dream: the secret gratification of an infantile and forbidden wish, lodged in the unconscious.

The term 'unconscious' must not be taken here as defining simply what is not present in the field of consciousness. It is to be understood in the context of the Freudian 'topographical' model of the psyche, where the unconscious is seen as a dynamic sub-system, a region or stratum of the mind which is part of a larger system of conflicting forces. In the first of these models (the second will concern us later), the unconscious is a dynamic sub-system containing instinctual drives attached to representations, especially childhood wishes, which try to get through to consciousness and be active, and which can only get through in disguise, as so-called 'compromise formations', symptoms, dreams, jokes and slips of the tongue, because they are not an acceptable part of 'normal' civilized behaviour. These drives or wishes strive for instant discharge, regardless of what they will meet with out in the world. In psychoanalytic terminology they are regulated by the 'primary process', a type of mental functioning whereby energy flows freely by means of certain mechanisms, seen to be operative not only in everyday life but also in works of art and literature. The classical psychoanalytic critic treated the literary text as analogous to the dream and believed that by detailed examination of its workings he could make it yield up the psychology of its creator. Here, then, a direct relation between text and author is presupposed and made the centre of inquiry.

It will become clear that there are stock objections to this approach but for the moment it is worth concentrating on the interest it nevertheless has for the literary critic. The classic example is a well-known study of the life and works of Edgar Allan Poe by Marie Bonaparte (Bonaparte 1949), a friend and disciple of Freud's. Bonaparte takes the characters in Poe's stories as imagos, that is, as internalized images which are the result of past experience, which have made their way from Poe's unconscious into his tales. Her basic contention is that Poe, through a fixation on his mother, was condemned to an eternal fidelity. In her analysis of his tales she wishes to show how the repressed emotion, or affect (as psychoanalysis terms any kind of affective state, however vague), is transferred to fictional figures and objects, and how any object can serve this purpose, be it the famous house of Usher, the sea or the earth's depths.

What is of interest to the literary critic is the way she avails herself of Freud's theory of dream interpretation in the carrying out of her task. According to Freud, 'a dream is a (disguised) fulfilment of a (suppressed or repressed) wish' (Freud 1953:160). The dream's wishes have to assume a disguise in order to achieve their aim and get through to consciousness. This means we have to distinguish between the manifest content, the dream-stories we remember, and the latent content, the 'dream-thoughts'. The dream-work, what the dreamer does, converts the latent 'forbidden' dream-thoughts into the manifest 'permitted' dream-stories, by a series of mental processes. Two of these processes, condensation and displacement, are worthy of special mention, particularly since, as will be seen, they have been reinterpreted by Roman Jakobson and Jacques Lacan as homologous with the rhetorical procedures of metaphor and metonymy. Condensation is necessary because the manifest dream has a much smaller content than the latent one. Composite figures are formed so that as little as possible is left out and hence the concept of 'over-determination', whereby several latent wishes converge on one manifest item. In the other activity, displacement, elements in the manifest dreams have replaced elements in the latent dream-thoughts via a chain of association for the purpose of disguise. The intensity of an idea becomes detached from it and passes on to other ideas, which in themselves are of little intensity. Displacement also describes the notion that the manifest dream has a different centre from the dream-thoughts and does not reflect their relative importance. A brief example of Bonaparte's application of these mechanisms to the literary text can be extracted from her analysis of Poe's story 'The Black Cat'. She argues that for the narrator, whom she identifies with the author, there is a displacement of his hatred for the mother seen as bad onto the all-black cat which bites him and which he duly mutilates and kills, whereas the succeeding cat enables him momentarily to regard it as the good mother, for it has, according to Poe, 'a large, although indefinite splotch of white, covering nearly the whole region of the breast' (Bonaparte 1949: 472-474). This splotch, Bonaparte argues, represents milk both by its colour and its position, and what is more, this second cat is found in a tavern (where one drinks), and is perched on a barrel of gin. One might therefore make the point for Bonaparte, that here is an example of condensation in that there are several images to do with drinking condensed into one scene. Of particular interest to literary critics is the notion that elements in the manifest dream have replaced elements in the latent dream-thoughts via a chain of association, for it is through such chains that figurative devices work. There is also the notion that the manifest dream has a different centre from the dream-thoughts and does not reflect their relative importance, which matches the literary critic's interest in implicit as distinct from explicit meanings.

Marie Bonaparte herself is clearly much more interested in scoring psychoanalytical points than in elucidating linguistic and literary processes. Literary critics in the past have not been slow to point out that she totally neglects formal and aesthetic factors and, consequently, all that these imply in terms of the part that consciousness plays in the creative process. Her analyses de-centre the text only in order to privilege the unconscious and this has also brought her into disrepute with later Freudian psychoanalysts who want to play down the role of the instinctual drives. Nevertheless, for the current de-centred reader working on the currently de-centred text which knows no split between latent and manifest Bonaparte's performance is not entirely irrelevant. For all her monotonous rehearsing of a predictable number of themes she makes us aware of the role that desire plays in the interconnections of imagery, which have a part in tropes and other rhetorical figures. Her explorations, however, are entirely confined to the relation between author and text.

Classical psychoanalysis and the reader

This deficiency was made good by the second phase of classical psychoanalytic criticism. This criticism arose in the 1950s and 1960s and resulted in some pioneering work on the relation between reader and text, following on from the work of I. A. Richards (discussed in Chapter 3). Its conceptions rested on the other topographical model of the psychic apparatus, often referred to as the 'structural model', in which Freud sees the component parts of the psyche as three groups of functions: the 'id', directly related to the instinctual drives: the 'ego', an agency which regulates and opposes the drives; and the 'superego', another part of the ego with a critical judging function. Psychoanalytic criticism based on ego-psychology, as distinct from id-psychology (as the earlier instinct theory come to be called), developed with the influence of a theory of creativity evolved by an American psychoanalyst, Ernst Kris (Kris 1952), a former member of Freud's circle in Vienna. Its most active exponent and developer, though not its first, is Norman Holland (Holland 1968), who takes up the question of what goes on between the reader and the text. He sees this relationship in terms of id-fantasies and ego-defences; that is to say, for Holland the source of the pleasure we get from literature lies in the transformation of our unconscious wishes and fears into culturally acceptable meanings. Like Bonaparte, Holland sees literary texts as concealments, coded systems that act as a disguise. But unlike Bonaparte, who viewed the text as evidence of the author's psychology, Holland sees it as the scene of a collusion between author and reader, upon which he founds an aesthetics of response. The form of the text is in fact defined as the very mode of concealment. What draws us as readers to a text is the secret expression of what we desire to hear, much as we protest we do not. The disguise must be good enough to fool the censor into thinking that the text is respectable, but bad enough to allow the unconscious to glimpse the unrespectable. Hence, as Holland himself comes to see, the role the reader plays in getting from the latent to the manifest is a curiously passive one, as the text appears to do all the work for him.

Holland's latest position is an attempt to redress the balance between reader and text. In this psychoanalysis has drawn attention to the most neglected relation in the literary process (see the five elements outlined in the Introduction). His focus has shifted from seeing the organizing principle in the text to seeing it in the reader, who gets to work on the text with his identity theme. Reading, says Holland, is first and foremost a re-creation of identity (Holland 1978:183ff.) The expectations the reader brings to the text are challenged by the encounter. Defensive strategies come into play to transform meanings so as to allow the adaptation of the reader's identity and yet confirm it in a reassuring unity. Holland thinks it valuable to compare the different responses of readers to the same text (Holland 1975), and to note the relation between their free associations to the story and their personalities, as revealed in free-association tests. But now the balance is completely reversed: nothing happens in the text and everything happens in the reader, whose reading serves to re-create for him his own unique identity. Thus Holland's own reading of Poe's 'The Purloined Letter' (Holland 1980) misses precisely what Lacan reveals with his, as will be seen: that a new reading is both private and public, that reading is an intersubjective process, in that it is the overtaking of another's meaning. The reading transaction which Holland performs with this text is that it is 'a story about hiding, especially the hiding of sexual secrets' (Holland 1980:368-9). This is only a thematization, one implication of the structure of desire which Lacan takes the trouble to display. It is true that Holland is concerned with a variety of different responses to the text, but if such 'transactions' are to be seen as purloinings of meanings, they are not so by the bare uniqueness of an act of reading. The term 'transaction' begs the question of the intersubjective nature of understanding, of the developing of another's meaning in a new and justifiable direction, with which Lacan is particularly concerned.

Classical psychoanalysis, however, does present us on the level of the 'transaction' between analyst and patient (the transference relationship which Holland has in mind) with insight into the structure of narrative, and this is perhaps the best trick it has produced so far in a game which finally involves author, reader and text. Both psychoanalysis and literature are concerned with narrative, with telling stories. Psychoanalysis reads the past in order to make sense of the present. Like a detective story it starts with effects and traces these effects back to origins. In tracing back the history of his patients is in order to discover what caused the neurosis, Freud found that the narrative was bound up with a fictional element, even though he was dealing with an actual case-history. Because memory aroused feelings not present to consciousness at the time, meaning was conferred 'nachträglich' (after the event), interpreting with the help of fiction. Recent theorists (Brooks 1979; Culler 1980) have made an analogy with the narrative theory of Russian Formalism and the narrative that goes on in the psychoanalytic situation. The Russian Formalists distinguish between *fabula* and *syuzhet, fabula* being the original sequence of events, and the *syuzhet,* being the sequence in which the events appear in the story (see Chapter 1). The reader, like the analyst, is confronted with the *syuzhet,* and this is all he has to reconstruct the *fabula.* The reader, like the analyst, has to find causes and connections and like the analyst, he has to work back through time in order to recover meaning. This is not simply the search for an event which starts off the sequence, for the teller of the story, be it the author or the patient, is himself engaged in an act of interpretation which involves the evaluation of past experience. Hence we may fairly conclude that the insights of psychoanalysis can provide far more than a simple code of meaning, for what is at stake here is common to *all* narrative: the endeavour to grasp reality through a fictitious construct. And this is where the new psychoanalytic criticism comes in.

The main contribution of classical psychoanalytic criticism was to point out the role of desire in the figuring and structuring of texts, and this links psychoanalysis with both rhetoric and narrative. Though a reader theory was seen to emerge this became oddly detached from any theory of the text. The contribution of the new psychoanalysis, to which I now turn, concern a new approach to the role of desire in the writing and reading process seen as a compound phenomenon, and this is turn depends on a new definition of the unconscious.

Lacan and structural psychoanalysis
(a) Language

The work of Jacques Lacan is a re-interpretation and a critique of classical Freudianism in the light of structuralist and post-structuralist theories. Lacan is not interested in an instinctual unconscious that precedes language. He maintains not only that the unconscious is structured like a language, but that it is a product of language. In order to understand this theory it needs to be placed in the context of Saussure's concepts of signifier and signified, of which Lacan makes so much use. Saussure introduces the idea of signifier and signified as one of words being used to divide up continuum, a flux. He talks of an 'indefinite plane of jumbled ideas', thus postulating a pre-linguistic stage here — a primordial state. He actually speaks of a realm of thoughts as 'chaotic by nature' (Saussure, 1974:112) before language has got to work on it. Saussure is not interested in the problem of how thoughts could exist before language. As has already been indicated earlier (pp. 39-41), Saussure is affirming a relation between the verbal sign and a portion of the chaos of experience. We are able to sort out the experience of sensations because we perform bonding between two continua. There are two continua, one of sounds and one of thoughts, both of which are chaotic. Language sorts out a part of the chaos of sounds and a part of the chaos of thoughts, and couples them: the signifier, which is the sound element, is matched with the signified, which is the concept (for a diagram see Chapter 2, p.40). With this Saussure considers the problem of the continuum as solved, for shortly afterwards we find him talking about a happy match of signifier and signified as the two sides of a single sheet of paper. The significant omission is how we get from the jumble to the distinction, how meaning is made. To put it another way, there is a difficult question here: how does a disorganized realm, whether experience or thought, become sorted out into discrete units? Saussure does not explain it: he just draws these dotted lines.

Lacan similarly has a concept of chaos, but it is not a chaos of thoughts. The most that can be said is that it is a state of organic need with a minimal instinctual guidance. The infant's experience is a jumble which Lacan punningly calls 'l'hommelette' (Lacan 1977b

:197). Two meanings in the pun are both relevant: *homme-lette* as 'little man'; and 'omelette' as 'shapeless mass' of the egg just broken in the pan corresponding to the jumble of organic need. It is upon this 'shapeless mass' that language comes to work. Its working is not, however, a straightforward achieving of fixity: the signifiers are not logically secure in their sorting of the shapeless mass. Lacan gives an account of how signifiers move about on the continuum, how meanings change.

Lacan develops Saussure's neat equation of signifier and signified by showing that a different signifier can apparently be applied to what is ostensibly the same signified, with a consequent difference in *interpretation:*

Saussure's analogy of the two sides of a piece of paper, the front (recto) being the thought or signified and the back (verso) being the sound or signifier does not fit this example. Indeed his piece of paper would have to have three sides: one recto, the concept 'door', and two versos, the sounds 'Ladies' and the sounds 'Gentlemen'. (Lacan is himself not making a distinction between the percept, the sight of the doors, and the concept what lies beyond the doors, but this does not invalidate his re-thinking of Saussure.) One might add that the same signifier can apply to different signifieds:

In this case we have two rectos, two signifieds, for one verso, one signifier and hence three sides again.

What these examples point to is that there is no secure bond between signifier and signified. Now Saussure knew perfectly well that meanings changed and he had found a place for meaning-change in his system which he called 'diachrony'. But the very name, 'through-time', shows that he only thought of it as a long-term historical development. His complementary notion, 'synchrony', refers to the interrelationships of all parts of the language system at one ideal point in time. One of the fundamentals of structuralism is this key emphasis on the interdependence of the parts of a language. In Chapter 4 attention has been drawn to Derrida's criticism of Saussure: that the synchrony/diachrony distinction does lead to his system having 'a certain logocentric resonance'. In both these notions, diachrony and synchrony, Saussure never breaks with his verso-recto match. For Saussure the signifier does not slide over the continuum of the signified.

Lacan, on the other hand, points to the sliding of the signifier over the continuum, over the field *from which* the signified is selected. The question may be asked what this field is and whether it is a realm of chaotic thoughts as Saussure says. Somewhere in the system a place has to be found for reality, but Saussure does not do this, whereas Lacan does make some attempt to give reality a place. He has a difficult concept called 'the Real'. The Real is that upon which language is at work; it is that which 'lies beyond the insistence of the signs' (Lacan 1977b:53-54). Lacan talks of a network of signs totally enveloping man, but also of 'interferences and pulsations' of desire (Lacan 1977a:68). Though desire 'determines' you, it is paradoxically that which escapes the logical rigidity of the signifying system. If desire can 'interfere' with the system, it partakes of the Real. It looks as though there are elements both internal to the subject—his desire— and external to the subject—the physical world—both of which can upset the signifying system.

The Real turns up in man's relation to desired objects. It makes its appearance because the signifying system is revealed as inadequate: the desired object is never what one thinks one desires. What one imagines, according to psychoanalysis, is always the primordial lost object, the union with the mother. To take an example, in Luis Buñuel's film, *The Obscure Object of Desire,* the desired love-object was represented by two actresses playing the one role. They had the same name, Conchita, but one could see that they were really different; what the women actually were—the Real—did not correspond to the imaginary picture the lover had of them. This is an analogy of what actually happens: the Real never fits comfortably into any conceptualization. Hence Lacan's point that the Real is impossible to grasp; it must be different from what words say it is.

Freud's view was that the unconscious existed before language took effect. Lacan sees the unconscious as coming into being simultaneously with language. When words fail to fulfil their promise of satisfaction, then the unconscious breaks out, making its appearance in the mis-match between language and desire. Desire, according to Lacan, 'is an effect in the subject of that condition which is imposed upon him by the existence of the discourse to cause his need to pass through the defiles of the signifier' (Lacan, 1977a:264). The discourse is the defile, the groove, the mould; it is 'imposing' a shape on our needs, which do not disappear but turn into desire. In the Freudian scheme the unconscious exists as a mass of instinctual representatives; in Lacan's scheme the unconscious is the result of the structuring of desire by language. The word does not capture the substance in that what has been named has only apparently been named. Desire invests the signifier with meaning, but it is only subjectively felt, not mutually acknowledged. The unconscious is desire which has been meant but not recognized.

A subject's use of words will thus be open to shifts for which his unconscious is responsible, what his desire directs. The 'it' of the unconscious—the true discourse—will always subvert the 'I'—the imaginary discourse. The 'I' thinks it is speaking univocally, but its rhetoric will always be figurative. Whereas Freud sees this in terms of condensation and displacement, for Lacan these figures are metonymy and metaphor, the terms he took from Jakobson. Lacan wishes to press home a linguistic parallel. Like the structuralists he would like to take linguistic theory as a starting-point. He sees an analogy between Jakobson's bipolar concept of metonymy and metaphor (linked to Saussure's syntagmatic and paradigmatic distinction, which has already been explained on pp. 41-2) and the Freudian pair condensation and displacement. The parallel upon which he relies is as follows: metonymy and displacement are both characterized by contiguity (item associated with item by being next to it in a chain); metaphor and condensation are characterized by similarity (item associated with item by likeness). As regards metonymy, the subject does not understand the chain of connections in his words as they proceed. There is an endless chain of signifiers in pursuit of a 'real' satisfaction, what Lacan calls 'lack'. As regards metaphor, desire is revealed by the metaphorical substitution for surface meaning of the repressed meaning. All the time what the subject wants continues to show itself. The metaphor can be regarded as the symptom which reveals the repressed desire, providing access to the unconscious across the boundary between signifier and signified. Just as in the case of a neurotic, physical symptoms provide clues via their body-language to unconscious concerns, so words can be similarly indicative of them. The unconscious signals that a wrong direction is being taken. For Lacan, hyperbolically speaking, every word is a Freudian slip, whether recognized or not, the point being, that the unconscious is present even when not recognized. It is in this sense that Lacan sees the unconscious as structured like a language.

(b) The subject

For Lacan the function of language is not to communicate but to give the subject a place from which he can speak. Freud did not give language this central place in the socializing process, being more concerned with a maturational sequence of instinctual development in the unconscious, leading from an oral to a genital phase. Hence the predictable themes uncovered by the classical psychoanalytic critic such as Marie Bonaparte. Lacan sees as all-important the domain of the signifier, where the naming of social roles goes on. Hence any Lacanian literary criticism will tend to focus on the *structures* of desire as determined by a signifying chain. Lacan maintains that a subject does not come into being until it has acquired a consciousness, that is to say until it has developed a concept of self. According to Lacan this happens in a mythic moment, which he calls 'the mirror stage', which we may take as a metaphor for a fictional self-concept, not requiring a concrete mirror or even a reflection, but merely pointing to an image which does not involve self-knowledge. The mirror stage is the pre-linguistic stage, and it requires a brief exposition; it will lead on to the 'Seminar on "The Purloined Letter"', central to this discussion, where Lacan illustrates what happens when the induction into language and its rules, what he defines as the 'Symbolic Order' takes over.

'The mirror stage' is a paper of Lacan's of 1949, a revision of an earlier version. In it he develops Freud's concept of the ego as it appeared in Freud's paper 'On narcissism' (Freud 1914c), and rejects the later concept that appears in 'The ego and the id' (1923b). The notion of the mirror stage came up through a comparison of apes and humans; they each react differently to their mirror image. The ape can pick out something that moves as it moves, but once it has mastered this idea it gets bored. The infant, on the other hand, sees the relation between the movements of the image and those of its own body. It is delighted with this discovery and leans forward to get the best possible view. But like a paranoid person it is unable to get away from the imaginary dimension and invests all its instinctual energy in images instead of objects. The thrust of Lacan's argument has been summarized and clarified many times, but I would like to show that once the context has been established, it becomes more possible to tackle Lacan's notoriously difficult prose for oneself, even in English translation. I will therefore cite two of the passages most important for my argument, preceding each one with a gloss which tries to keep close to the original, while transposing it into more general terms.

The joyful assumption of a specular image on the part of the child, before he can speak, is an outstanding example of how the self comes into being at its very beginning within a conceptual scheme, *before* it can achieve a clearer self-concept through mutual correction from others and *before* language has provided it with the general term 'I' and it has become a subject, that is, it can reflect upon itself:

> This jubilant assumption of his specular image by the child at the *infans* stage, still sunk in his motor incapacity and nursling dependence, would seem to exhibit in an exemplary situation the symbolic matrix in which the *I* is precipitated in a primordial form, before it is objectified in the dialectic of identification with the other, and before language restores to it, in the universal, its function as subject. (Lacan 1977a:2).

The child proceeds 'in a fictional direction'; that is to say that he will have to resort to fantasy to overcome his alienation from his own reality. Like a graph that approaches zero, but never reaches it, his self-concept will never match up to his own being. The *Gestalt* that he has picked out in the mirror is both smaller and more stable than he is and is something outside him that is having an effect upon him without his understanding it. It gives him the illusion that he has control over his body when he has not:

> The important point is that this form situates the agency of the ego, before its social determination, in a fictional direction, which will only rejoin the coming-into-being of the subject asymptotically, whatever the success of the dialectical syntheses by which he must resolve as *I* this discordance with his own reality.
>
> The fact is that the total form of the body by which the subject anticipates in a mirage the maturation of his power is given to him only as a *Gestalt,* that is to say, in an exteriority in which this form is certainly more constituting than constituted, but in which it appears to him above all in a contrasting size that fixes it and in a symmetry that inverts it, in contrast with the turbulent movements that the subject feels are animating him.

Lacan's point is that the ego is constituted by an identification with another whole object, an imaginary projection, an idealization ('Ideal-I'), which does not match the child's feebleness. The ego is thus not an agent of strength, but the victim of an illusion of strength, a fixed character-armour, which needs constant reinforcement. This alienated relationship of the self to its own image is what Lacan calls the domain of the Imaginary.

(c) The Text

Lacan's theory of the subject and its undermining of a stable self has brought about a radical change in the relation between psycho-analysis and literary criticism. As outlined in the Introduction, changes in literary theory in the twentieth century have produced transformations in critical practice at large. The theory of classical psychoanalysis set itself the task of using texts as clues to the author's psychology, or to the psychology of his characters. Lacan's work calls in question both this theory and its practice by undertaking a thoroughgoing reassessment of the role of language. He has not summarized a literary theory for us; in this he is unlike Freud and Bonaparte, and also unlike the theorists discussed in the rest of this book. Therefore, in order to elicit a theory, it is necessary to examine Lacan's 'Seminar on "The Purloined Letter"' in some detail. It could be said that here theory and practice coincide: in analyzing a text, Lacan uses that very text to throw light on all texts. With the help of such new theoretical understanding approaches may indeed be made to actual texts, but it is as a result of the light that such approaches cast on language and communication as such that they are valuable. This does not exclude the possibility that a literary merit may be displayed in the text to which the old type of interpretation was impervious. However, it must be stated at the outset that Lacan himself is not interested in performing a literary analysis. As Derrida has pointed out in his critique, Lacan has left out the literary text's frame. There are a number of purely psychoanalytic issues in the seminar which it is not my province to explore. There are also some meta-theoretical questions about the actual writing of the seminar itself: Derrida has attempted a deconstruction of it, which Barbara Johnson deconstructs in turn, and I shall comment on these at the end. What the seminar will mainly serve to illustrate is the new psychoanalytic structural approach to literature, whereby analogies from psychoanalysis are used to explain the workings of the text as distinct from the workings of a particular author's, character's or even reader's mind. Here then is the barest summary of the sequence of events in Poe's tale. It is the story of an incriminating letter, twice stolen, initially sent to an exalted personage whom Lacan calls 'the queen'. When the king comes unexpectedly into the royal boudoir, she leaves the letter on the table in full view, thereby hoping that it will be overlooked. Minister D appears on the scene, works out the situation, steals the letter in full view of the queen and leaves another in its place. She is powerless in the presence of the king, but later she asks the prefect of police to find the letter. The prefect systematically searches the minister's apartment but fails to find the letter. He then consults Dupin, an amateur detective renowned for his analytic ability. At their next meeting Dupin miraculously produces the letter and gives it to the prefect in exchange for a large sum of money. How has he done it? He deduced that the minister, like the queen, would leave the letter *unconcealed* as the best way of hiding it. And so he noticed it, casually stuck in a card-rack, hanging from the mantlepiece. He then arranged a second visit, and waiting until the minister's attention was distracted by a pre-arranged noise, he stole the letter and left one which looked the same in its place.

Lacan's main concern is to bring out the repetition of a structure. Just as for Freud there was a repetition of patterns of behaviour within the course of a single individual's life—which he illustrates in his essay 'The Uncanny' with his reading of Hoffmann's *The Sandman* (1919: 219-256), so for Lacan in the plot of Poe's story there is a recurrence of an ambiguous relationship affecting the positions of three persons. This recurrence underpins the peculiar ironies of the tale. It is not the mere repetition of a theft which is significant, but the total situation in which the theft takes place: in each case there are three participants who succeed one another by stepping into three functional positions in a pre-determined structure.

Lacan points out that there are two scenes; the first, which he calls the 'primal scene', starts off the sequence (Lacan 1976: 41). This takes place in the royal boudoir, and the participants are the king, the queen and the minister. I will draw out what happens in the scheme of a triangle (as illustrated by Shoshana Felman in her lucid article (1979: 136-7)), a form which conveniently makes clear the multiple relationships of the three persons, and can be matched with the oedipal triangle, though this is not explicit in Lacan.

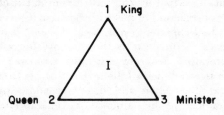

According to Lacan (1976: 44), there are three glances: 'the first is a glance that sees nothing' (the king), 'the second, a glance which sees that the first sees nothing and deludes itself as to the secrecy of what it hides' (the queen), and 'the third sees that the first two glances leave what should be hidden exposed to whomever would seize it' (the minister). The operation is that the minister takes the letter the queen has received and puts another, a blank letter, in its place.

Lacan sees the second scene as the repetitive scene. This takes place in the minister's flat, and the participants are the police, the minister and Dupin.

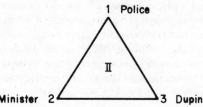

Here the police are in the first position, in the place formerly occupied by the king, and like the king, they see nothing. The minister is in the second position and makes the same mistake that the queen formerly made, that is, he deludes himself as to the secrecy of what he hides. And Dupin is in the third position: like the minister in the first scene he sees that what should be hidden is left exposed. The operation is that Dupin takes the letter from the minister and puts another in its place, this time not a blank letter, a subtlety on which I will be commenting.

A further schematization (produced by Felman) goes like this:

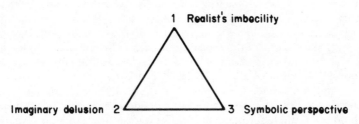

Though Felman does not elaborate this, her schematization is very suggestive. Position 1 might be seen as that of pure objectivity: the king is the authority figure lost in the sense of his own supremacy, 'invested with the equivocation natural to the sacred, with the imbecility which prizes none other than the subject' (Lacan 1976: 69), and the prefect (in scene 2) likewise thinks he has arrived at all knowledge through defining and labelling all the space, measuring and quantifying. Position 2 might be seen as that of pure subjectivity: the queen, and the minister in scene 2 think they are in possession of a pure private meaning. 1 and 2 each believe that the letter or signifier has only one interpretation, the one they themselves are making, but a subject in position 3 understands both their interpretation and his own.

Lacan is here playing on the word 'letter' and making it into a pun. As a letter in the story it has a literal meaning, but its metaphorical meaning is a signifier in a system in use in the world. To make it plain, to use *letter*, originally meaning 'written or printed character' for a letter as an item of correspondence is a familiar metonym, for the letter (as item of correspondence) in the story comes to mean by metaphorical shift a signifier. The way the letter is treated in the story is *like* the way a signifier is treated in the world.

In a psychoanalytic reading the purloined letter becomes a metaphor for the unconscious, thus a signifier of unconscious desire. The ground of this metaphor is the similarity between the structural positioning of those in the story who pass the purloined letter on and those in life who are determined by a single signifier in intersubjective discourse, a signifier invested with their desire without their being aware of it. This same structure recurs in psychoanalysis itself, where a symptom is repeated in a variety of displacements, unrecognized by the patient. Dupin, in returning the letter to the queen, is like an analyst, who rids the patient of a symptom and who pockets a considerable sum of money at the end of the treatment. As analyst, Dupin is in a *position* to understand in what way the second scene is a repetition of the first. In the psychoanalytic interview both patient and analyst are subject to the phenomenon of transference, in which each is affected by the role a past significant figure played in his life. The patient, by virtue of having succumbed to his symptoms, is of course more at the mercy of past events than the analyst, but it is one of the revisions of Lacan's Freudianism, at least in theory, that the analyst is not to be regarded as 'the-subject-who-is-supposed-to-know' (Lacan 1977b: 230), unlike the so-called 'shrink' on the American scene, who knows it all. And thus Lacan is clearly delighted to note that Dupin too is trapped in the circuit by not being able to leave the letter blank and using it to settle an old score against the minister. Dupin is also 'purloining' the letter, by making clear to the minister that he, Dupin, momentarily has the power that the minister hoped to gain over the queen. All this enables Lacan to read the story as an allegory of psychoanalysis. But the story also functions as an allegory of reading, because it shows, as has already been argued, that both literary and psychoanalytic narrative depend on structures of repetition in order to make sense of experience retrospectively. It is the second scene in the story which allows for an understanding and re-interpretation of the first, because it illustrates how we understand and evaluate the events of the past only when we find ourselves in the position of repeating certain scenarios. For the literary critic this is a story about the place of fiction in reality and about the way that persons are plotted.

Lacan is interested in a structure of desire which triangulates and sorts out a set of characters. This structure only repeats itself through the difference of its characters, who move into one another's positions, and as they move, the letter too moves to a different place. For Lacan what the story shows is the effect of the transmission of signifiers in an unconscious process of exchange, and hence no one gets to know the text of the letter, neither its content nor its addresser. His exegesis makes plain that texts have in them that which we most *want*, that which we desire and are in need of. This want is not to be found in a hidden meaning, as the old psychoanalytic criticism of the Bonapartian type would have it, but in a rhetorical displacement, which is lying around, like the letter, for those that have the eyes of a Dupin. Just as Dupin and the minister, who also happen to be poets in

Poe's story, are capable of disrupting the 'readable' given interpretation, so the reader can disrupt the constraints of the text. But the metaphor of disruption is not altogether appropriate. Lacan is showing that in the redirection of desire in the text the unconscious is revitalizing language. Owing its origin to language, the unconscious, linguistic in its very nature as Lacan sees it, shows itself to be creative within the structure.

For this, the quotation from Goethe's *Faust*, which Lacan uses as epigraph to his seminar, is a case in point:

Und wenn es uns glückt,
Und wenn es sich schickt,
So sind es Gedanken.

Taken quite out of its context it is here made to work for Lacan, who, one might say, has purloined the letter from Goethe. Epigraphs, by their very placing, are often used with special emphases that to some degree subvert the usual meaning. Lacan has here gone further in actually punning on Goethe's words, a trick that is analogous to the purloining he has described. This epigraph can now be understood as an utterance which has general implications for Lacan's theory of language: words are not the property of those who use them. In the quotation, 'es', instead of the simple pronoun 'it', can be taken as the Freudian term for the core of the unconscious. Each of the first two lines is thus overdetermined in meaning. Line 1, as well as meaning 'if fortune is kind to us', also means 'if "es" (that is the unconscious) attains its desire'. Line 2, as well as meaning 'and if fate is kind', or 'if it is deemed proper', also means 'if "es", the unconscious (the letter) sends itself' ('schicken'=to send), that is to say, desire circulates, or becomes a locus for everyone's unconscious. (Lacan's way of saying this is 'the unconscious is the discourse of the Other'). Then the final line, 'so sind es Gedanken', as well as meaning *both* 'then thoughts will result' and 'then thoughts will have brought it ("es") about', also means 'then desires will have a chance of satisfaction', through the investing of signifiers, that is through allowing desire to follow the path of the signifier. For a Lacanian psychoanalytic criticism a text will be first and foremost a discourse of desire, with the result that the emphasis will be not on an appropriation of the author's meaning but on an expropriation by the reader.

Indeed Lacan's reading of Poe's story has such an implication for the reading and writing process in general. We might therefore construct a model of the reading process in keeping with Lacan's de-centering of the subject and take the text as circulating like the letter. The authorial ego, seen as omniscient by past critics, would initially be at the top of the triangle. The so-called competent reader (or whatever idealization is applied to the concept 'reader'), he who tries to recover a stable meaning, even if he allows that there might be several such stable meanings, would be in position 2, and this would include the classical psychoanalytic critic who wants to recover a latent stable meaning. The third position is the deconstructionist's position, which is that of a reader who discovers instabilities in both these positions and who produces an innovative reading which takes into account the problematic relationship between author and text, and between reader and text, in terms of their intentional perspectives. These perspectives are upon reality. What issues from the conflict of readings of the text is the question of which perspective is most viable, how reality is to be viewed. Thus this escapes the dilemma of whether the relationship between the text and reality is 'representational or genetic' (see Introduction, p.10). Three 'readers' are trying out representation after representation in order to test their view of the world.

The triangular structure within Poe's text has in fact shown itself to continue outside it and will serve to exemplify the model of the reading process just sketched in. As a result of his reading Lacan goes into Dupin's place, that is position 3, and becomes ripe for deconstruction. Derrida obliges with the plainly ironic title, 'The purveyor of truth' (1975). He says that Lacan is himself idealizing the signifier by giving it a materiality it does not possess. Lacan has jumped to the immediate and predictable conclusion of the psychoanalyst: the letter is the phallus and master-signifier of desire. According to Derrida, Lacan is guilty of 'phallogocentricism' (coined from 'logocentricism', *logos* at the centre). For this psychoanalytic interpretation to apply, says Derrida, the letter has to be thought of as entire. To assume the wholeness of the letter, however, is exactly contrary to what all signifiers, in Derrida's view, are subject to, namely 'dissemination', the constant dispersing and re-forming of meaning.

Barbara Johnson in turn displaces Derrida from position 3 (Johnson 1979). Derrida, she argues, repeats Lacan's error, for he too idealizes the signifier in privileging 'dissemination'. Where Derrida accuses Lacan of being too objectivist, in making the word too determining, Johnson accuses Derrida of being too subjectivist, in letting the word become too equivocal. Her paper is entitled 'The frame of reference'; she knows that every utterance is an attempt to frame the world, which includes the people who frame it, *a fortiori* the self. Johnson strives for a synthesis via a series of paradoxes concerning the impossibility of a meta-language. Since no final capturing of the self by the signifier is possible, it is precisely here that the subject is left vulnerable to subversion by another. If there were no undermining of a subject's self-definition, the result would be an infinite regress: if the subject had defined himself completely, he would have to include his defining of himself completely, and this would have to include his defining of himself including his defining of himself completely, *ad infinitum.*

This series of counter-assertions raises the problem of what in fact does distinguish Lacan from Derrida as regards the relevance of their theories of language to literary texts. Both Lacan and Derrida are questioning structuralism from within, though both remain structuralists in accepting the diacritical nature of language. Both are throwing doubt upon the security of the match between signifier and signified upon which Saussure founded his theory. Lacan sees the use of the signifier as always leading to an awareness of lack: the subject becomes aware of his alienation from what was originally represented. Derrida sees the signifier as failing to retain the match with the signified, because of a continual slippage of meaning, owing to 'différance'. Lacan and Derrida are also similar in attributing a 'radical alterity' to the unconscious, which brings about in language an 'incessant synthesis which is constantly led back upon itself' (Derrida 1973: 152). Both would claim that the 'alterity' extends to all discourse, but each in his own way sees the literary text as more open to ambivalence than other forms of discourse; each makes his *own* discourse show awareness of its own ambivalence through indulging in various forms of word-play. There is a difference, however, in the kind of deconstruction Lacan performs on a literary text, as his reading of Poe shows; unlike Derrida, he is not out to demonstrate how the text simultaneously affirms and undermines itself as a logocentric form of discourse. In ignoring the text's literary frame, he is leaving aside the persuasive force of the author's rhetoric of intention, in which he is not interested. His interest is focussed on a language effect not accounted for by traditional notions of ambiguity: the compulsive repetition of a structure of unconscious desire, in the constant attempt to invest the signifier with lost meaning. Hence it might be pointed out that, whereas Derrida's emphasis is on author, text and language, Lacan's is on reader, text and language.

It can be seen that structural psychoanalytic criticism has gone beyond the interpretation of a particular text. It has opened out onto a wider discourse, with a philosophical relevance the founder of psychoanalysis could not have envisaged. His assorted followers and revisionists are busily engaged in purloining his letter with that peculiar psychoanalytic hindsight he called 'Nachträglichkeit'. And Lacan's treatment of Poe's story is also an example of this. With his new psychoanalytic reading he has made a contribution to the understanding of literary texts. Just because his analysis is about *interpretation,* does not mean that it is not an interpretation. One can argue that Poe has some reason to feel grateful to Lacan, for he has shown that Poe's story has a generality Poe himself could not have known. The one thing Poe would not have dreamt of, rhetorically speaking, is that his story would one day become the primal scene of a meta-critical debate. Perhaps, if he were now given the choice, he would settle for this in place of the usual canonization of the Poe-et.

Further Reading

My account has been collated with the help of the works already mentioned in the references of the text and has been slanted to fit the requirements of this particular book; a further aid has been the invaluable dictionary by J. Laplanche and J. B. Pontalis, *The Language of Psychoanalysis*. For a more psychoanalytically biased account see 'Towards a reorientation of psycho-analytic literary criticism', by Alan Roland, in *Psychoanalysis, Creativity, and Literature: A French-American Inquiry*, ed. Alan Roland, pp. 248-270. This paper, and another in the same book by André Green, entitled 'The double and the absent', pp. 271-292, explore an important direction in the development of an intersubjective psychoanalytic criticism which no longer seeks to master the text: that of the English School of 'object relations', which concerns theories of creativity and playing evolved by Melanie Klein and D. W. Winnicott respectively. (See also 'Transitional objects and transitional phenomena', in D. W. Winnicott, *Playing and Reality*). Further psychoanalytic background to a specifically Lacanian psychoanalysis can be found in a difficult but most evocative collection of clinical reports of the Lacanian School (including a transcript of a psychoanalytic interview conducted by its founder), entitled *Returning to Freud: Clinical Psychoanalysis in the School of Lacan*, ed. and tr. by Stuart Schneiderman.

A useful general background to Freud is provided by a collection of essays published in the *Twentieth Century Views* series, namely *Freud*, ed. Perry Meisel; see especially the contribution by another important Freudian revisionist critic, Harold Bloom. Freud's own writings on literature and the arts are listed in volume XXI of the *Standard Edition*, but much more relevant both for a linguistically orientated literary criticism and for a psychoanalytic theory seeking to account for inter-subjective processes is his *Jokes and their Relation to the Unconscious*, S.E., VIII. For an understanding of the concept *Nachträglichkeit* and its relevance to interpretation as a retrospective activity, see 'Remembering, repeating and working-through', *S.E.*, XII, pp. 145-156, and 'From the history of an infantile neurosis' ('The wolfman'), S.E., XVII, pp. 1-122.

Further theoretical background for a text-based psychoanalytic criticism can be found in *The Literary Freud: Mechanisms of Defence and the Poetic Will*, ed. Joseph H. Smith, in *Psychoanalysis and the Question of the Text*. ed. Geoffrey H. Hartman, and in *Psychology and Literature, New Literary History* (1980). For the necessary sociological and political perspective see Sherry Turkle, *Psychoanalytic Politics: Freud's French Revolution*. For a most illuminating ideological perspective see the chapter entitled 'Advertizing and the "Mirror Phase"' in Judith Williamson, *Decoding Advertisements*.

Finally, some approaches to critical practice. For the old approach, based on Freudian themes of the maturational process, see Bruno Bettelheim, *The Uses of Enchantment: The Meaning and Importance of Fairy Tales*, and Frederick C. Crews, *The Sins of the Fathers: Hawthorne's Psychological Themes*, both good of their kind and useful for the understanding of some of the premises of classical psychoanalysis. Examples of a new critical practice are provided by the following: Shoshana Felman, 'Turning the screw of interpretation', in *Literature and Psychoanalysis: The Question of Reading*. Otherwise, *Yale French Studies*, No. 55/56 (1977), 94-207, which makes reader theory central to an analysis of Henry James's *The Turn of the Screw;* Neil Hertz, 'Freud and the sandman', in *Textual Strategies*, ed. Josué V. Harari, is based on Harold Bloom's theory of the anxiety of poetic influence; *Urszenen: Literaturwissenschaft als Diskursanalyse und Diskurskritik*, ed. Friedrich A. Kittler and Horst Turk, combines psychoanalysis with discourse analysis, thus taking into account the *position* of the author vis-à-vis the current ideology, and includes a reading of E. T. A. Hoffmann's *The Sandman* and of Goethe's *Werther*, in German; finally Meredith Anne Skura, *The Literary Use of the Psychoanalytic Process*, which is interesting for its eclectic use of modern psychoanalytic approaches, using examples from English and American authors.

6 Marxist Literary Theories

David Forgacs

The field

Marxist approaches to literature occupy a wide field. Marxism is a theory of economics, history, society and revolution before it has anything much to do with literary theory. There has been no need for it to be bound to any one theory of art or any one kind of criticism. Although there has been a kind of tradition in Marxist literary criticism, a degree of going 'back to sources' in Marx and Engels's scattered writings on literature and a tendency among later critics to build on earlier ones, Marxism has also been harnessed to quite divergent critical approaches and literary theories.

This is one reason why my title speaks of literary 'theories' in the plural. Marxist literary theorists do not constitute a school like the Moscow and Petersburg exponents of Formalism, the Prague structuralists or the *Tel Quel* theorists in Paris. There are other reasons too. Marxism is a living body of thought and a set of real political practices. It is both influenced by changes in the world and aims to intervene to change the world. During this century there have been many developments, rifts and reassessments in Marxism, and these have reproduced themselves to an extent in work on literature produced by Marxists. Finally, Marxist thinking, however rigorous in itself, tends to have a hybrid character. Marxism has taken shape by scrutinizing and sharpening itself not only on the real world and not only on its own texts but also against non-Marxist thinking. Marx's own thought developed in a critical dialogue with that of thinkers like Hegel, Ricardo and Proudhon. Similarly, Marxist literary theories have developed alongside, and in dialogue with, very different non-Marxist approaches which have to some extent influenced their form. As we shall see, Lukács had an 'interlocutor' in Hegel, the Bakhtin school had theirs in Russian Formalism and Macherey and Kristeva have had theirs in French structuralism.

Not all Marxists who write about literature put forward a literary theory. Bertolt Brecht's brilliant writings on the theatre were mostly pragmatic, concerned with how to make a revolutionary art. The Soviet theory of socialist realism, launched in the thirties, was more a set of prescriptive rules for the kind of writing deemed to be desirable by the party and a set of yardsticks for criticizing 'decadent' literature than a literary theory as such. It is not that these things do not have

134

theoretical implications, but it is difficult to do them justice without bringing into play a detailed historical context. I have narrowed the field by excluding them here.

My aim in this chapter is to offer a broad sample of the strategies developed by Marxists for explaining literature in relation to society. Since other modern literary theories are dealt with amply elsewhere in this book, I deal only partially with fusions and cross-fertilizations between Marxist and other modern approaches. An attempt to cover more recent conjunctions between Marxism and structuralism or psychoanalysis in depth would have involved unwieldy repetition of material contained in the other chapters. I have therefore indicated in the Further Reading where some of these developments can be sought.

Some Marxist concepts

Despite their diversity, all Marxist theories of literature have a simple premise in common: that literature can only be properly understood within a larger framework of social reality. Marxists hold that any theory which treats literature in isolation (for instance as pure structure, or as a product of a writer's individual mental processes) and keeps it in isolation, divorcing it from society and history, will be deficient in its ability to explain what literature really is. This premise already tells us part of what distinguishes Marxist theories from many others. But it does not tell us very much, and by itself it does not account for what makes these theories Marxist. There are other 'sociological' approaches to literature, non-Marxist ones, which share the same premise. Erich Auerbach's criteria for studying Western literature in *Mimesis* (Auerbach 1971) would be one example, and our premise really applies to a whole spectrum of historical criticism emerging before Marx or Marxist influence in nineteenth-century Europe.

Where Marxist theories of literature differ from these other approaches is in having available to them a number of specific concepts and ways of seeing the world which assign a structure to it. For Marxists, social reality is not an indistinct background out of which literature emerges or into which it blends. It has a definite shape. This shape is found in history, which Marxists see as a series of struggles between antagonistic social classes and the types of economic production they engage in. The shape is also found in any given moment of society, because particular class relationships and particular political, cultural and social institutions are related to the system of economic production in a determinate way. Both the structure of history and the structure of society are what Marx and Engels called *dialectical,* a term which draws attention to the dynamic and opposed forces at work within them. The term 'dialectic' also refers to a *method* by which history and society can be analyzed in order to reveal the true relationship between their component parts. Marx for instance proceeded dialectically when he studied political economy. He did not start by looking at population or economic production in general, because these concepts were too broad and included other things which were logically prior to them. He looked instead at social classes and socially determinate economic production—capitalism—before moving to more general things.

Although social reality has a structure for a Marxist, it is not given at the outset where or how literature fits into this structure. One might, for instance, start by looking at the structure of history and society and then see whether the literary work reflects or distorts this structure. But one could just as easily start from a general concept of literature, then move to writers and texts and out to society; or start from a specific text and move to the author, the author's class and the role of this class in society. Each of these procedures has in practice been adopted by different Marxists, and this list of options is by no means exhaustive. The fact that there is little consensus on how to proceed is partly a result of the problematical status of the object—literature—itself. Does literature mean literary texts, a particular use of language, or a certain kind of cultural product? But the lack of consensus comes also from the kind of differences among Marxists I referred to at the start. We shall see that Lukács and several other theorists dealt with in this chapter understand the dialectic as being a universal kind of system called the 'totality' in which all parts of reality and consciousness are interrelated. Yet not all Marxists share this view or place so much emphasis on this philosophical approach.

One part of this structured view of reality which has had an indisputable impact on Marxist literary theory is the model of *base* and *superstructure* which Marx succinctly outlined in his 1859 foreword to *Towards a Critique of Political Economy* (Marx and Engels 1962:363). One of the things which distinguished Marx's view of history and society from that of his predecessors and contemporaries was the emphasis it placed on the socio-economic element in any society as an ultimate determinant of that society's character. 'Socio-economic' means the social relations created by the kind of economic production preponderant in a given society. In a capitalist society, this is the relationship between capitalist and proletarian. It is founded on exploitation and is thus a relationship of potential or actual conflict. This basic economic structure (or *base*) engenders a number of social institutions and beliefs which act to regulate or dissipate the conflict and keep the mode of production in being. Under a capitalist economy, these may be a bourgeois parliament and judiciary, an education system geared broadly to the needs of capitalist production, and the values which uphold these institutions. All these elements which arise on the socio-economic base Marx calls the *superstructure* of society.

Despite the fact that this picture of causation in society was an important part of what made Marxism new, Marx was not consistent about how rigidly he meant it to be taken. Engels stressed in 1890 that neither he nor Marx had ever intended the base to be seen as the sole or simple determinant of everything else in society. He said that the process of causation was a complex one, that the different elements of the superstructure interacted and influenced historical change (Marx and Engels 1956:498). Because of this margin of uncertainty about the model of base and superstructure, Marxist thinking about it has admitted of differing interpretations. Broadly speaking, we can distinguish two periods here. From the 1870s to the First World War, the majority of Marxists took the determinist view that the base simply caused the superstructure and the superstructure reflected the base (a view known as 'vulgar Marxism'). Since Lenin, however, most Western Marxists have placed more emphasis on the way changes in the superstructure (for instance political organization and party action) can influence and accelerate changes in the base. Nevertheless, there has been little real agreement even among twentieth-century Marxists on how these two levels interact.

All this has had considerable importance in Marxist literary theory because literature is one of the things Marx situated in the superstructure of society. Thus if one theorist takes a vulgar Marxist view and sees a fairly direct and one-way determination of literature by the socio-economic base, while another stresses the complexity of the causation, two very different theories of literature and criticism result. The first of these approaches probably corresponds to the image many people still have of Marxist criticism, but the second corresponds more accurately to the reality of Marxist literary theory in the West this century.

A final element which bears crucially on most Marxist thinking about literature is the concept of *ideology*. The term is a difficult one to define satisfactorily, but it generally conveys the sense of a collective representation of ideas and experience as opposed to the material reality on which experience is based. It does not necessarily refer to the system of values held or put in circulation by the ruling class to establish consensus in society. Nor is it necessarily a 'false consciousness', a phrase used by Engels. It has however been used frequently by Marxists in both these senses. Part of the difficulty comes from the fact that Marx and Engels offered different definitions of ideology over a period in which their ideas developed significantly.

Two points can be stressed here to help clarify matters. Firstly, ideology in Marxism tends to be contrasted with a more objective

137

kind of knowledge. This can be illustrated by the way Marx sees the capitalist economy. When we look at the economy we may see only a circulation of commodities (Marx also calls this view a 'fetishism' of commodities). But if we try to understand how the economy really works, approaching it dialectically, we will see that this circulation of things is only an ideological representation of relations between people—workers and bosses—where surplus value is extracted from the worker's labour by the capitalist. People represent these relations to themselves ideologically, and in this case involuntarily, as a circulation of things, and this prevents them from breaking through to an understanding of the contradiction between classes on which the relations are objectively founded. The ideological view here is perhaps not so much a false or illusory one as a partial one. It is bound up with what Marx calls *reification*, the process by which a world of human relationships appears as a set of relationships between things. Similarly, the process by which a worker relinquishes his labour power to the capitalist in exchange for wages and becomes the appendage of a machine is part of what Marx called *alienation*. We shall find the concept of an ideological or reified or alienated view which needs to be broken through by a dialectical view in the literary theories of Lukács and Adorno.

Secondly, Marx explicitly situates literature within a larger *ideological* superstructure along with religion, philosophy, politics and legal systems (Marx and Engels 1962: 363). In this usage there is no suggestion that an ideology is a distortion of material reality. Marx however stresses that changes in these ideological forms cannot be determined with the same kind of scientific precision as changes in economic production. He also argues in another context that changes in art, in ideology, do not necessarily correspond evenly to changes in the socio-economic base. Rather, the development of the arts can be 'out of all proportion to the general development of society, hence also to the material foundation' (Marx 1973: 110). These observations, as well as the concept of ideology itself, challenge Marxists to develop theories of literature. If ideology is a representation, so too—it may be argued—is literature. The prospect of finding how these two kinds of representation might be related opens up a wide avenue of inquiry.

Having examined these Marxist concepts, we can now return to the premise I began with and see how literary theorists have built upon it in practice. In what follows, I subdivide Marxist approaches into five *models* which they have devised for linking literature to social reality. These models are not always watertight compartments and in some cases the theories flow into one another. Yet there is a sufficient difference of emphasis between each model to justify the subdivision, and sometimes this difference is quite great.

138

The reflection model

One of the most influential of these theoretical models has been that which sees literature as reflecting a reality outside it. It is this model which Lenin used when he wrote about Tolstoy as the 'mirror of the Russian revolution' (Lenin 1967: 28). This model may seem simple or primitive but it need not be so. It should be remembered that before the 'structuralist revolution' the majority of literary theorists treated works as somehow referring to a reality outside them. All early Marxist thinking on literature, as well as some of its modern versions, draws on an aesthetic tradition which stretches from Aristotle to the nineteenth century and sees art as mimesis, an imitation of life. This view retained its hold over Marxist thinking for a long time, because Marx himself had maintained, against Hegel, that external reality is prior to ideas in the mind, that the material world is 'reflected in the mind of man and translated into forms of thought' (Marx 1976: 102).

The most fully worked-out version of the reflection model in modern Marxist aesthetics is that of the Hungarian thinker Georg Lukács, an important figure in the international communist movement from the twenties till his death in 1971. Lukács did not see literature reflecting reality as a mirror reflects the objects placed in front of it; literature is a knowledge of reality, and knowledge is not a matter of making one-to-one correspondences between things in the world outside and ideas in the head. Reality is indeed out there before we know it in our heads, but it has shape, it is what Lukács insists is a dialectical totality where all the parts are in movement and contradiction. To be reflected in literature, reality has to pass through the creative, form-giving work of the writer. The result, in the case of a correctly formed work, will be that the form of the literary work reflects the form of the real world.

Before looking at what Lukács understands by a 'correct' form, let us examine his notion of *form* itself. This term, in his usage, should be distinguished from the same term used by the Russian Formalists, where it refers to the sum of devices in a text. Shklovsky could, for instance, see Sterne's disruptions of narrative conventions in *Tristram Shandy* as a way of bringing form to the fore: 'By violating the form, he forces us to attend to it' (Shklovsky 1965b: 30). An early work by Lukács, however, calls Sterne's writings 'formless' because they are full of 'unselected matter' and their narratives are theoretically infinite: they impose no bounds, no shape on the world (Lukács 1974: 143). Clearly, 'form' means different things in each case.

Lukács's view of form is the older one. It is rooted in nineteenth-century aesthetics. He did little more here than take over a concept of form used by Hegel, who wrote of characters and their actions in epic literature as means of giving 'form' to history. Form for Lukács is not itself something technical or linguistic, as it was for the

Formalists and later for the structuralists. It is, rather, the aesthetic shape given to a content, a shape manifested through technical features such as narrative time and the interrelationship of characters and situations in a work. When Lukács for instance deals with Balzac's novel *Les Paysans* in *Studies in European Realism* he sees a significant form in the triangular configuration of three social classes: landed aristocracy, bourgeoisie and peasantry (Lukács 1972: 28-29). In order to see this kind of relationship between characters as form, Lukács, like Hegel before him, needs to make an implicit distinction between reality as it could have been embodied in literature and reality as it actually is embodied. Form in this respect is nothing other than the content of a literary work when it assumes a meaningful configuration.

What, then, is a *correct* form? For Lukács it is one which reflects reality in the most objective way. He considers the form of the early nineteenth century novel (Scott, Balzac, Tolstoy) to be the most correct for embodying a knowledge of the contradictory content of capitalist society as it develops. This notion of correctness depends on Lukács's view that the reality which literature either manages or fails to reflect is a social and historical reality with a dialectical shape. The 'increased' realism of the later nineteenth-century writers, Flaubert and Zola, is for Lukács really a lapse away from realism into a kind of writing which reflects reality falsely, a writing which concentrates on insignificant minutiae or offers too subjective a picture of the world. By the time of Proust, Joyce and the avant-gardes we have, according to Lukács, 'the complete dissolution of all content and all form' (Lukács 1976: 172).

What Lukács was criticizing in Zola or Proust was the presence of, in his terminology, 'unmediated' totalities. In simple terms, these are representations of the world which give an inflated emphasis to one aspect of reality at the expense of others. A properly 'mediated' totality, by contrast, is a representation which reveals the true relationship between the human subject and the objective world, as well as between the various parts of the world itself. In Lukács's view, Zola portrays a world made up of a wealth of detail but he displays these unsorted individual facts as if they constituted a whole reality. Proust and Joyce proceed in a similar way, and Joyce also falls into another kind of error: that of displaying a world made up of abstract universals as if it were a whole reality. For Lukács these unmediated totalities were more than just distorted perceptions. They had a political significance, since unmediated totalities were reifications, ideological deformations of reality which falsified the objective situation of a society founded on the contradiction between classes.

Lukács's judgement of what a correct form is, and his consequent criticisms of naturalism, subjectivism, allegory and myth, were influenced by the way in which he saw history moving. In Stalin's analysis of world history from the mid-thirties, which Lukács broadly accepted, the spread of world revolution had suffered a setback since the end of the First World War and the rise of fascism. Lukács's response to this diagnosis was to look back over the long period of history and culture which began with the Industrial Revolution and the spread of modern capitalism, a period whose crisis point had not yet been reached in the West. He found the apex of this movement of history in the literature and culture of the early period of post-French Revolution Europe, and a subsequent decline into naturalism, subjectivism and symbolism after the revolutions of 1848. Before 1848, writers and critics were inside the process of history, active participants struggling to make sense of it and *narrate* it. Afterwards they became observers and salaried members of the system and were content to *describe* the world. (See the two important essays 'The writer and the critic' and 'Narrate or describe?' in Lukács 1970.) All of Lukács's work as a Marxist shows a nostalgia for this period of critical, militant, creative European culture, the ideal progenitor, as he saw it, of socialist culture. This nostalgia is complemented by a hatred for the irrationalist tradition in thought and art which he saw as alienated from reality and culminating in fascism.

We should now be in a position to see how Lukács's dialectic and his reading of history underpin his reflection model. The critic who approaches a literary work with this model cannot see it as a reflection by making back-and-forth comparisons between elements in the work (say a character or a scene or a descriptive detail) and elements in the world. What is being reflected in a correct work and failing to be reflected in an unmediated one is a whole objective *form* of reality, something which is far less immediate and tangible. A work which *appears* to be like life will thus not necessarily be realistic for Lukács, and a work which manifestly *distorts* appearances will not necessarily be unrealistic. He insists that the literary work is a 'self-contained whole' (1970: 47). He sees the exaggerations in Balzac's situations, characterizations and style not as Flaubert and Zola saw them, namely as obstacles to a more developed realism. They are, rather, the very means of Balzac's social realism: it was through these literary inflations and condensations and generalizations that Balzac achieved 'typicality' in his realism (1970: 50).

Typicality, or the concept of the *type,* is a central component of Lukács's reflection model. Art, in his mature aesthetic theory, is a kind of knowledge which centres on the 'particular', and particularity *(Besonderheit)* in literature is contained for Lukács in what Engels had called 'the truth in reproduction of typical characters under typical circumstances' (Marx and Engels 1956: 478-79). The type is not, Lukács insists, a mere statistical 'average' (Lukács 1972: 6). It is the character or situation in the literary work which brings together the general movement of history and a number of unique, individual traits into a distinctive particularity. The type gives the work the 'three-dimensionality' which for Lukács is the essence of realism (1976: 6).

Lukács's argument that the type is not the same as the average or the mean might seem puzzling, so let us see how his literary theory would judge an 'average' person like Leopold Bloom in Joyce's *Ulysses* and a rather un-average person like Waverley in Walter Scott's book of the same name. Bloom may certainly be felt to possess behaviour traits typical of many married men or advertising reps or lower middle-class Jews. But in Lukács's terms these traits of Bloom's are not portrayed as typical of the historical situation of his class, and Bloom is not presented as being bound up in a general dialectical movement of history.

Waverley is ostensibly less lifelike than Bloom. He starts out in adult life with his head full of literary recollections and fantasies, so that his life, Scott says, is 'a dream'. Yet in Lukács's terms, Waverley is located within the form of the novel (between his Tory uncle on the land, his Whig father in town and the life of adventure of the Jacobite rebels he joins) in such a way that he draws together and reveals the conflicts between three historically significant social groups. Himself a 'middle-of-the-road hero' (Lukacs 1969: 71) in the sense that the action of the novel revolves around him as a passive 'hub', Waverley, like all Scott's central characters, has the function of bringing into contact with each other 'the extremes whose struggle fills the novel, whose clash expresses artistically a great crisis in society' (1969: 36). Waverley is thus not a historically significant type in himself but a vehicle for presenting typicality, the fusion between the individual and the general in history.

Moreover, Joyce's more naturalistic treatment of time (making the action of the novel take place in a single day) appears from Lukács's point of view as less realistic that Scott's more conventionalized foreshortening, since Scott's method allows him to depict a general movement of history. Similarly, the other time-scale in *Ulysses*—that of myth—is in Lukács's terms trans-historical, too broad to show a typical stretch of history.

Lukács's reflection model, it should now be clear, is in no way a primitive or a crude one. He never takes the view that a literary work is simply a mirror held up to nature, and his theory centres precisely on making distinctions between 'accurate' and erroneous reflections, between 'critical' realists like Balzac and Scott and naturalists or modernists like Zola and Joyce. His idea that the literary work is simultaneously both a 'self-contained whole' controlled by 'specific, objective laws' of its genre (1970: 54) and a reflection of the world is not a matter of conceptual acrobatics or confusion on his part. It can be seen as an attempt to bring together in a single explanation two feelings about literature that many people undeniably hold: that it is about real life, and that it is also some kind of autonomous reality itself, with particular formal characteristics of its own. Since the principal correspondence established by Lukács's reflection model is that between the form of the literary work itself and the structure of reality, it appears to be precisely those 'objective laws' of the work's form which enable it to make an accurate reflection of the world. It is Lukács's emphasis on form in this sense which quite clearly constitutes his novelty within the tradition of Marxist literary criticism that he developed.

One of the 'classics' of this tradition is the letter by Engels I have already quoted which expounds Engels's idea of realism in relation to Balzac. Engels noted that although Balzac was politically a reactionary, a supporter of the Bourbon restoration after 1815, who sympathized in his work with the nobility, he in fact also satirized this very class and showed admiration for his political opponents, the republicans. Engels says of this that Balzac 'was compelled to go against his own class sympathies and political prejudices, that he *saw* the necessity of the downfall of his favourite nobles...and that he *saw* the real men of the future'. This, Engels concludes, is 'one of the greatest triumphs of Realism' (Marx and Engels 1956: 480). Many Marxists have understood this letter to be saying in theoretical terms that realism triumphs over ideology, over political views that are quite consciously held and are even given considerable space in the literary work. Realism seems here to involve a kind of superior vision which sees the truth and movement of history even as the writer's sympathies barricade him against it. What Engels's letter does not attempt to explain is how this can happen, how the writer's work can run counter to his prejudices while the writer, and even large parts of the work itself, remain rooted in these prejudices. The letter seems to beg for some theory of ideology in relation to literature, some explanation of how ideology is confuted by the 'triumph of Realism' in the literary work.

Lukács seems to offer an answer to this. In his essay of 1934 on *Les Paysans*, he picks up Engels's observations by saying that what Balzac intended to write was not what he actually wrote (Lukács 1972: 27). At the same time, he goes further than Engels in theoretical terms by demonstrating that the *form* of Balzac's novel corresponds to reality and by suggesting that it is through this formal reflection that the work goes counter to Balzac's ideology. He compares *Les Paysans* with two of Balzac's more utopian novels about rural France, which he shows to be more transparently ideological because they do not fully portray the relationships between the different classes in conflict in the countryside. The theoretical implication of this would seem to be that Lukács greatly plays down the role of the *author* in the process of reflection. It is not Balzac who reflects accurately in *Les Paysans*, because the same Balzac could write utopian novels which reflect inaccurately: it must therefore be the form of *Les Paysans* itself.

In practice, however, Lukács is less clear and consistent than this about the role of the author in his theory. In the same essay on *Les Paysans* he appeals to the creative perspicacity of the author to explain the work's realism. Balzac sees with 'incorruptible eyes' the way French capitalism is moving (1972: 38). Indeed, as Lukács argues in his important theoretical essay of 1954 'Art and objective truth', 'objectivity of form is an aspect of the creative process' itself (1970: 53). This weakens Lukács's suggestion that Balzac's work itself goes against Balzac's ideology and appears to put him in a theoretical difficulty: that of explaining whether the realism comes from Balzac's creative skills, his honesty in recording what he sees, or from something in the form of his novels themselves.

I have now illustrated what Lukács understands by reflection, form, correctness, realism and typicality. Although in many ways his reflection model holds together in his hands almost to perfection, we can see that it raises some theoretical difficulties. If we try and compare it against other kinds of literary theory, we can see what it leaves out and what it includes. Firstly, it is not a theory of literature in general but a theory of realist literature and also a theory, with rare exceptions, of the novel. Lukács focuses on the novel because he develops Hegel's view that the novel is *the* modern literary form, an attempt to reconstitute the totality of man and the world contained in the epic when this totality is no longer possible under capitalism but can be so again (for Lukács) under socialism.

Secondly, it is not strictly speaking a descriptive theory but an evaluative one. Lukács's reflection model provides him with a way of making a basic value-judgement: realistic or non-realistic. To reach this judgement he needs to make a number of descriptive distinctions between correct and incorrect form, the presence or absence of types, the true or the unmediated totality, yet the value-judgement is no mere optional addendum to the theory: it lies at its centre.

Thirdly, it is not a theory which has much to do with language. Lukács tends to deal with language only as a function or vehicle of some higher principle of form (in his sense) like a character or a genre. He does not, in other words, see language as the substance of literary works but as the transparent medium of these opaque forms.

Fourthly, it is not (as we have seen with the case of Balzac) a theory which assigns a clear and consistent role to the author, because it tends to draw away from the author to the reflection of the world in the literary work itself, yet without undermining the creative presence of the author, and indeed suggesting in many places that accurate reflections are a sign of the author's artistic greatness.

On the other hand, some very clear theoretical principles emerge from Lukács's theory, and perhaps I can draw attention to its particular strengths by isolating two. Lukács's literary theory is, in the first place, based on the assumption that literary history is not an autonomous evolution, what later Russian Formalists like Tynyanov called a relatively closed 'series', but is inseparable from history in general. The critic must therefore bring both kinds of history to bear on a given work in order to make sense of its form. Lukács applies this principle to brilliant effect when he deals with Stendhal, Balzac and Tolstoy *(Studies in European Realism)*, as well as with a writer's whole output *(Goethe and His Age)* and a literary genre *(The Historical Novel)*. At the same time, because of the evaluative basis of his theory, he can apply the same principle in a reductive way to writing he does not consider realistic *(The Meaning of Contemporary Realism)*. In the second place, the critic's job in Lukács's theory is to show if and how reality is reflected in a work not as a simple mirror image but as an autonomous structure, something necessarily self-contained, with its distinctive resources of form: characterization, action and scene, narration and description, compositional structure and narrative time.

The production model

The French Marxist Pierre Macherey has developed a model of the relationship between the literary work and reality which differs significantly from Lukács's reflection model. It can be helpful to see this model as taking off from Lukács's, since it proposes an alternative to what looked so seamless in Lukács: the correct literary form as a bond between the realist work and historical reality; and it opens up some of the seams that Lukács's model leaves: the relationship between author and text, between ideology and realism.

Macherey's most substantial theoretical work is *A Theory of Literary Production*. As the title implies, this book is concerned with how literary works are made. But Macherey gives 'production' a quite specific meaning. He sees literature as like productive labour, where raw materials are worked into an end-product. He sees the author not as a creator (a concept which suggests that literary works are fashioned from nothing, or from some shapeless clay) but as someone who works pre-existing literary genres, conventions, language and ideology into end-products: literary texts. Anything that enters the text will tend to be changed into something else when the text is written, just as, for example, the steel which goes into making an aircraft propellor changes its appearance and function after being cut, welded, polished and fitted onto the aircraft with other components.

If we leave out the mention of ideology, there should be nothing particularly unfamiliar about Macherey's production model. His view of the author as a producer is not unlike the Formalists' view of the writer as a craftsman, the user of devices. It also resembles Barthes' emphasis in *S/Z* on the production of the text and on writing as a practice using codes, some of which may come from other texts. Although Macherey's book, which appeared in 1966, predated *S/Z* and was in many ways a critique of early structuralist approaches, Macherey shared a common cultural climate with structuralism and was one of the theorists to develop the view of the author as someone who works upon a world of signs and codes from the inside, so that he or she is 'written' by language in the act of writing it. Yet Macherey at the same time gives his production model a distinctive twist which places it squarely within the scope of Marxist literary theories. He does this by bringing into play a theory of reading which sees texts as necessarily *incomplete* and contradictory and which is crucially concerned with *ideology.*

The essays on Jules Verne and Balzac contained in Macherey's book illustrate his approach. In both cases, he tries to show that, although the author starts with a project by which he intends to create a unified and coherent text, this coherence was not and could not have been achieved in practice. According to Macherey, Verne's project was to show how industry and science conquer nature and transform it. Balzac's project, as he explicitly stated in his general preface to the *Comédie Humaine,* was to observe society and to judge it. Neither of these projects worked out as the authors intended.

In Macherey's analysis of Verne's *The Mysterious Island,* he starts by pointing out that Verne tries to update the theme of *Robinson Crusoe* by having a little society of castaways (unlike the solitary Crusoe) who are forced to put the natural wealth of the island to their social use (again unlike Defoe's hero, who had a wreck full of socially made products conveniently to hand offshore). But as the story progresses, Verne's castaways find that they are not alone and are not the first colonists. Captain Nemo is living under the volcano and his men have been on the island. A bullet is found in a dead pig; the castaways are provided by Nemo with a chest full of goods. For Macherey, what is happening here is that one of the aspects of the old Robinson Crusoe theme that Verne had started by leaving out (the wreck full of socially produced goods) is brought back (the chest supplied by Nemo). Verne's project is undermined by his own text. The modernized Robinson Crusoe theme is broken into by the old Robinson Crusoe theme. The narrative, in Macherey's words, is 'faulty'.

The result of this for Macherey is that what Verne's novel actually reveals is something it had not intended. Verne would like to believe that the pioneering conquest of new worlds by science and industry, part of the ideology of colonial imperialism of his time, can be achieved in the kind of artificial pre-social conditions set up in the Crusoe story. From a Marxist point of view this is impossible, since society has to be not only already in existence but also quite economically developed before science and industry can come into being. What Macherey says about Verne is implicitly based on a criticism Marx was fond of making of early bourgeois economists who did not see that Defoe's story was a myth. They used the image of Crusoe on his island to present their picture of primitive economic man without realizing that Defoe's hero is really bourgeois man. He does not in fact start with 'nothing' but with socially made products and learned economic practices, such as book-keeping (Marx 1976: 170).

Now although Macherey treats the 'fault' in Verne's text as if it is a kind of parable of what Marx is talking about, he is not saying that Verne somehow possessed a Marxist knowledge of bourgeois society and imperialism. This would be an absurd claim to make, and Macherey is quite explicit that Verne's novel does not actually say anything about bourgeois society which reveals a theoretical (shorthand for Marxist) understanding of it (Macherey 1978: 239). But the text's contradictions, which the faulty narrative displays, allow an informed reader to bring a theoretical understanding to bear upon it.

Macherey's procedure with Balzac is similar, although where Verne's narrative was 'faulty', Balzac's text is 'disparate'. This is because Balzac bases himself on two projects—to observe and to judge—which are quite different and which demand different kinds of writing. On the one hand, Balzac writes out a copy of the world, peopled with a rich array of recurring characters who move around in a variety of settings. On the other hand, he uses rhetorical exaggerations and artificial comparisons to convey his moral and ideological judgements. Both of these projects are carried out by similar means, using literary resources like the type, the scene, the description. Yet Macherey asserts that they do not come together in a coherent blend; he shows that the two projects contradict each other in the text itself. In *Les Paysans,* which he looks at in detail, the peasants are described as savages and compared to redskins (and therefore 'judged'), yet they are also pictured realistically ('observed') in their early nineteenth-century French rural milieu. Balzac tries to blend these two images of the peasants, but the literary methods he uses in fact allow us to distinguish them. For Macherey, two different kinds of 'utterance' correspond to the two projects: fictional utterances (in the 'observations') and ideological utterances (in the 'judgements').

Since Balzac's *Les Paysans* was one of the novels discussed by Lukács, it is worth asking at this point how Macherey's approach to it differs from Lukács's. Lukács told us that Balzac's picture of French rural society was 'meticulously complete' (Lukács 1978: 30), that Balzac described 'faithfully' (1978: 39) the historical necessity of the downfall of the rural nobility and the exploitation of the peasant smallholders by the bourgeoisie. Lukács in other words sees Balzac's novel as complete and coherent, and he identifies the means of Balzac's objectivity in certain broad features of the novel's form. But he does not explain how Balzac came to 'betray' the reactionary beliefs which were apparent in the novels that lacked this particular form.

Macherey's argument, based on the production model, is that Balzac's ideology enters the text as one of its constituent elements and even produces specific and 'detachable' ideological utterances (Macherey 1978: 297). But the novel is not an expression of Balzac's ideology or a reflection of the society around him; it is a fictional 'working' or production of both these things. Ideology, as well as reality, enters the text (Macherey states that 'A good novelist without an ideology is inconceivable' (1978: 261)), but once it is in the text it is set to work with other elements, 'hollowed' as ideology and transformed into fiction, and thus is no longer the same thing as it was before. The text is far from being coherent or 'complete'.

This transformation of ideology is the part of literary production Macherey is most closely concerned with. He describes literary production in a later work as a 'staging' of ideology, which suggests that ideology is produced and transformed by the writing of fiction in the same sort of way that the script of a play is transformed on stage. Verne's ideological project is changed when it enters the faulty narrative. Balzac's ideological utterances conflict with other elements of his disparate narrative and are themselves transformed into something else, changed by fiction. Macherey understands ideology in *A Theory of Literary Production* to be a compact system of *illusory* social beliefs. It is complete in itself, but only on the condition that there are certain things it cannot see or say. Literature 'produces' ideology by writing it out. It gives it a shape and contours it could not possess as ideology, since illusions are insubstantial. In doing so, the text 'hollows' the ideology, separates its fictional version from the same ideology before it entered the text. In Macherey's words: 'there is a conflict within the text between the text and its ideological content' (1978: 124); 'literature challenges ideology by using it' (1978: 133).

Before looking more closely at Macherey's concepts of ideology and fiction, let us return to the role of the reader and critic in his literary theory. I said that Macherey has a theory of reading and that in his essay on Verne he points out that the reader has to bring to the text the theoretical knowledge the text and its author did not possess. Macherey's idea that reading involves 'theorizing' what we read may strike many people as being odd and counter to the notion that critical reading is simply a highly sensitized perception of what a text contains. The easiest way to explain Macherey's view and show how it is bound up with a Marxist theory is to look at what it is based on: an idea of 'symptomatic reading' developed by the French philosopher Louis Althusser, with whom Macherey had collaborated in a project called *Reading Capital.*

Put simply, Althusser's idea is as follows: when we write, we do not just record what we see and fail to record what lies outside our field of vision; rather, we see all the elements of reality about which we write, but our written text cannot always make the right connections between them. A text thus tends to present reality partially or incoherently, leaving gaps. Through these gaps, however, an informed reader can see what the text was hiding from itself. Althusser understands the progress of scientific knowledge as one in which an informed reader (in his case, the Marx of *Capital*) explains the necessity for a given writer's (Adam Smith's or Ricardo's) lapses by superimposing a new conceptual framework on the text he reads. Althusser puts this in the form of a paradox: 'What classical political economy does not see, is not what it does not see, it is *what it sees*' (Althusser and Balibar 1970: 21).

Althusser is talking here about the way breakthroughs are made in scientific understanding. Marx is a good example, because large stretches of *Capital* are indeed critical dialogues with economic theorists like Smith and Ricardo in which Marx breaks through to a new theory by reading, citing and criticizing their texts. The name 'symptomatic' for this kind of reading shows the influence of the psychoanalytical theories of Lacan. Marx, like a psychoanalyst, reads 'symptoms' in an incomplete or elliptical text, which is like the patient's account of a dream, and explains why the text contains lapses and gaps from the point of view of his own theory. As Macherey applies the theory of symptomatic reading in his book, it involves superimposing a coherent theoretical framework (Marxist theory) on the gaps and silences in a given writer's texts. I have illustrated this in his procedure with Verne. 'What is important in the work', Macherey writes, 'is what it does not say' (1978: 87).

Macherey's theory of reading literature is a challenging one which goes against many other ideas of what criticism is or should be concerned with doing. Most notably, it rejects the idea that criticism is interpretation. 'Interpreting' a text implies getting out of it things that are within it and are not obvious to a casual reader. This in turn implies that what is in the text is somehow complete and coherent, with a meaning that simply needs to be revealed. But Macherey's view of writing as production, when combined with his view that writing is necessarily a partial or incoherent rendering of reality, makes it meaningless for a critic to approach a text in this way. Moreover, for all the similarities Macherey's work may display with certain kinds of structuralist literary theory, his work departs from them by

149

suggesting that it is not sufficient to find out how texts create meaning. The literary theorist must also *explain* the text in the light of a theoretical understanding of a reality which includes author, text, reader and theorist: and 'theoretical' here, as for Althusser, means Marxist.

Theory, then, is in Macherey's approach something which the *critic* alone possesses. In the author and the text we find fiction and ideology, but not a theoretical picture of reality. Ideology, as we have observed, was something illusory for Macherey which became transformed by fiction, 'produced' in the text. The reader as theorist (the critic) needs to stand at a distance from both the ideology and the fictional text to watch and understand these transformations. Macherey is rather unclear about what 'fiction' means in this case. It appears to have the simple technical sense of the elaboration of literary raw materials, presumably in prose, so that it is more or less synonymous with 'prose-writing' in a literary context. But at a philosophical level (and Macherey after all is using philosophical concepts here like illusion, truth and reality) the status of 'fiction' is more ambiguous. Given Macherey's sharp contrast between ideology (or illusion) and theory (or science), fiction seems to stand between ideology and theory as a kind of halfway house. It would appear not to share the illusory nature of ideology, because Macherey says that it is precisely the production of ideology by fiction that sets it a distance from itself and reveals gaps in it. At the same time, fiction does not seem to partake of theory, working to criticize ideology, since it only serves to hollow the ideology, to create the gaps and silences in the text, and it needs the intervention of the theorist to explain the presence of these silences. Macherey seems to add confusion by stating that 'Fiction, not to be confused with illusion, is the substitute for, if not the equivalent of, knowledge' (1978: 64).

Macherey's theory thus does not seem to be problem-free, but we should not lose sight of where it is innovative. I have already shown that it overthrows intrepretive criticism because of its theory of reading and the incomplete text. I have also indicated an important part of where it breaks with Lukács's Marxist criticism: in replacing reflection with production and in replacing the notion of the complete or coherent text with that of the incomplete one. A few more points could be added. Firstly, although Macherey restricts the application of his model to narrative fiction there seems to be no reason why it could not be applied to poetry and drama too. It is not intrinsically committed to the novel for aesthetic or historical reasons as Lukács's theory was. To be applied in this way, the concept of 'fiction' would need to be refined by testing it against other kinds of text.

Secondly, it is not an evaluative theory but a descriptive one.

Macherey does not ask, like Lukács, whether a particular work is good (correct, accurately realistic) but what it is like. He frees Marxist literary theory from evaluation because he does not see literary works as containing a *knowledge* of reality which the critic can judge as being either correct or not. He sees them rather as productions or workings of things in reality, and knowledge in his approach is something the *critic* brings to bear on them. Thirdly, although it is not a theory which could be said to be based on language, it assigns an important place to the language of the literary text. It is fictional language and a number of specifically literary resources which bring about the production or transformation of ideology. Fourthly, and finally, it eclipses the creative presence of the author by presenting the author as someone not fully aware of what his own text is doing.

Before moving on from Macherey to a third model, it must be stated that Macherey himself has not developed his own work on literature quite along the lines he suggested in *A Theory of Literary Production*. After writing this book, he turned away from his production model with its emphasis on the way literature is produced from raw materials, and began considering literature as part of the education system, one of the apparatuses the State uses to prop up its domination in society (Macherey and Balibar 1974). One of the effects of such a move, and of similar moves by other Marxists and sociologists who deal with literature, is that it tries to make us understand and question the values our society ascribes to literature, by treating certain texts as constituting a cultural tradition, and by reading and teaching them in a particular way. Such an approach in practice dissolves literary theory away as an autonomous discipline and makes it part of a political criticism of culture. Although this approach obviously has profound repercussions across the whole field dealt with in this book, I cannot really treat it in depth in the present context. I have indicated at the end of this chapter where Macherey's later approach and some kindred developments can be found.

The genetic model (Skip to 159)
A long tradition of Marxist literary theory has been concerned with the question of how literature, along with the other arts, came to develop out of social life and of what causes literary works to assume the form they do. The model used in this approach can be called 'genetic' because it deals with origins, causes and determinations. One of its more interesting modern versions is that of the Rumanian-born sociological theorist Lucien Goldmann, who worked in France and died in 1970.

Goldmann, who wrote both on philosophy and literature, was struck by the fact that the 'objective meaning' of a literary or philosophical work 'was often not completely clear for the author himself' (Goldmann 1964: 8). Both Hume and Descartes, for instance, believed in God, yet their philosophical writings were, respectively, wholly sceptical and wholly rationalist. A similar insight led Wimsatt and Beardsley to the idea of the 'intentional fallacy' and to basing literary criticism on the text alone. Yet Goldmann's alternative to the biographical approach of correlating the literary work with the author's life and personality was not to centre on the text but to correlate the work's structure with what he came to call the 'mental structure' of the author's social group. He was influenced here by Lukács's insistence that reality and thought constituted a dialectical totality in which everything was interconnected. With such a view, it became meaningless for him to talk about a text 'in itself'. For Goldmann, literary works arise out of social consciousness and behaviour, and it was the way they are linked to society that he sought to establish.

What does Goldmann mean by 'mental structure' and the structure of a literary work? He is not thinking of linguistic structures but of patterns of ideas and concepts. He believes that 'certain privileged social groups' (1977: 76) possess a superior form of ideology he calls a 'world view' *(vision du monde)*. A world view is the expression of those groups in society 'whose thought, feeling and behaviour were oriented toward an overall organization of interhuman relations and of relations between men and nature' (Goldmann 1977: 76). These social groups can either be 'revolutionary' or 'reactionary' classes (Goldmann 1964: 17). A world view expresses itself as a mental structure and this structure is given what Goldmann terms 'coherence' by the work of great writers and philosophers who represent the social group.

Goldmann's approach thus has much in common with older views of literature as a form of expression. Yet it differs from most expression theories by seeing the literary work as the expression not of the author's self but of the social class of which the author is a member. Goldmann stressed that the origin of a work's mental structure lies in social behaviour, and he saw social behaviour arising not from the will of separate individuals but from two or more individuals acting as one: for instance when they cooperate to lift a heavy load. He thus took the basic unit of social activity to be what he called the 'transindividual subject'. Literary works consequently became for him in a sense *collective* products of social groups. Goldmann did not go so far as to eliminate the role of the individual author altogether. Instead, he saw the great writer as elaborating the mental structure of the group so that his work could relay back to the group a sharpened awareness of that structure. A writer does not simply reproduce the collective consciousness in a mechanical way but rather advances very considerably the degree of structural coherence which the collective consciousness itself has so far attained only in a rough and ready fashion. Thus the work constitutes a collective achievement through the individual consciousness of its creator, an achievement which will afterwards reveal to the group what it was moving towards without knowing it (Goldmann 1973: 115).

Most of these views were developed in practice in Goldmann's major work *The Hidden God,* originally published in 1955. This is a remarkably ambitious project which explores the mutual connections between a social group, a religious movement, the philosophy of Pascal and the plays of Racine. In each of these things Goldmann finds a particular form of world view, the 'tragic vision', in which 'man appears torn between contradictory obligations that the world prevents him from reconciling' (Goldmann 1969: 109). The social group (the *noblesse de robe* of seventeenth-century France) is torn between its dependence on the absolutist rule of the monarch and the pull of bourgeois individualism. The religious movement (Jansenism) is torn between the absolute authority of a hidden God and the rationalism of the human world. These same contradictions are at the heart of the thought of Pascal and the dramas of Racine, both of whom were Jansenists and members of the *noblesse de robe.* Goldmann presents these contradictory obligations as two corners of a triangle—God and the world—which exert a magnetic pull on the third—man or the 'tragic' individual. In Racine's *Phèdre,* for instance, God is represented by the pagan gods Venus and the Sun, who act as Phèdre's moral conscience. The world is represented by characters like Hippolyte and Thésée, who lack awareness and have no 'reality or value' (Goldmann 1964: 378) but who provide the occasion for Phèdre, the tragic character, to recognize the error of her incestuous love and bring her back to truth.

The kind of conflict Goldmann sees as dramatized in *Phèdre* might also have been identified by a traditional psychoanalytic approach. Yet this approach would have related it to a conflict either in the mind of the character Phèdre herself or in that of Racine. Goldmann differs by relating the triangular structure in which this conflict is fought out in Racine's plays to the mental structure of the *noblesse de robe* and the Jansenists, in other words to things in society. And he relates the structure, not the substance. On the face of it, the substance or content of a Christian doctrine like Jansenism and that of Racine's pagan plays could hardly be more dissimilar. Yet by looking behind the overt content to the mental structure of the shared tragic vision, Goldmann finds that they have the same *form.* He later gives this sameness of form the label 'homology'.

As we have seen, Goldmann's mental structures are not linguistic structures but interrelationships of concepts. As in Lukács's theory, language is not given either a distinct or a central role in Goldmann's work. In his studies of Racine's plays, he sees the mental structures as being *represented* by characters, some of whom (like the gods, who are necessarily hidden) are present in the text but not on the stage. Goldmann's 'structure' here is therefore very like the 'form' which Lukács perceived in the configurations of representatives of social classes in a novel. Goldmann did in fact assert that literature was a language, but what he meant was that literature was 'reserved for the expression and communication of certain particular contents' and that these contents were, precisely, world views (Goldmann 1964: 313). This is, of course, quite different from the structuralist view which sees meaning itself as a product of language. Goldmann's is a variant of the more conventional view that Jacques Derrida calls 'logocentrism'. For him, language, and therefore literature, is a vehicle for expressing a reality already in existence; the reality exists prior to the literary work in the world view and its mental structure. It is this older sense of 'structure' Goldmann employs when he calls his approach 'genetic structuralism', not that of the Parisian structuralists, whom he generally criticized.

If Goldmann sees the structure of the literary work as 'homologous' with the mental structure of the social group, where does the specific nature of the literary work lie in his model? It lies precisely in the 'coherence' that the author's work gives to the preexisting mental structure. As he states: 'World-views are social facts. Great philosophical and artistic works represent the coherent and adequate expressions of these world-views' (Goldmann 1969: 120). There is a clear criterion of value involved here. Not only are those literary works which express a world view also 'aesthetically satisfying' (Goldmann 1964: 14); works which do not give a fully balanced expression of the world view are also somehow lacking. In Racine's *Iphigénie*, for instance, Goldmann finds a conflict between a tragic universe and a providential universe with no mediating element between them. This destroys 'the unity which alone can make a work of art absolutely valid' (Goldmann 1964: 361). Racine, according to these criteria, wrote only four plays which are 'completely coherent' (Goldmann 1964: 361).

How does all this look when we compare Goldmann's model with Lukács's and Macherey's? The early Lukács was a very strong influence on Goldmann, and Goldmann to a large extent owes his notion of homology to what he saw as Lukács's search for the relationship between art and social consciousness 'not in the contents but in *the categories which structure one or other of them*' (Goldmann 1973: 118). It is true that both Lukács and Goldmann posit a more or less direct formal correspondence between the literary work and social reality. Yet Goldmann's model is less centred on the notion of reflection than on the process of expression, and this is what makes it genetic. Indeed his later emphasis on the way the individual writer 'advances' and gives coherence to group consciousness is designed as a rejection of reflectionist theories (Goldmann 1973: 115). Again, although both Lukács and Goldmann see reality and thought as a dialectical totality, Lukács looks for the way the literary work reflects or fails to reflect the totality, whereas Goldmann studies more precise connections between the work and the author's social group, which constitute only a part of the totality. This makes Goldmann's approach more sociological than Lukács's. In other words, he looks first at groups within society rather than starting with a whole society, and his concept of social class is more restricted and specific than Lukács's.

Goldmann's model differs quite markedly from Macherey's. Its emphasis is on expression rather than production and on the coherence of what is expressed rather than its incoherence. This underlies what one critic of Goldmann has called, with Macherey in mind, his model's 'too trimly symmetrical' nature. (Eagleton 1976a: 34). Goldmann's world views are the expression of social classes and great literary works are in turn the coherent expressions of world views. World views are for Goldmann privileged forms of ideology, 'global' rather than partial ones, so he is stressing the coherence with which ideology can be given shape in literature. Macherey on the other hand sees an ideology as sufficient unto itself in the practical world but radically undermined when it enters a literary text, where it leaves gaps that the critic has to explain.

If we wish to assess the validity of the genetic model, I suggest we should grasp what Goldmann's work teaches us but at the same time start separating its potential applicability from the way it is actually used in Goldmann's hands. Goldmann was an innovator in his attempt to see how various parts of the superstructure (literature, philosophy, politics, religion) were related to each other and, in turn, to class relationships. Since it is probably true to say that Marxism lacks an adequate theory of the superstructure, this attempt should not be slighted, despite the fact that Goldmann's Marxism was not particularly rigorous. In its innovations, the model overcomes the vulgar Marxist view that the economy directly causes the literary work and attempts to work out a more accurate map of the intermediary levels between them. But there is also much in Goldmann's approach that is grounded in conventional literary studies and much that is simply rather vague or questionable: the notions of coherence and unity, the evaluative equation between fully expressed world views and aesthetic quality, the notion that characters stand primarily for abstract concepts.

MARXIST LITERARY THEORIES

The negative knowledge model

We saw how Lukács's reflection model forced his criticism to adopt a kind of 'either-or' strategy. He could either demonstrate the grasp of the totality in a classic realist work or reject the unmediated totality of the non-realist work, whether it were naturalist, symbolist or lyrical and subjective. In his book *The Meaning of Contemporary Realism*, written in 1956 at the start of the process of de-Stalinization in the Soviet Union, Lukács began more openly to criticize the limitations of the socialist realism, which had been promoted by Soviet cultural apparatchiks since the early thirties, and to reconsider modernist writers like Joyce and Beckett. Yet the net result of this reassessment was really that he vindicated what he had been saying all along about the superiority of critical realism or authentic socialist realism over other forms of writing. It did not affect the basic premises of his aesthetics and literary theory.

An attack on this book was written by the Frankfurt School Marxist Theodor W. Adorno, who died in 1969. Adorno complained of Lukács's dogmatism and tried to show how Lukács was trapped within a 'vulgar-materialist' view of the work of literature as the reflection of objective reality (Adorno 1977: 153). We need not be concerned here with all the details of Adorno's critique, much of which takes Lukács to task for using an erroneous, pre-Marxist kind of dialectic. What makes Adorno's approach immediately interesting is that it tries to assign a definite value to modernist writing, in opposition to a literary theory which had been weighted heavily against modernism.

Despite Lukács's view that the literary work reflected reality by using its own distinctive formal resources, he treated the reflection itself as being similar to the way reality was reflected in human consciousness. Adorno criticizes Lukács precisely because he transfers 'to the realm of art categories which refer to the relationship of consciousness to the actual world, as if there were no difference between them' (Adorno 1977: 159). Adorno's own view is that art and reality stand at a distance from each other and that this distance gives 'the work of art a vantage-point from which it can criticize actuality' (Adorno 1977: 160).

For Adorno, this critical distance comes from the fact that literature (his word is art, but he means it to include literature) has its own 'formal laws'. He does not spell out precisely what these formal laws are, but he does give two important indications of the kind of thing he means. Firstly, he talks of the 'procedures and techniques' which in modern art 'dissolve the subject matter and reorganize it' (1977: 153). Secondly, he says that art is the 'essence and image' of reality rather than its photographic reproduction (1977: 159). An image in a work of art comes for Adorno from the artist (the subject) absorbing in the creative process what he perceives in reality (the object): 'In the form of an image the object is absorbed into the subject' (1977: 160).

With this emphasis on formal laws of art as a matter of procedures and techniques and as a fusion of subject and object, Adorno explains how the writers Lukács castigates for their 'subjectivism' in fact set themselves at a distance from reality, so that their work effectively criticizes it. Proust and Joyce both use the interior monologue, which in Lukács's view was a technique which placed an inflated emphasis on the thinking subject in the novel, detaching him from the social reality he inhabits and thus detaching the literary work from realism. Adorno however insists that the interior monologue, far from cutting the literary work off from reality, can expose the way reality actually is. The separation from the world and the emphasis on subjectivity which comes from the interior monologue are a true picture of reality in its 'universal atomistic state', where 'alienation rules over men, turning them into mere shadows of themselves' (1977: 160). At the same time, the emphasis on the subject is also an *appearance* and not, from a Marxist perspective, how things really are, since in reality 'the social totality has precedence over the individual' (1977: 160). A great modernist work, for Adorno, is precisely that which manages to reveal this contradiction between appearance and reality. When Proust and Joyce use the interior monologue, they both show the subject as alienated, cut adrift from society, yet at the same time they place the subject in a social context which reestablishes the correct perspective in which the individual subject is only a part of the totality. Proust and Joyce thus *expose* the contradictory reality they inhabit (that the alienated condition is a real one, but that the alienated individual is still objectively bound up with the social totality). They do not, as Lukács maintained, just reflect the alienated and subjective side of things, without being able to transcend it by adopting the true perspective which comes from a correct realist form.

Adorno's concept of reality is not itself a very different one from Lukács's. Like Lukács, Adorno takes reality to be not the empirical world we see through our eyes or through the camera lens but the dialectical totality, a structure which can only be perceived by a process of thought linking things together and seeing how they effectively are. Like Lukács too, Adorno emphasizes the alienated nature of reality in contemporary Western society, a world where people appear to be at the mercy of the mechanical laws of the market and of a rationalized and bureaucratic State. Where Adorno differs from Lukács is in the role he attributes to art in this reality. Lukács held that the only way for art to break through the crust of reified appearances was for it to reflect the correct form of the totality. Adorno rejects this, not only because he insists on the work's formal laws (Lukács himself, after all, emphasized the 'objective laws' of literature) but also because he stresses the distance between the work

157

and reality. He says that 'art exists in the real world and has a function in it' and yet it is 'the antithesis of that which is the case' (1977: 159). The literary work does not give us a neatly-shaped reflection and a knowledge of reality but acts within reality to expose its contradictions. Adorno says, 'Art is the negative knowledge of the actual world' (1977: 160).

'Negative knowledge' does not mean knowledge of nothing, non-knowledge. It means knowledge which can undermine and *negate* a false or reified condition. This kind of negation is what Adorno finds at work in Proust or Joyce's use of the interior monologue, and it is what he has in mind when he talks about the vantage-point from which art criticizes actuality. Adorno and his associates in the Frankfurt Institute for Social Research developed a theory of culture which argued that, as capitalist society had become increasingly rationalized, culture itself had become an industry. Any work of literature or art which had a 'positive' content, which tried to put forward an antagonistic political message in simple and lucid language, would instantly be negated by the culture industry, which is geared precisely to neutralizing criticism against the social order. Adorno thus came to put a premium on formally 'difficult' texts and to criticize as pointless 'committed' literature, like the novels of Sartre or some of Brecht's plays.

What are the practical implications of such a view for literary theory? Firstly, by emphasizing the 'formal laws' of literature as something which set it at a distance from the form of the real world, Adorno moves sharply away from the models of Lukács and Goldmann, who both treat the form of the work and the reality outside it as 'homologous'. Yet he does not overthrow, as Macherey does, Lukács's idea that literary works contain a knowledge of reality. In a sense, he turns it upside down by making this knowledge a negative rather than a positive one. He therefore places a central emphasis on the antagonistic, critical role played by the literary work which respects its own laws of form.

Secondly, when he deals with literary works, Adorno adopts the view that the work must be read attentively in order to bring out what we could call the 'double-reality' it contains. Just as Adorno says it is not sufficient to see how Proust and Joyce reproduce an alienated condition, but that one must also see how their work transcends this condition by placing the individual subject within a social totality that takes 'precedence' over him, so he can see a similar double-reality in the work of Kafka, which he studies in his book *Prisms* (Adorno 1967). Kafka, Adorno says, presents a kind of copy of an alienated or reified totality, as many of his critics have noted. But he also uses formal devices in his text, disruptions of conventional narrative time for instance, which show that this alienated reality has weak points and cracks in it. By both reproducing and exposing the way reality is, Kafka's books work to give a negative knowledge of it, to negate it.

Thirdly, Adorno's model breaks the kind of collusion there was in Lukács's model between literary theory, evaluation and a certain kind of text. He opens up modernist writing to Marxist literary theory by showing that a different kind of relationship between the text and reality is possible: one of critical distance and negative knowledge rather than reflection. In practice, Adorno is an evaluative critic too; he has his own great writers and his own targets. Yet despite his critique of commitment in literature and his general distaste for the kinds of realism defended by Lukács, his literary theory is not actually made for modernism alone. Indeed his point that art always has its own 'formal laws' means that it would be illogical for his theory to deny these formal laws to non-modernist works. He concedes as much when he argues against Lukács that 'there is no way of preserving the antithesis between realist and "formalist" approaches' (Adorno 1977: 163). All art stands at a distance from reality. Where an approach like Adorno's might be pushed further, indeed, is towards finding out just where texts like Balzac's, based on assumptions of mimesis, differ from modernist ones, which are to varying extents anti-mimetic, and where on the other hand they share certain formal principles and a distance from reality.

Language-centred models
In most of the models I have discussed so far, language has not been assigned a central, or even a distinctive role. Only Macherey can be said to have given language real prominence in his theory; even so, it is not language itself which really stands at the centre of Macherey's model, but the production of ideology by the text.

In many ways, this state of affairs is understandable. Rather than asking why Marxists have failed to make language central, it might make more sense to ask why they should have tried to do so. We saw that Marxists have available to them a dialectical view which assigns a structure to society and also a base and superstructure model which, however one interprets it, links and yet separates literature from non-literary things in the material world. As many Marxist theorists apply these views, literature comes to refer to or develop something outside it which is not a linguistic reality and which seems indeed to be more fundamental and real than language. Language may have a place in the process, but to assign it the central place looks like an inversion of priorities, if one is attempting to explain how a whole social structure includes literature, and where literature is distinct in society.

For a model to become centred on language while remaining Marxist, a new conception of the importance of language in the social process is therefore needed. The language-centred model I shall deal mainly with in this last section puts forward such a conception. It was developed by the so-called Bakhtin school, a group of Soviet scholars active from the last period of Russian Formalism in the early twenties who were influenced by the Formalists' work as well as by Marxism. The precise authorship of some of the principal works of the school is a matter of dispute. I shall for convenience refer to these works here by the name of the author under which they originally appeared: either that of Mikhail Bakhtin, Pavel Medvedev or Valentin Vološinov.

The basic assumption by which these theorists bring language to the centre is that society itself is not separable from language. They see language as the material medium in which people interact in society, and they see ideology as made of language in the form of linguistic signs.

If we take ideology first, we can see where this idea leads in Marxist terms. By saying that everything ideological is a sign (Vološinov 1973: 9), Vološinov departs from the view that ideology is something which exists solely in consciousness. This view was based on Marx himself, since Marx talked about parts of the ideological superstructure like politics, religion and art as forms in which men become 'conscious' of and fight out the struggle at the material centre of civil society, in other words the socio-economic base (Marx and Engels 1962: 363). It is this view too which models like Lukács's, Goldmann's and Adorno's draw on. Vološinov therefore breaks quite clearly with a philosophical tradition in Marxism when he calls ideology a 'material segment' of reality (Vološinov 1973: 11). The ideological sign shares the material nature of other parts of reality, although it is also distinct. Medvedev for example distinguishes between ideologies—which are material, social and made of signs—and those material things which are either not social (such as natural physical bodies) or do not signify anything (like the instruments of production). This view of ideology radically affects the base and superstructure model. With it, the structure of society does not involve direct reflections or repercussions from the material level (the base) onto ideas, forms of consciousness (in the superstructure); instead, there is an unbroken *material* chain between the levels.

The Bakhtin school's view of language was itself a novel one. Vološinov was writing his *Marxism and the Philosophy of Language* at a time when idealist linguists like Karl Vossler were developing a view of language as an individual creative activity and as something which resided largely in the mind. Vološinov took over this emphasis on creativity, but he saw language as a social activity and thus the creativity became a matter of arousing the hearer's attention and maintaining interest in a dialogue. Saussure's theories were also starting to become known at this time, yet Vološinov did not accept for his purposes Saussure's view that the primary object of the linguist's attention was the 'abstract' language system, the *langue;* nor did he accept the other part of Saussure's couplet, *parole,* because like Vossler's view it emphasized the individual language user, not the social reality of speech. Vološinov held that Saussure's view of language was 'perfectly legitimate within the range of the specific tasks linguistics sets for itself' (Vološinov 1973: 99). Yet the Bakhtin school theorists were not concerned with linguistics in this sense but with the study of language within real social situations, with what they called the study of 'utterance' or 'word' (the Russian term *slovo,* which has connotations of both 'word' and 'discourse', is a central one in the Bakhtin school writings). 'Word' is always a dialogue, and dialogue and the stretch of discourse, rather than individual speech or the components of a sentence, is really the basic unit of language in the Bakhtin school approach. As Vološinov puts it: 'word is a two-sided act. It is determined by *whose* word it is and for whom it is meant' (Vološinov 1973: 86).

This conception of language, and the related view of ideology as a material embodiment of social interaction, lay at the basis of the literary theory of the Bakhtin school. This theory had three main applications: as a theory of the literary work, as a procedure for analyzing discourse, and as a theory of literature as a practice. It is the last of these which has the greatest theoretical importance within Marxist literary theory, and I shall therefore deal only briefly with the other two.

The theory of the literary work is developed in Medvedev's book *The Formal Method in Literary Scholarship,* first published in 1928, and for our purposes it is perhaps sufficient to note two things about it. Firstly, this book, as its title shows, is in large part a critique of Russian Formalism. Medvedev takes over many of the Formalists' objections to earlier literary studies which did not assign a distinct status to literature, but he does not agree with the Formalists that the distinctiveness of literature lies in its 'literariness', or with their strict separation of literary studies from other disciplines. The specific nature of literature lies, for Medvedev, in its being a distinct form of ideology and at the same time a reflection of other ideologies. The study of literature thus needs to become a branch of the study of ideologies in general.

Secondly, Medvedev takes issue with earlier sociological theories of reflection and with the vulgar Marxist view of literature as a direct reflection of socio-economic reality. His alternative is not to deny that literature is a reflection, but to see it as a 'staggered' reflection of reality, a reflection at two removes. The literary work, itself a form of ideology, reflects another ideology; this ideology in turn reflects the

socio-economic base. If we correlate what we find in the literary work
directly with reality or life, we jump a stage in the reflection process
and falsify both the literary work and its indirect relationship to
reality. It is impermissible, Medvedev says,

> for a Marxist to draw direct conclusions about the social reality of a
> given epoch from secondary reflections in literature... For a
> genuine sociologist, of course, the hero of the novel or an event of
> plot tell much more as elements of artistic structure (i.e. in their
> own artistic language) than can be learned from naively projecting
> them onto life (Medvedev/Bakhtin 1978: 21).

Medvedev's approach was a highly innovative one for its time, and
there is still much to be learned from his attempt simultaneously to
circumscribe the specific artistic nature of the literary work and to
allow the work to be related back to the ideology which informs its
every element through a staggered process of reflection. Medvedev's
revised reflection model reveals many 'asymmetries' between the
literary work and reality, yet I feel it has in many respects been
superseded by models like Macherey's which seize on more drastic
asymmetries (notably between the author and ideology in the text
itself), the possibility of which Medvedev's model does not broach.

The second application of the Bakhtin school theory is as a
procedure of analyzing literary discourse. The main point that needs
to be stressed here is that although the Bakhtin school model is
centred on language, it is not a conventional linguistic model; the
reality of language for the Bakhtin school is, as I noted, discourse and
dialogue. Bakhtin argues in his book of 1929 *Problems of Dostoyevsky's
Poetics* that the analysis of discourse (which he calls 'stylistics' here)
'should be based not only, and even *not as much* on linguistics as on
metalinguistics which studies the word not within the system of
language and not in a "text" which is removed from dialogical
intercourse, but rather precisely within the sphere of dialogical
intercourse itself, i.e. within the sphere of the genuine life of the
word' (Bakhtin 1973: 169). Bakhtin criticizes the view of language as a
'thing', an object, rather than as a medium of human interaction. This
was also one of Medvedev's grounds for criticizing the Formalists
(Medvedev/Bakhtin 1978: 152-53).

What Bakhtin calls 'metalinguistics' (a term which, following Julia
Kristeva's suggestion, we can amend to 'translinguistics', to avoid
confusing it with its more accepted sense) becomes in his hands a
procedure for breaking the language of a literary narrative down into
different types of utterance, each of which is more or less a form of
dialogue. This might appear odd, since large stretches of narrative
would seem to be written in the single narrator's voice. Yet Bakhtin's
translinguistics draws attention to techniques like free indirect
discourse (where the vocabulary and prosody of a character's speech

are rendered without quotation marks in what is nominally the narrator's voice) to show that narrative discourse can contain a dynamic interaction between two or more voices. A similar schema of different types of discourse is found in Vološinov's *Marxism and the Philosophy of Language,* where it is used to show how certain kinds of discourse predominate in given historical periods. In periods under stable hierarchical societies, for instance, authors tend to accept the dogmatic authority of utterances which they quote or report, since what is quoted has an 'official' or a sacred character for them. In societies in transformation, by contrast, reported speech is infiltrated by the author's retorts and comments, so that the author effectively challenges quotations.

These procedures for analyzing discourse are important in our context for the bearing they have on the third application of the Bakhtin school approach: the conception of literature as a practice. Just as Vološinov's 'sociolingual' schema draws attention to the way an author infiltrates his voice into quotations in periods of social transformation, so Bakhtin's book on Dostoyevsky, as well as his later study of 1940, *Rabelais and His World,* is concerned with the related idea that the language of a literary work can involve a subverting of stability, authority and convention, which gives it a social significance. This significance can be explained if we look at the work in relation to the period in which it is written and understand the norms of literary discourse that it violates.

Bakhtin argues in the first of these books that Dostoyevsky institutes a new genre, the 'polyphonic' novel, which is characterized by the multiplicity of voices present in it, none of which are subjected to the authoritarian control of the writer himself. 'Dostoyevsky, like Goethe's Prometheus, creates not voiceless slaves (as does Zeus), but rather free people who are capable of standing beside their creator, of disagreeing with him, and even of rebelling against him' (Bakhtin 1973: 4). This multiplicity of voices is not manifested as a multiplicity of styles. Dostoyevsky's characters do not speak in markedly different styles, as Tolstoy's do; they gain their freedom from each other and from their author through the way their speech is 'situated' in relation to the author's speech. Tolstoy's characters, on the other hand, despite their differentiated styles, are in fact more controlled by their author than the characters of Dostoyevsky. This makes Tolstoy's novels 'monologic', dominated by the author's authoritarian voice, where Dostoyevsky's are 'polyphonic'. The fact that monologue and polyphony are not to do with style but with the relations between author's and characters' voices brings out what Bakhtin means when he claims that his approach is not a linguistic but a translinguistic one.

This approach is a markedly different one from those we have looked at so far. Rather than seeing literature as a knowledge of reality, Bakhtin sees it as a practice of language within reality. This distinguishes his model from those of Lukács and Adorno, where the literary work gives the theorist a knowledge, albeit a negative one in Adorno's case, of the real world. A practice in language is also quite different from an expression of ideas through the medium of language, the basis of Goldmann's genetic model. For Macherey, I need only reiterate the point that he is most closely concerned with the way literature produces something anterior to it, and his model has to centre on the critic's theory to see the difference between an ideology as it is in a project, and the way it is actually produced in the text. All this is quite unlike Bakhtin's view.

When Bakhtin draws attention to Dostoyevsky's technique of 'polyphony' he is not concerned with what the themes of Dostoyevsky's novels, or their form or content, tell us about reality, but with the social significance this technique of discourse possesses. Polyphony for Bakhtin is a new genre, and he does not see a genre merely as a category the literary theorist uses to distinguish types of literature like tragedy, comedy, lyric or novel. The real significance of a genre is to be found in two things: the fact that it 'conceptualizes' reality, and the way it stands in relation to other literary genres. Seeing genres primarily as means of conceptualizing reality means for Bakhtin that a genre is not something circumscribed only to literary texts, but is bound up with the way we present the world to ourselves through language. 'One might say', he writes, 'that human consciousness possesses a series of inner genres for seeing and conceptualizing reality' (Bakhtin 1973: 134). Indeed, literary genres provide us with ways of conceptualizing in language that we did not possess before, and in this sense life can be said to imitate literature: 'the genres of literature enrich our inner speech with new devices for the conceptualization of reality' (Bakhtin 1973: 134).

The practical significance of a genre also lies in the way it relates to other genres. Bakhtin sees the novel not, like Lukács, as a modern attempt to reconstitute the epic but as a supremely open and unregulated genre. Its history is that of a continuous mixing of other genres, a rupturing by parody or by new kinds of discourse of the more hierarchically structured reality conceived of in other genres such as, precisely, the epic (Bakhtin 1976). Dostoyevsky's polyphony is a way of conceptualizing a reality which gives freedom to the individual character by subverting the authoritarian and monologic discourse of Tolstoy and other nineteenth-century novelists. Rabelais transposes and develops the anti-authoritarian practices of the language of the carnival and the popular festivity, which play freely with language to parody the languages of the Church and the magistrates. With these views, Bakhtin gives a privileged place in literary history to what he calls the 'Menippean' tradition (from

Menippus, the hero of Lucian's fantastic dialogues) of 'carnival' literature, in which he includes the Socratic dialogue, the dialogue with the dead, the parody and the personal satire. These all involve types of literary discourse in which the individual character has free play against the author, an interlocutor, or social rules and conventions.

From a Marxist viewpoint one could quite reasonably object that Bakhtin's emphasis on rebellion and the freedom of the individual literary voice against constituted authority has an anarchist and libertarian ring that makes it resemble the ideas of Proudhon more than those of Marx. It is quite true that Bakhtin's Marxism appears consistently more diluted and utopian in these works, particularly the later one on Rabelais, than the dialectical method of poetics put forward in *The Formal Method*. Yet my contention would be that this does not necessarily diminish the importance of his view of literature for Marxist literary theory. It is not the precise significance that Bakhtin ascribes to the Menippean tradition or to free indirect discourse that counts, but the fact that he can see a significance in these things at all. When, for instance, he treats Dostoyevsky's polyphony as a more radical language practice than Tolstoy's 'monologue', he swings a Marxist approach away from an identification between a 'progressive' ideology (as Tolstoy's, in comparison with Dostoyevsky's, could be said to be) and a 'progressive' work. He also detaches it from the kind of procedure Lenin and Lukács apply to Tolstoy, namely the search for the objective social realism which emerges in spite of Tolstoy's evangelical utopianism. It is not so much what the work reflects, either about the author or about the objective shape of the world, that matters for Bakhtin, but what the work is as a practice in language.

The Bakhtin school as a whole, then, can be seen as instituting an approach which breaks away from a view of literature as a clear or direct reflection of reality, attempts to rethink the meaning of ideology and its function in literature, and treats literature as a practice rather than a form of knowledge or expression. Although the Bakhtin school theorists use a non-Saussurean view of language, there is much in their approach which allows it to be adapted to a structuralist approach.

Julia Kristeva, a literary theorist first active in the climate of sixties structuralism and semiotics in France, makes just such an adaptation. She emphasizes the revolutionary nature of literary language, as one which renders explicit the total signifying process *(significance)* of language, something that is not acted out in automatized practical language. Kristeva basically retains Bakhtin's emphasis on literature as a practice, and the social significance which Bakhtin gave it, while bringing to Bakhtin's view a structuralist concept of the text and of the role of the subject (the writer) within language.

Kristeva developed these theoretical views in her book *Semeiotikè* and applied them to poetry in *La révolution du langage poétique*. It is interesting to note in this context that Kristeva deals in the second of these works with the period of history—the latter half of the nineteenth century—where Lukács saw writers becoming more detached from reality because of their increased professionalization within a rationalized State. Kristeva, whose book looks in some detail at French society in this period, as well as dealing with Mallarmé and Lautréamont, notes exactly these things too. Yet she comes up with an opposite view to Lukács's of the effective role of symbolist poetry in this process. Mallarmé himself had an elitist conception of poetry, and during the revolutionary upheaval of the Paris Commune he retreated from the 'invasion' of politics into his private life as a pure *littérateur*. Yet for Kristeva these biographical facts are important only in that they indicate how Mallarmé refused any institutional authority. Mallarmé's *texts*, on the other hand, are objectively revolutionary because they oppose the 'fetishization' of poetic language created by the bourgeois regimes of the Second Empire and the Third Republic, which reduced poetic discourse to an embellishment of life, as well as being distinct from the 'delirium' of the Romantic and bohemian poets. They are revolutionary texts because they act out the tension between the subject and language, within which the subject is inserted. As Kristeva puts it, 'the transformation of poetic language . . . consists in its becoming a practice of this dialectical condition of the subject in language' (Kristeva 1974: 80).

The mention of 'dialectic' in this context illustrates how a structuralist can relate the Marxist view of the human subject, as dialectically inserted into a world of object reality, to the post-Saussurean view of the subject as inserted into an objective structure of language. In fact, the marriage between structuralist and Marxist concepts which this seems to augur is not necessarily a smooth or simple one. Structuralist approaches were in the sixties a constant target of criticism for many Marxists on the grounds of their allegedly ahistorical nature (the emphasis on synchrony at the expense of diachrony) and the alleged 'reification' by which they made language and sign-systems appear to replace or exclude a material, non-linguistic reality. Such criticisms were in turn rebuffed by post-structuralists, who argued like Derrida that it made no sense to distinguish between language and a pre-existing reality, since all social processes and thought were constituted in and through language. Hence the marriage is more accurately speaking a rapprochement, and the problem remains for Marxists either to maintain a division between a world of signs and a material world of non-signs, or to overcome the 'logocentrism' inherent in this division and remodel the older Marxist conception of the social structure into that of a structure centred on language. Kristeva, for her part, is rather inexplicit and perhaps inconsistent about the way the two structures relate to one another. In *Semeiotikè* she argued that all intellectual disciplines and areas of social activity need to viewed as signifying systems, that history for instance should be treated as a set of texts rather than as a 'history without language'. In *La Révolution du langage poétique* she in practice limits herself to relating the revolution in language to 'socio-economic revolution' in the form of a 'correspondence' (Kristeva 1974: 14).

In many ways Kristeva's is an appealing approach. It not only brings back modernist texts, and in a quite different way from Adorno's model, from the limbo into which Lukács had cast them. It also suggests a more complex and contradictory set of links and mediations between literature and society than many other models by arguing that a revolution in language can correspond to a social revolution without being directly connected to it and without the author needing to be politically aware in a conscious and practical sense. As in Bakhtin's view of the Menippean tradition (which Kristeva incidentally picks up and extends to writers like Joyce) there is something reductive about Kristeva's 'correspondence', a tendency to exclude the real context in which poetry like Mallarmé's is valued, taught, sold and read as well as aspects of its language. Yet there is something very productive about this use of the language-centred model; it indicates how language can be made the starting point of a broader sociological investigation of literature in society and it opens up Marxist literary theory to areas such as the language of poetry from which many earlier models had closed if off.

Further reading
This chapter has not dealt in any detail with early Marxist writings on literature. Specifically on Marx, the reader will find Mikhail Lifshitz, *The Philosophy of Art of Karl Marx,* a useful introduction which can now be supplemented by S. S. Prawer's informative *Karl Marx and World Literature.* There is naturally no substitute for reading the texts of Marx and Engels themselves, and the fundamental anthology here is Baxandall and Morawski's *Marx Engels on Literature and Art.* Two broad surveys which take the early tradition of Marx and Engels through to Lukács and beyond are Henri Arvon's *Marxist Esthetics* and Peter Demetz's *Marx, Engels and the Poets.* Prior to Lukács, Lenin's statements of the reflection model are the classic ones, and can be found in his articles on Tolstoy in *On Literature and Art,* along with his views on literary partisanship and party literature. Trotsky's *Literature and Revolution,* first published in 1923, contains a suggestive critique of Russian Formalism from a genetic viewpoint, and some of his later writings on literature can be found in *Leon Trotsky on Literature and Art.* The founding documents of socialist realism are contained in Gorky *et al., Soviet Writers'*

Congress 1934. For a Western concept of committed literature, see Jean-Paul Sartre's *What is Literature?* Important theoretical essays by Brecht are contained in the excellent edition *Brecht on Theatre.* A useful anthology covering Marx, Engels, Plekhanov, Lenin, Trotsky, Lukács, Brecht and others is David Craig's *Marxists on Literature.*

Most of Lukács's writings with relevance to literature are currently available in English, with the exception of his late *Ästhetik* which develops the reflection theory at length. Works by Lukács not cited in this chapter include the early *Theory of the Novel* and the later *Essays on Thomas Mann.* There is a perceptive treatment of Lukács's concept of realism in George Bisztray, *Marxist Models of Literary Realism.* The philosophical side of Lukács is dealt with well in István Mészáros, *Lukács's Concept of Dialectic,* and there is a wide-ranging collection of essays in G. H. R. Parkinson (ed.), *Georg Lukács, The Man, His Work and His Ideas.*

Macherey's production model is sympathetically expounded by Terry Eagleton in *Marxism and Literary Criticism,* along with a critique of Lukács and Goldmann. Eagleton himself integrates Macherey's insights with an original version of the genetic model in his *Criticism and Ideology.* Macherey's earlier ideas are echoed in Althusser's 'A letter on art in reply to André Daspre' in *Lenin and Philosophy,* and Althusser develops similar aesthetic positions in his chapter on 'The "Piccolo Teatro"' in *For Marx.* Macherey's later positions and elements of a self-criticism are to be found in his presentation with Etienne Balibar of Renée Balibar's *Les Français Fictifs.;* in 'Problems of reflection' in F. Barker *et al.* (eds.) *Literature, Society and the Sociology of Literature 1976;* and in 'An interview with Pierre Macherey' in *Red Letters,* no. 5. Macherey's later views are echoed by Tony Bennett in the latter part of his *Formalism and Marxism.* The later Macherey's emphasis on the way values are ascribed to literature has a British variant in Raymond Williams, whose more recent works along these lines include *Marxism and Literature, Problems in Materialism and Culture* and statements in *Politics and Letters.*

An influential early version of the genetic model is that of Georgei Plekhanov in *Art and Social Life.* An interesting though more utopian version is outlined by Christopher Caudwell in *Illusion and Reality.* Goldmann's later work *Towards a Sociology of the Novel,* which I have not discussed here, is a revealing text in which he lapses into more vulgar Marxist positions almost despite himself. Raymond Williams criticizes vulgar Marxism and develops a concept of 'structure of feeling' as a mediation between socio-economic structure and cultural products in *The Long Revolution.* These views are now updated in his *Marxism and Literature,* which also has a chapter aiming to clarify the concept of ideology. Another useful work on ideology is the volume produced by the Centre for Contemporary Cultural Studies of Birmingham University, *On Ideology.*

The negative knowledge model is applied to literature by Adorno in *Prisms,* which also contains an important theoretical first chapter. For an overall view of the Frankfurt School and Adorno with comments on his aesthetics see respectively Martin Jay's *The Dialectical Imagination* and Gillian Rose's *The Melancholy Science.* There is a thoughtful treatment of Adorno in relation to literary theory in Fredric Jameson's *Marxism and Form.* Adorno's critique of Lukács and his essay on committed literature are to be found in the volume *Aesthetics and Politics,* a collection of valuable critical exchanges among

Marxists including Brecht, Benjamin and Lukács. Adorno's associates included Herbert Marcuse—whose *The Aesthetic Dimension* develops the view of the autonomous work of art negating a repressive society—and Walter Benjamin, for whom I have not had adequate space in this chapter. Benjamin's work is of fundamental importance within Marxist thinking on literature and art. His 1934 lecture 'The author as producer' and a number of valuable texts on Brecht are collected in *Understanding Brecht*. See also the selection *Illuminations*, the study *Charles Baudelaire* and *The Origin of German Tragic Drama*. Benjamin's views are sympathetically treated in Cliff Slaughter's *Marxism, Ideology and Literature*, along with a critique of Althusserian criticism.

Julia Kristeva's work remains largely untranslated. Among the works I have not cited is *Le Texte du roman*, which develops the semiotic concept of intertextuality stated in *Semeiotikè*. Kristeva's application of Lacan and Althusser is developed in English with original additions in Rosalind Coward and John Ellis, *Language and Materialism*. See also the essay 'Ideology, subjectivity and the artistic text' by Steve Burniston and Chris Weedon in the already cited volume *On Ideology*, and Colin MacCabe's *James Joyce and the Revolution of the Word*. Catherine Belsey's *Critical Practice*, still within this framework, incorporates the insights of Macherey and, like Eagleton's *Criticism and Ideology*, includes a well-handled critique of older Anglo-Saxon critical assumptions and practices. Much of the more recent British writing along language-centred lines is to be found uncollected in the reviews *Ideology and Consciousness* and *Screen*. A different, and earlier, language-centred model is developed in Galvano Della Volpe's *Critique of Taste*. For a presentation of his ideas, see David Forgacs, 'The aesthetics of Galvano Della Volpe' in *New Left Review* 117.

References

ADORNO, THEODOR, 1967. *Prisms,* London (tr. from *Prismen: Kulturkritik und Gesellschaft,* Frankfurt: 1955).

1977. 'Reconciliation under duress' in *Aesthetics and Politics,* London (tr. from 'Erpreßte Versöhnung', *Noten zur Literatur* vol. II, Frankfurt: 1961).

ALTHUSSER, LOUIS, 1971. *Lenin and Philosophy and Other Essays,* London (miscellaneous articles written 1964-9).

1977. *For Marx,* London (tr. from *Pour Marx,* Paris: 1965).

and Balibar, Étienne, 1970. *Reading Capital,* London (revised, abridged and tr. from *Lire le Capital,* Paris: 1965-8).

ARVON, HENRI, 1970. *Marxist Esthetics,* Ithaca, N.Y. (tr. from *L'esthétique marxiste,* Paris: 1970).

AUERBACH, ERICH, 1971. *Mimesis,* Princeton, N.J. (first published in German 1946).

BAKHTIN, MIKHAIL, 1968. *Rabelais and his World,* Cambridge, Mass. (first published in Russian in 1940).

1973. *Problems of Dostoyevsky's Poetics.* Ann Arbor, Mich. (first published in Russian in 1929).

1976. 'Epos e romanzo', in *Problemi di teoria del romanzo,* ed. V. Strada, Turin (dates from 1938, published in Russian in 1970).

BANN, STEPHEN and BOWLT, JOHN E., 1973. *Russian Formalism,* Edinburgh.

BARTHES, ROLAND, 1963. *Sur Racine,* Paris.

1966. *Critique et vérité,* Paris.

1967a. *Système de la mode,* Paris.

1967b. *Elements of Semiology,* London (tr. from *Eléments de sémiologie,* Paris: 1964).

1970. 'Science versus literature', in Lane 1970: 410-16.

1972. 'To write: an intransitive verb', in Macksey and Donato 1972: 134-56.

1975a. *S/Z,* London (tr. from *S/Z,* Paris: 1970).

1975b. 'An introduction to the structural analysis of narrative', *New Literary History* 6:2, 137-72, (tr. from 'Introduction à l'analyse structurale des récits', *Communications* 8, 1-27 (1966)).

1976. *The Pleasure of the Text,* London (tr. from *Le plaisir du texte,* Paris: 1973).

1977. *Roland Barthes by Roland Barthes,* London (tr. from *Roland Barthes par Roland Barthes,* Paris: 1975).

BEARDSLEY, MONROE, 1958. *Aesthetics: Problems in the Philosophy of Criticism,* New York.

BELSEY, CATHERINE, 1980. *Critical Practice,* London.

BENJAMIN, WALTER, 1970. *Illuminations,* London (tr. of articles from *Schriften,* Frankfurt: 1955).

1973a. *Charles Baudelaire: A Lyric Poet in the Era of High Capitalism,* London (tr. from *Charles Baudelaire: Ein Lyriker im Zeitalter des Hochkapitalismus,* Frankfurt: 1969).

1973b. *Understanding Brecht,* London (*Versuche über Brecht,* Frankfurt: 1966).

1977. *The Origin of German Tragic Drama,* London (tr. from *Ursprung des deutschen Trauerspiels,* Frankfurt: 1963).

BENNETT, TONY, 1979. *Formalism and Marxism,* London.

BENOIST, JEAN-MARIE, 1976. *La révolution structurale,* Paris.

BENVENISTE, EMILE, 1971. *Problems in General Linguistics,* Miami (tr. from *Problèmes de linguistique générale,* Paris: 1966).

BETTELHEIM, BRUNO, 1978. *The Uses of Enchantment: The Meaning and Importance of Fairy Tales,* Harmondsworth, Middx.

BISZTRAY, GEORGE, 1973. *Marxist Models of Literary Realism,* New York.

BLOOM, HAROLD, *et al,* 1979. *Deconstruction and Criticism,* London.

BLOOMFIELD, MORTON, 1976. 'Stylistics and the theory of literature', *New Literary History* 7:2, 271-311.

BONAPARTE, MARIE, 1949. *The Life and Works of Edgar Allan Poe,* London (tr. from *Edgar Poe: Étude psychanalytique,* Paris: 1933).

BRECHT, BERTOLT, 1978. *Brecht on Theatre,* London (selections from German texts published between 1930 and 1964).

BRIK, OSIP, 1977. 'The so-called formal method', *Russian Poetics in Translation* 4, 90-1, (first published in Russian in 1923).

1978. 'Contributions to the study of verse language', in Matejka and Pomorska 1978, 117-25 (first published in Russian in 1927).

BROOKS, CLEANTH, 1947. 'Literary criticism', in *English Institute Essays 1946,* New York, 127-58.

1949. *The Well Wrought Urn,* London.

1950. 'The quick and the dead: a comment on humanistic studies', and 'The critic and his text: a clarification and a defense', in *The Humanities: An Appraisal,* ed. J. Harris, Madison, Wisc., 1-21 and 40-8.

1951. 'The formalist critics', *Kenyon Review* 13, 72-81.

1962. 'Literary criticism: poet, poem and reader', in *Varieties of Literary Experience,* ed. S. Burnshaw, New York.

BROOKS, PETER, 1979. 'Fictions of the wolfman', *Diacritics* 9:1, 72-83.

BROWER, R., VENDLER, H., and HOLLANDER, J. (eds.), 1973. *I. A. Richards: Essays in His Honor,* New York.

DE BUFFON, GEORGES, 1978. *Discours sur le style,* Hull (first published in 1753).

BUTLER, CHRISTOPHER, 1980. 'I. A. Richards and the fortunes of critical theory', *Essays in Criticism* 30, 191-204.

CAUDWELL, CHRISTOPHER, 1946. *Illusion and Reality,* London (first published in 1937).

CHATMAN, SEYMOUR, 1966. 'On the theory of literary style', *Linguistics* 27, 13-25.

(ed.), 1971. *Literary Style: A Symposium,* New York and London.

and Levin, S. R., (eds.), 1967. *Essays on the Language of Literature,* Boston, Mass.

COHEN, JEAN, 1966. *Structure du langage poétique,* Paris.

COLERIDGE, SAMUEL TAYLOR, 1817. *Biographia Literaria,* London.

COMTE, AUGUSTE, 1830-42. *Cours de philosophie positive* (6 vols.), Paris.

COWARD, ROSALIND and ELLIS, JOHN, 1977. *Language and Materialism: Developments in Semiology and the Theory of the Subject,* London.

CRAIG, DAVID, (ed.), 1975. *Marxists on Literature: An Anthology,* Harmondsworth, Middx.

CREWS, FREDERICK, 1966. *The Sins of the Fathers: Hawthorne's Psychological Themes,* New York.

CULLER, JONATHAN, 1975. *Structuralist Poetics,* London.

1976. *Saussure,* London.

1980. '*Fabula* and *syuzhet* in the analysis of narrative', *Poetics Today* 1:3, 27-37.

DELLA VOLPE, GALVANO, 1978. *Critique of Taste,* London (tr. from *Critica del gusto,* Milan: 1960).

DE MAN, PAUL, 1971. *Blindness and Insight,* New York.

DEMETZ, PETER, 1967. *Marx, Engels and the Poets: Origins of Marxist Literary Criticism,* Chicago (tr. from *Marx, Engels und die Dichter,* Stuttgart: 1959).

DERRIDA, JACQUES,

1973. *Speech and Phenomena,* Evanston, Ill. (tr. of *La voix et le phénomène,* Paris: 1967, and 'La différance' in *Théorie d'ensemble,* Paris: 1968).

1975. 'The purveyor of truth', *Yale French Studies* 52, 31-113, (tr. from 'Le facteur de la vérité', *Poétique* 21, (1975)).

1976. *Of Grammatology,* Baltimore, Md. (tr. from *De la grammatologie,* Paris: 1967).

1978. *Writing and Difference,* London (tr. from *L'Écriture et la différence,* Paris: 1967).

1981. *Positions,* London (tr. from *Positions,* Paris: 1972).

EAGLETON, TERRY, 1976a. *Marxism and Literary Criticism,* London.

1976b. *Criticism and Ideology,* London.

EIKHENBAUM, BORIS, 1963. 'How Gogol's *The Overcoat* is made', *Russian Review* 20, 377-99 (first published in Russian in 1919).

1965. 'The theory of the "formal method"', in Lemon and Reis 1965: 99-139 (first published in Russian in 1926).

1978. 'O. Henry and the theory of the short story', in Matejka and Pomorska 1978: 227-70 (first published in Russian in 1925).

ELIOT, T. S., 1953. *The Sacred Wood,* London (first published in 1920).

1955. *The Use of Poetry and the Use of Criticism,* London (first published in 1933).

1957. *On Poetry and Poets,* London.

1972. *Selected Essays,* London (first published in 1932).

EMPSON, WILLIAM, 1950. 'The verbal analysis', *Kenyon Review* 12, 594-601.

1965. *Seven Types of Ambiguity,* Harmondsworth, Middx. (first published in 1930).

EPSTEIN, E. L., 1978. *Language and Style,* London.

ERLICH, VICTOR, 1980. *Russian Formalism: History — Doctrine,* The Hague (first published 1955).

FELMAN, SHOSHANA, 1977. 'Turning the screw of interpretation', *Yale French Studies* 55/56, 94-207.

1980. 'On reading poetry: reflections on the limits and possibilities of psychoanalytic approaches', in Smith 1980.

FOKKEMA, D. W., and KUNNE-IBSCH, E., 1977. *Theories of Literature in the Twentieth Century,* London.

FORGACS, DAVID, 1979. 'The aesthetics of Galvano Della Volpe', *New Left Review* 117.

FOUCAULT, MICHEL, 1970. *The Order of Things,* London (tr. from *Les mots et les choses,* Paris: 1966).

FOWLER, ROGER, 1966a. 'Linguistics, stylistics; criticism?', *Lingua* 16, 153-65.

(ed.), 1966b. *Essays on Style and Language,* London.

FREEMAN, D. C., (ed.), 1970. *Linguistics and Literary Style,* New York.

FREUD, SIGMUND, 1953. *The Standard Edition of the Complete Psychological Works* (24 vols.), London (tr. from *Gesammelte Werke* vols. I-XVIII, London and Frankfurt: 1940-68).

1900. *The Interpretation of Dreams,* in Freud 1953, Vol. IV.

1905. *Jokes and their Relation to the Unconscious,* in Freud 1953, vol. VIII.

1914. 'On narcissism: an introduction', in Freud 1953, vol. XIV, 67-102.

1919. 'The uncanny', in Freud 1953, vol. XVII, 217-56.

1923. 'The ego and the id', in Freud 1953, vol. XIX, 3-66.

GARVIN, PAUL, (ed.), 1964. *A Prague School Reader on Esthetics, Literary Structure and Style,* Washington, D.C.

GENETTE, GÉRARD, 1966. 'Structuralisme et critique littéraire', in *Figures,* Paris, 145-70.

1969. *Figures II,* Paris.

1972. *Figures III,* Paris.

1980. *Narrative Discourse,* Oxford (tr. from 'Le discours du récit' in Genette 1972).

GOLDMANN, LUCIEN, 1964. *The Hidden God,* London (tr. from *Le dieu caché,* Paris: 1955).

1969. *The Human Sciences and Philosophy,* London (tr. from *Sciences humaines et philosophie,* Paris: 1952).

1973. 'Genetic structuralism in the sociology of literature', in *Sociology of Literature and Drama,* eds. Elizabeth and Tom Burns, Harmondsworth, Middx.

1975. *Towards a Sociology of the Novel,* London (tr. from *Pour une sociologie du roman,* Paris: 1964).

1977. *Cultural Creation in Modern Society,* Oxford (tr. from *La création culturelle dans la société moderne,* Paris: 1971).

GORKY, MAXIM, *et al,* 1977. *Soviet Writers' Congress 1934: The Debate on Socialist Realism and Modernism* (first published as *Problems of Soviet Literature,* ed. H. G. Scott, London: 1935).

GREEN, ANDRÉ, 1978. 'The double and the absent', in *Psychoanalysis, Creativity and Literature: A French-American Inquiry,* ed. Alan Roland, New York, 248-70.

GREIMAS, A.-J., 1966. *Sémantique structurale,* Paris.

GUIRAUD, PIERRE, 1975. *Semiology,* London (tr. from *La sémiologie,* Paris: 1971).

HALLIDAY, M. A. K., 1964. 'Descriptive linguistics in literary studies', in *English Studies Today* s.III, Edinburgh, 25-39.

1967. 'The linguistic study of literary texts', in Chatman and Levin 1967: 217-23.

1971. 'Linguistic function and literary style: an inquiry into the language of William Golding's *The Inheritors',* in Chatman 1971: 330-68.

HARTMAN, GEOFFREY H., (ed.), 1979. *Psychoanalysis and the Question of the Text,* Baltimore, Md. and London.

HAWKES, TERENCE, 1977. *Structuralism and Semiotics,* London.

HERTZ, NEIL, 1979. 'Freud and the sandman', in *Textual Strategies,* ed. J. V.

Harari, London, 296-321.

HIRSCH, E. D., 1976. *Validity in Interpretation*, New Haven, Conn.

HJELMSLEV, LOUIS, 1963. *Prolegomena to a Theory of Language*, Madison, Wisc. (first published in Danish in 1943).

HOLLAND, NORMAN, 1968. *The Dynamics of Literary Response*, Oxford.

1975. *Five Readers Reading*, New Haven, Conn. and London.

1978. 'A transactive account of transactive criticism', *Poetics* 7, 177-89.

1980. 'Re-covering "The Purloined Letter": Reading as a personal transaction', in *The Reader in the Text*, ed. Susan Suleiman, Princeton, N.J., 350-70.

ISER, WOLFGANG, 1978. *The Act of Reading*, London (tr. from *Der Akt des Lesens*, Munich: 1976).

JAKOBSON, ROMAN, 1956. 'Two aspects of language and two types of aphasic disturbance', in Roman Jakobson and Morris Halle, *Fundamentals of Language*, The Hague, 53-82.

1963. *Essais de linguistique générale*, Paris.

1968. 'Poetry of grammar and grammar of poetry', *Lingua* 21, 597-609.

1973. *Questions de poétique*, Paris.

and JONES, L. G., 1970. *Shakespeare's Verbal Art in 'Th'Expence of Spirit'*, The Hague and Paris (French version in Jakobson 1973: 356-77).

JAMESON, FREDRIC, 1971. *Marxism and Form: Twentieth-Century Dialectical Theories of Literature*, Princeton, N.J.

1972. *The Prison-House of Language*, Princeton, N.J.

JAUSS, HANS ROBERT, 1974. 'Literary history as a challenge to literary theory', in *New Directions in Literary History*, ed. Ralph Cohen, London, 11-41 (tr. from *Literaturgeschichte als Provokation der Literaturwissenschaft*, Constance: 1967, chs. 5-12).

JAY, MARTIN, 1973. *The Dialectical Imagination: A History of the Frankfurt School and the Institute of Social Research 1923-50*, London.

JOHNSON, BARBARA, 1979, 'The frame of reference' in Hartman 1979: 148-71 (abbreviated version of *Yale French Studies* 55/56, 457-505).

KITTLER, FRIEDRICH A., and TURK, HORST, (eds.), 1977. *Urszenen: Literaturwissenschaft als Diskursanalyse und Diskurskritik*, Frankfurt.

KOLAKOWSKI, L., 1972. *Positivist Philosophy from Hume to the Vienna Circle*, Harmondsworth, Middx.

KRIEGER, MURRAY, 1956. *The New Apologists for Poetry*, Minneapolis, Minn.

KRIS, ERNST, 1952. *Psychoanalytic Explorations in Art*, New York.

KRISTEVA, JULIA, 1959. *Semeiotikè: Recherches pour une sémanalyse*, Paris.

1974. *La révolution du langage poétique*, Paris.

LACAN, JACQUES, 1976. 'Seminar on "The Purloined Letter"', *Yale French Studies* 48, 38-72 (tr. from 'Le séminaire sur la lettre volée' in *Écrits*, Paris: 1966).

1977a. 'The mirror stage', in *Ecrits*, London, 1-7 (tr. from 'Le stade du miroir', in *Écrits*, Paris: 1966).

1977b. *The Four Fundamental Concepts of Psycho-Analysis*, London (tr. from 'Les quatre concepts fondamentaux de la psychanalyse', *Le séminaire de Jacques Lacan* XI, Paris: 1973).

LANE, MICHAEL, (ed.), 1970. *Structuralism: A Reader*, London.

LAPLANCHE, J., and PONTALIS, J. B., 1973. *The Language of Psycho-Analysis*, London (tr. from *Vocabulaire de la Psychanalyse*, Paris: 1967).

LEAVIS, F.R., 1937. 'Literary criticism and philosophy: A reply', *Scrutiny* 6, 59-70 (also in Leavis 1978: 211-22).

1962. *The Great Tradition*, Harmondsworth, Middx. (first published in 1948).

1978. *The Common Pursuit*, Harmondsworth, Middx. (first published in 1962).

LEMON, LEE T., and REIS, MARION J., (eds.), 1965. *Russian Formalist Criticism: Four Essays*, Lincoln, Nebraska.

LENIN, VLADIMIR ILYICH, 1967. *On Literature and Art*, Moscow.

LEPSCHY, G. C., 1972. *A Survey of Structural Linguistics*, London.

LÉVI-STRAUSS, CLAUDE, 1968. *Structural Anthropology*, London (tr. from *Anthropologie structurale*, Paris: 1958).

LEVIN, S. R., 1977. *Linguistic Structures in Poetry*, The Hague (first published in 1962).

LIFSHITZ, MIKHAIL, 1973. *The Philosophy of Art of Karl Marx*, London (first published in Russian in 1933).

LUKÁCS, GEORG, 1963. *The Meaning of Contemporary Realism*, London (tr. from *Wider den missverstandenen Realismus*, Hamburg: 1958).

1968. *Goethe and his Age* (first published in Hungary in 1946).

1969. *The Historical Novel*, Harmondsworth, Middx. (tr. from *Der historische Roman*, Berlin: 1955).

1970. *Writer and Critic*, London (miscellaneous articles 1936-54).

1972. *Studies in European Realism*, London (tr. from *Essays über Realismus*, Berlin: 1948).

1974. *Soul and Form*, London (first published in Hungary in 1910).

1976. 'Il romanzo come epopea borghese' in *Problemi di teoria del romanzo*, ed. V. Strada, Turin (first published in Russian in 1935).

LYONS, JOHN, 1968. *Introduction to Theoretical Linguistics*, Cambridge.

MACCABE, COLIN, 1978. *James Joyce and the Revolution of the Word*, London.

MACHEREY, PIERRE, 1968. 'A propos du processus d'exposition du *Capital*', in *Lire le Capital*, Paris.

1974. 'Présentation' of Renée Balibar, *Les français fictifs*, Paris.

1977. 'An interview with Pierre Macherey', by C. Mercer and J. Radford, *Red Letters* 5, 3-9.

1978. *A Theory of Literary Production*, London (tr. from *Pour une théorie de la production littéraire*, Paris: 1966).

MACKSEY, RICHARD, and DONATO, EUGENIO, (eds.), 1972. *The Structuralist Controversy: The Languages of Criticism and the Sciences of Man*, Baltimore, Md.

MARCUSE, HERBERT, 1978. *The Aesthetic Dimension*, Boston, Mass. (tr. from *Die Permanenz der Kunst*, Munich: 1977).

and ENGELS, FRIEDRICH, 1956. *Selected Correspondence*, Moscow.

1962. *Selected Works Volume I*, Moscow.

MARX, KARL, *Grundrisse*, Harmondsworth, Middx. (tr. from *Grundrisse der Kritik der politischen Ökonomie* (1857-8), Berlin: 1953).

1976. *Capital Volume I*, Harmondsworth, Middx. (tr. from *Das Kapital: Kritik der politischen Ökonomie I*, Hamburg: 1867).

1973. *Marx Engels on Literature and Art*, New York.

MATEJKA, LADISLAV, and POMORSKA, KRYSTYNA, (eds.), 1978. *Readings in Russian Poetics* (rev. ed.), Ann Arbor, Mich.

MEDEVEDEV, P.N. and BAKHTIN, M.M., 1978. *The Formal Method in Literary*

Scholarship: An Introduction to Sociological Poetics, Baltimore, Md. (first published in Russian in 1928).

MEISEL, PERRY, (ed.), 1981. *Freud: Twentieth-Century Views,* Englewood Cliffs, N.J.

MÉSZÁROS, ISTVÁN, 1972. *Lukács's Concept of Dialectic,* London.

MILL, JOHN STUART, 1961. *Auguste Comte and Positivism,* Ann Arbor, Mich. (first published in 1865).

MORRIS, C. W., 1938. *Foundations of the Theory of Signs,* Chicago (also in Morris 1971: 13-71).

1939. 'Esthetics and the theory of signs', *Journal of Unified Science* 8, 131-50 (also in Morris 1971: 415-33).

1946. *Signs, Language and Behavior,* New York (also in Morris 1971: 72-397).

1971. *Writings on the General Theory of Signs,* The Hague.

MUKAŘOVSKÝ, JAN, 1936. 'L'art comme fait sémiologique', in *Actes du VIIIe Congrès International de Philosophie,* Prague, 1065-72.

1938. 'La dénomination poétique et la fonction esthétique de la langue', in *Actes du IVe Congrès International des Linguistes,* Copenhagen, 98-104.

1970. *Aesthetic Function, Norm and Value as Social Facts,* Ann Arbor, Mich. (first published in 1936).

1976. *On Poetic Language,* Lisse (first published in 1940).

OGDEN, C. K., and RICHARDS, I. A., 1936. *The Meaning of Meaning,* London (first published in 1923).

OHMANN, RICHARD, 1964. 'Generative grammars and the concept of style', *Word* 20, 423-39.

OSBORNE, H., (ed.), 1972. *Aesthetics,* Oxford.

O'TOOLE, L. M., and SHUKMAN, ANN, 1977. 'A contextual glossary of formalist terminology', in *Russian Poetics in Translation* 4, 13-48.

PARKINSON, G. H. R., (ed.), 1970. *Georg Lukács, the Man, his Work and his Ideas,* London.

PETTIT, PHILIP, 1976. *The Concept of Structuralism,* London.

PICARD, RAYMOND, 1965. *Nouvelle critique ou nouvelle imposture,* Paris.

PLEKHANOV, GEORGEI V., 1953. *Art and Social Life,* London (first published in Russian 1912-13).

POULET, GEORGES, 1969. 'Phenomenology of reading', *New Literary History* 1:1, 53-68.

PRAGUE LINGUISTIC CIRCLE, 1929. 'Thèses', *Travaux du Cercle Linguistique de Prague* 1, 5-29 (also in Vachek 1964: 33-58).

PRAWER, S. S., 1976. *Karl Marx and World Literature,* Oxford.

PROPP, VLADIMIR, 1968. *The Morphology of the Folktale,* Austin, Texas (first published in Russian in 1928).

PSYCHOLOGY AND LITERATURE, 1980. *New Literary History* 12.

RANSOM, JOHN CROWE, 1941. *The New Criticism,* Norfolk, Conn.

RICHARDS, I. A., 1926. *Science and Poetry,* London.

1934. *Coleridge on Imagination,* London.

1967. *Principles of Literary Criticism,* London (first published in 1924).

1970. *Practical Criticism,* London (first published in 1929).

RIFFATERRE, MICHAEL, 1959. 'Criteria for style analysis', *Word* 15, 154-74 (also in Chatman and Levin 1967: 412-30. French version in Riffaterre 1971: 27-63).

1960. 'Stylistic context', *Word* 16, 207-18 (also in Chatman and Levin 1967: 431: 41. French version in Riffaterre 1971: 64-94).

1964. 'The stylistic function', in *Proceedings of the Ninth International Congress of Linguists,* The Hague, 316-23 (French version in Riffaterre 1971: 145-58).

1966. 'Describing poetic structures: two approaches to Baudelaire's "Les Chats"', *Yale French Studies* 36/37, 200-42 (French version in Riffaterre 1971: 307-64).

1971. *Essais de stylistique structurale,* Paris.

ROBEY, DAVID, (ed.), 1973. *Structuralism: An Introduction,* Oxford.

ROLAND, ALAN, 1978. 'Towards a reorientation of psychoanalytic literary criticism', in *Psychoanalysis, Creativity, and Literature: A French-American Inquiry,* ed. Alan Roland, New York. 248-70.

ROSE, GILLIAN, 1978. *The Melancholy Science: An Introduction to the Thought of Theodor W. Adorno,* London.

SARTRE, JEAN-PAUL, 1978. *What is Literature?,* London (tr. from 'Qu'est-ce que la littérature?', *Situations II,* Paris: 1948).

SAUSSURE, FERDINAND DE, 1978. *Course in General Linguistics,* London (tr. from *Cours de linguistique générale,* Paris: 1916).

SCHILLER, J. P., 1969. *I. A. Richards's Theory of Literature,* New Haven, Conn.

SCHNEIDERMAN, STUART, (ed.), 1980. *Returning to Freud: Clinical Psychoanalysis in the School of Lacan,* New Haven, Conn.

SEBEOK, THOMAS, 1971. *Style in Language,* Cambridge, Mass. (first published in 1960).

SHKLOVSKY, VIKTOR, 1965a. 'Art as technique', in Lemon and Reis 1965: 3-24 (first published in Russian in 1917).

1965b. 'Sterne's *Tristram Shandy:* stylistic commentary', in Lemon and Reis 1965: 25-57 (first published in Russian in 1921).

1973a. 'On the connection between the devices of *syuzhet* construction and general stylistic devices', in Bann and Bowlt 1973: 48-72 (first published in Russian in 1919).

1973b. 'The resurrection of the word', in Bann and Bowlt 1973: 41-7 (first published in Russian in 1914).

SKURA, MEREDITH ANNE, 1981. *The Literary Use of the Psychoanalytic Process,* New Haven, Conn. and London.

SLAUGHTER, CLIFF, 1980. *Marxism, Ideology and Literature,* London.

SMITH, JOSEPH H., (ed.), 1980. *The Literary Freud: Mechanisms of Defence and the Poetic Will,* New Haven, Conn. and London.

SPITZER, LEO, 1948. *Linguistics and Literary History,* Princeton, N. J.

1954. 'On Yeats's poem "Leda and the Swan"', *Modern Philology* 51, 271-6 (also in Spitzer 1962: 3-13).

1962. *Essays on English and American Literature,* Princeton, N. J.

STEMPEL, W. D., (ed.), 1972. *Texte der russischen Formalisten, II: Texte zur Theorie des Verses und der poetischen Sprache,* Munich.

STRIEDTER, JURIJ, (ed.), 1969. *Texte der russischen Formalisten, I: Texte zur allgemeinen Literaturtheorie und zur Theorie der Prosa,* Munich.

STURROCK, JOHN, (ed.), 1979. *Structuralism and Since,* Oxford.

TAINE, HIPPOLYTE, 1863. *Histoire de la littérature anglaise* vol. I, Paris.

TATE, ALLEN, 1959. *Collected Essays,* Denver, Col.

1970. *Essays of Four Decades,* London.

TODOROV, TZVETAN, (ed.), 1965. *Théorie de la littérature: Textes des Formalistes russes,* Paris.

1969. *Grammaire du Décaméron,* The Hague.

1973a. *Poétique,* Paris (first published in 1968).

1973b. 'The structural analysis of literature; the tales of Henry James', in Robey 1973: 73-103 (another version in Todorov 1977a).

1977a. *The Poetics of Prose,* Oxford (tr. from *Poétique de la prose,* Paris: 1971).

1977b. *Théories du symbole,* Paris.

TOMASHEVSKY, BORIS, 1978. 'Literature and biography', in Matejka and Pomorska 1978: 47-55 (first published in Russian in 1923).

TROTSKY, LEON, 1960. *Literature and Revolution,* Ann Arbor, Mich. (first published in Russian in 1923).

1970. *On Literature and Art,* New York.

TURKLE, SHERRY, 1979. *Psychoanalytic Politics: Freud's French Revolution,* London.

TURNER, G. W., 1973. *Stylistics,* Harmondsworth, Middx.

TYNYANOV, YURY, 1978a. 'On literary evolution', in Matejka and Pomorska 1978: 66-78 (first published in Russian in 1929).

1978b. 'Rhythm as the constructive factor of verse', in Matejka and Pomorska 1978: 126-35 (first published in Russian in 1924).

1978c. 'The meaning of the word in verse', in Matejka and Pomorska 1978: 136-45 (first published in Russian in 1924).

and JAKOBSON., ROMAN, 1977. 'Problems of research in language and literature', *Russian Poetics in Translation* 4, 49-51 (first published in Russian in 1928).

UITTI, KARL, 1969. *Linguistics and Literary Theory,* Englewood Cliffs, N. J.

UNIVERSITY OF BIRMINGHAM, CENTRE FOR CONTEMPORARY CULTURAL STUDIES, 1978. *On Ideology,* London.

VACHEK, J., 1964. *A Prague School Reader in Linguistics,* Bloomington, Ind. and London.

VOLOŠINOV, VALENTIN, 1973. *Marxism and the Philosophy of Language,* New York (first published in Russian in 1929).

WALSH, W., 1980. *F. R. Leavis,* London.

WELLEK, RENÉ, 1937a. 'Literary criticism and philosophy', *Scrutiny* 5, 375-83.

1937b. 'Literary criticism and philosophy' (correspondence), *Scrutiny* 6, 195-6.

1960. 'Leo Spitzer (1887-1960)', *Comparative Literature* 12, 310-34.

1963. *Concepts of Criticism,* New Haven, Conn.

1966. *A History of Modern Criticism 1750-1950* vol. IV, London.

1970. *Discriminations: Further Concepts of Criticism,* New Haven, Conn.

and WARREN, AUSTIN, 1963. *Theory of Literature,* Harmondsworth, Middx. (first published in 1949).

WILLIAMS, RAYMOND, 1975. *The Long Revolution,* London (first published in 1961).

1977. *Marxism and Literature,* Oxford.

1979. *Politics and Letters,* London.

1980. *Problems in Materialism and Culture,* London.

WILLIAMSON, JUDITH, 1980. *Decoding Advertisements,* London and Boston, Mass.

WIMSATT, W. K., 1958. *The Verbal Icon,* New York.

and BROOKS, CLEANTH, 1957. *Literary Criticism: A Short History,* New York.
New York.
WINNICOTT, D. W., 1974. *Playing and Reality,* Harmondsworth, Middx.

Index

Concepts

actualization, 45
   see also foregrounding
aesthetics, 1, 10, 18
affect, 25, 115
   see also emotive
alienation, 138, 157
ambiguity,
   in Derrida, 108-9
   in Jakobson, 53
   in New Criticism, 71
   in psychoanalytic theory, 113, 131
   in Russian Formalist theory, 30
   in structuralist theory, 90
American criticism and scholarship, 70-83
associative, *see* paradigmatic
author, 8-9
   in Freud, 114-16
   in Goldmann, 151-2
   in Lacan, 129-30
   in Lukács, 144-5
   in Macherey, 146
   in New Criticism, 75
   in I. A. Richards, 68-9
   in Russian Formalist theory, 23-6
   in structuralist theory, 99
automatization, 19-33 *passim*
   see also defamiliarization

base and superstructure, 8, 136-7, 138, 155, 159, 160, 161-2, 167
British criticism and scholarship, 2, 4, 65-6, 70-1

class struggle, 135
codes, 87, 101-2
coherence, 75-6, 77, 90, 152, 154-5
combination, axis of, 49
   see also contiguity, syntagmatic
commodity fetishism, 138, 166
communication, 7-8, 29-30, 38, 44, 69-70, 125
complexity, 75
conative, 44, 67
condensation, 115-16, 122
connotation, 30, 77, 81, 90
   see also denotation
context, 45
contiguity, 49
   see also combination, syntagmatic
criticism, 1-2, 5, 7, 12-13, 14-15, 73, 89, 96-100, 101-4

deconstruction, 110, 112, 125, 130, 131
defamiliarization, 10, 19-34 *passim*, 44-5, 46, 68, 75
   see also automatization, deviation
deformation, 47
   see also defamiliarization, deviation, violation
denotation, 77, 81
   see also connotation
deviation, 9, 35, 46, 57, 59, 75, 87, 96-7, 109, 112
   see also defamiliarization, violation

Theorists